His Hand On My Shoulder

by

Don W. Samuelson

His Hand On My Shoulder

Copyright © 1993, Don W. Samuelson

First Edition
All Rights Reserved

Edited by
Dwayne Parsons
Janet Mershon & Marianne Love
with reader's assistance from
Joe Stilwell
Donna Foth Collins
Darleen Hauk
Chip and Linda Keen

Published in Idaho
by
ParBest & Dickoens

Library of Congress Card Catalog Number 92-063318
ISBN 0-9635441-0-1

Forward by Marianne Love

Jacket Design by Steve Dilts

ParBest & Dickoens
P.O. Box 1614
Sandpoint, ID 83864-0869
(208) 265-5245
(208) 263-4771 FAX

Table of Contents

Dedication

All four of my Grandparents emigrated from Sweden in the 1860's and 70's. They were married in Illinois where my parents were born and raised. I too was born in Illinois and spent the first thirty-two years of my life in that state.

In 1944 I became concerned about the way World War II was progressing so I enlisted in the United States Navy. I was sent to the Farragut Naval Training Station in the panhandle of Idaho, between Sandpoint and Coeur d' Alene.

I fell in love with Idaho, her beautiful lakes, mountains and down to earth friendly people.

First of all I would like to dedicate this book to my wonderful supportive family: Ruby, wife and companion for the past fifty-six years; our son Stephen (Steve) who was my hunting partner, fishin', hiking and prospecting buddie; our daughter Donna who was my lake fishing partner, mountain hiking partner and my campaign chairman when I ran for the Senate the first time.

Second, I would like to dedicate this book to all of the fine people that supported me and worked with me during my sixteen years in politics.

To my many friends throughout this beautiful state of Idaho and many others scattered around the United States, I dedicate these chapters humbly and with deep appreciation for the love and kindness shown me, and for the opportunities they have helped to provide for my comfort and pleasure.

October 25, 1992
Don W. Samuelson

Forward

I grew up on a farm on North Boyer Road, one mile north of Sandpoint, Idaho. Just down Boyer toward town sits a one-level, flat-roofed, rock house. It's one of the more unique homes in our neighborhood. Not only does the structure have an interesting history and an unusual look, but it's also the home of a man who has lived a fascinating, adventurous and good life.

Don Samuelson has been our neighbor down the road for as long as I can remember. His son Steve and I used to ride the bus to Lincoln School. I vaguely recall his daughter Donna, who was a few years older than I. His bubbly and pretty wife Ruby used to come to our house on Saturday mornings to purchase her weekly quart of rich, thick Guernsey cream from my mother. Don has always impressed me as a gentle giant of a man, a good father, and a loving husband.

During his mid-seventies, Don decided to write his memoirs. He asked me to help with the editing. When I first started working with him, I visited his home. A quick glance around the house and his shop convinced me that Don had not spent much time twiddling his thumbs. Pictures of big game in Africa, photographs of his years in Idaho politics, and case after case of jewelry surrounded by colorful rocks and gems collected over the years told me this man possessed a wealth of experiences to share with young people, his contemporaries, and anyone interested in the politics of Idaho and the Western United States.

Don developed the first hunter safety course in Idaho and the United States. Add to that his career as a gunsmith and tackle repairman at his Pend Oreille Sports Shop. He's an accomplished jeweler, collector of Indian artifacts, early American phonographs, music boxes, coins, and stamps. He has also worked with the Boy Scouts and has hunted most of the big game available to sportsmen in Idaho and the Northwest. His service in the Idaho State Senate from 1960 to 1966 gave him a prominent name in Gem State politics.

His main claim to fame, however, occurred in 1966 with his triumph in the Idaho governor's race. Don served one term. He met defeat at the hands of Cecil Andrus in 1970. After that, as regional representative of the U.S. Department of Transportation, he oversaw the construction of the Alaska Pipeline. In addition, his political life has allowed him to meet presidents, senators and astronauts. A close friendship still exists with Donald Slayton, one of the original seven astronauts and James Lovell, a visitor to the moon. The group spent seventeen days together on safari in Africa.

Don began his life on a farm in Illinois, and he has consistently stuck by values learned in his early childhood. Most important, he maintains, is that one should be able to face himself in the mirror each morning with pride and a clear conscience. "I've always been able to do that," he boasts.

A trip through Don's rock house on North Boyer and his shop reveals a life's journey of adventure, public service, and creative pursuits. Now, he has put those memories into words. Don's autobiographical work as follows will certainly deal with the politics which made him famous, but more importantly, it includes vignettes of the man, his family, and his love of life.

— Marianne Love

A Little of What's Been

This is not intended to be simply an autobiography. My goal, instead, is to provide an account of changes in family life-styles, business in general and in government and transportation as I've seen it, and to comment about the public's attitude toward ethical and moral changes I have been witness to and participated in throughout the first seventy-five years of my life.

During the past three-quarters of a century, I have held many challenging jobs and have operated several business ventures — all successfully. Throughout those same years, I have encountered a number of close shaves that could have resulted in serious injury or death. In the following chapters, I plan to relate some of these experiences in detail and in the sequence in which they happened.

I have survived a number of incidents that could have had very adverse effects upon my future, as well. During each experience, however, it seemed someone was watching over me and protecting me. As I reflect, I have a deep, sincere feeling that the Good Lord had other tasks for me to accomplish. With this in mind, and considering that these incidents were spaced at fairly regular intervals, I have decided that my life has been guided and guarded with His hand on my shoulder.

The two primary experiences of living through the Depression and of surviving World War II have continued to influence my philosophy of business and government at all levels as well as my feelings about the lives of every day people. That philosophy has always been, "You can't borrow yourself out of debt."

When I was a scoutmaster, I tried to impress upon the boys that it takes a lifetime to build a reputation but only one illegal, unethical or immoral act to destroy it. With that in mind, I have always tried to treat others the way I would like to be treated.

In some ways it seems, I have always had an extra sense of perception. I can see results of proposed projects before they are built or even laid down on paper. In my hobby of making gold and silver jewelry, I can picture the piece in detail before I ever make it. During my political career, I could read proposed legislation and see the good or bad impact a given bill might impose on the people or the State as far as five, ten or even twenty years out. I used to become quite frustrated over the fact that my colleagues in the Senate didn't seem to realize the future consequences of some of the bills they passed.

So, I have had several puzzling experiences which have led me to the belief that I possess a sixth sense. This is especially true with traumatic experiences where something has happened to someone close to me in friendship or as a family member.

On several occasions, I awakened from sound sleep to rush into our son's bedroom to find him in a diabetic coma. He had contracted diabetes when he was only six years old. His bedroom was in the far end of our house and when these incidents occurred, he did not make enough noise to be heard.

Another time, in December of 1966, after being elected Governor of Idaho, I headed for Boise, leaving my wife Ruby in Sandpoint to pack our personal belongings and clear out the house. My father was living with us at the time and he and Steve, who was by then in college at the University of Idaho, and Ruby set out for Boise shortly after the moving truck had picked up our household items. It was the dead of winter with snow everywhere, so I told them to stop in Riggins and not attempt the drive through the canyon between Cascade and Horseshoe Bend at night. But they were eager, and after arriving in Riggins, decided to continue on.

I was sound asleep in our new apartment in Boise. Suddenly at three o'clock in the morning, I woke with a start, shaking all over. I could not go back to sleep.

About thirty minutes later, the phone rang. It was Ruby telling me they had hit black ice and turned the car over on its right side at the edge of the bridge on the Payette River.

Fortunately, they had not been hurt. As close as we could tell, though, I had awakened, shaking, in the same instant of the wreck a hundred miles away.

On another occasion, I was with my mother in a Galesburg, Illinois hospital when she passed away. I was holding her hand and an odd feeling went through me the instant she passed on.

On yet another occasion, I was in Boise while my father was in a rest home in Genneseo, Illinois. He had a heart attack and died just a short time before his eighty-fourth birthday. I didn't even know he was ill at the time, but the same odd feeling came over me on the day of his death.

I knew that I would win the election for Governor in 1966, despite the press that said otherwise and the political heads who said I wouldn't make it. Before any votes were cast, I knew of my success. In the same way, I knew the morning before the vote was tallied that I was going to lose the re-election bid in 1970, in spite of the polls that showed me ahead.

Again, I believe the Good Lord had His hand on my shoulder, because after the defeat I was offered a job with the United States Department of Transportation by Governor Volpe of Massachusetts, who was at the time Secretary of Transporation. I accepted and found it to be a very interesting position.

Ruby and I have been witness to a lot of change, weathered our share of storms and enjoyed many good times along the way during our marriage, which at the time of this writing has been fifty-six years. Considering what appears to be an increasing instability in marriages, we feel very fortunate that ours has survived.

There is no doubt in my mind that the experiences of living through the Depression, World War II and some other genuinely tough times have created in us an appreciation of the value of all things, including family and life itself.

From the very beginning of my life, I was taught to be honest and fair in all dealings as well as open, above board and truthful. I sincerely believe that all these traits and circumstances have molded me into the conservative individual that I am and into a good business man, as well.

I ran my businesses to make an honest living and to give good service to my customers — not to make millions of dollars. I also tried to treat all my customers like good friends, regardless of their political, social or religious beliefs.

Though I am Republican, Ruby and I have many good friends who are Democrats. Both she and I believe in the philosophy of the Republican Party, but by the same token support others in their right to believe in their own choice of philosophy. The two-party system we have in this country, after all, is what sets us apart from the many other countries in the world.

I hope my narrative as follows relates these many influences on my life in an accurate manner. It is also my desire that others will gain insight through this high-lighting of my personal experiences and perhaps make wiser decisions than they might otherwise have made — especially the young, who have so much to look forward to and so much to say about what is to come.

Chapter 1

The Early Years

I was born on grandfather Samuelson's farm in Henry county, Illinois, where my father raised corn, oats, barley and hay of clover and alfalfa. The farm covered one hundred sixty acres, all of it plowed and put into small grain crops, except for twenty acres that went into pasture. This twenty-acre plot started at our barnyard and dropped down a draw about a quarter-mile long. There was a thirty-foot steel windmill in the center of the draw and about a hundred and fifty feet from the creek at the bottom.

The windmill pumped water from that well up to a huge concrete water tank that was exposed on both sides of the fence. The animals from the pasture used one side and the other was for the horses we kept in the barn for plowing, cultivating, mowing and harvesting. When we were not busy with these things, we'd turn those horses out to the pasture. We always watered the horses at that tank after we came out of the fields, before unharnessing them in the barn.

The long, sloping hill of that draw was our favorite sledding area in the winter. We enjoyed the quarter-mile ride down to the creek but did not like the quarter-mile long trudge back, pulling the sled. I still have fond memories of that hill. When there was a thin coat of crusty snow, we could really pick up speed on the slide down. That was quite a thrill, I'll tell you!

Our family home was almost a two-story house. I say "almost" because the two rooms upstairs had low, slanting ceilings unlike the houses of today. Those upstairs rooms were heated by a register in the ceiling downstairs which opened into the upstairs floor. One of those rooms was a bedroom, while the other, being immediately at the top of the stairs, was our playroom for a few years. It would double as a guest room when we had company or a quarters for hired men who worked for dad once in a while in the summers.

There was a big wood stove standing in the living room which heated

1

the entire house, with the only exception being the kitchen. My folks, like most Swedes back then, put the coffee pot on the kitchen stove when they started the cooking fire in the morning. That blue and white spotted enamel pot would still be there with hot coffee in it when we went to bed at night, serving twelve to fifteen cups throughout the day.

We could always count on coffee and cookies to be served about ten o'clock in the morning and again at around three in the afternoon when dad was close to the house or when one of our neighbors stopped in for a visit, or to help the folks with an extra hand.

Downstairs, there was a single bedroom, the living room, a dining room and the kitchen. In those days, the bathroom was a two-holer in the backyard. For obvious reasons, it was located about fifty feet away.

Our wash area was usually in one end of the kitchen where we had a wash basin in a sink with a small hand pump that brought rain water in from the cistern under the house. Our Monarch wood kitchen-range had a reservoir on one side which also held water and kept it warm. We used that for washing our faces and hands before eating or when we came in from working in the fields or doing chores.

The water in the cistern came from rain and snow that drained off the roof through the eave troughs (they now call them gutters) into the downspouts that directed the flow to the tank.

There were no washing machines then, so mom washed everything by hand with a scrub board and several wash tubs. The water was heated in a large copper boiler on the wood stove. In the winter, that boiling laundry water steamed-up all the windows in the house. In the summer, the heat from that stove was almost unbearable — even with the doors and windows wide open.

It was quite a job to keep enough wood cut and split for two stoves, and the kitchen stove was in operation 12 months out of the year. Adding to the chore, the kitchen stove wood had to be split rather fine in order to fit into the burning cavity.

We generally did our wood cutting in the winter using cross-cut saws. This was long before the advent of chain saws, buzz saws and tractors, so every single piece of sixteen-inch wood was cut with a cross-cut. And these were two-man cross-cut saws. Later in my youth, when I was big enough to handle it, I would cut wood with my father on the other end.

We were a man and boy team and I vividly remember being scolded by him.

"What you are *supposed* to do," he said, "is pull the saw toward you and the other fellow pulls it back. You are not supposed to push it back and you should never put any downward pressure on the saw." I learned my lesson quickly.

We had mostly hardwoods like maple, oak, elm and hickory which with their hardness and fine grain, did not cut very fast. Nevertheless, I enjoyed cutting wood. Besides working with my father, I also helped my grandfather Johnson off and on.

Houses were not insulated in those days and that made my opportunities for cutting wood more than plentiful, to say the least.

But back at the start, when I was only about two and a half, my folks moved to the Palmer place about two miles down the road but still seven miles from town.

I can't remember a reason for moving there, because the Palmer place was the same size as our original farm and its house and out-buildings were comparable. Possibly, dad thought it had better soil...I just don't know. We stayed there for three years and then moved back to the Samuelson farm.

By then our family had grown by one more. My sister Aileen was born on July 17, 1916. I was only three years old at the time, so don't remember much about our relationship in those first few years except that when she was about two, our folks gave her a small piano.

It was only about 16 inches tall, maybe ten-inches wide and twenty-inches long or so. Made of wood, it looked and played like a big piano.

At that age, my sister stayed in the house with mom but, being five, I stayed outside from morning 'til night.

I remember Aileen having a toy set of irons similar to the ones mom used to press clothing. Mom kept Aileen's irons on the back of the stove where they would stay warm but not hot enough to burn my little sister. While mom was ironing, she would give Aileen a handkerchief or some other small piece of linen so that she could iron with mom.

With my dad as busy as he was in the fields, I was a bit of a loner as a young boy. He was usually in the fields already when I got up, so I'd play by myself around the barnyard. Later, when I was older, I would wander over into the timbered areas, or play in the pastures and explore along the creek.

While we were still at the Palmer farm, dad bought me a dark brown Shetland pony, we named Bluebell. He was young, pretty spirited and would test me constantly to see how far he could go. I took a few spills off his back, but never broke a bone, never got seriously hurt.

I remember the butter churn at the Palmer farm, also. Mom churned the butter in a tall crock churn with a stomper-type agitator. I enjoyed working the churn until the cream started to go into butter. Then mom had to take over and finish it because it would get too hard for me to handle at that age.

I liked feeding the hens and their chicks, especially. This was a time before incubators had come on the market, so the folks would collect a dozen eggs or so and place them in special nests in a separate room at one end of our chicken house. Then they would select a hen that appeared to want to sit on the eggs. During the spring of the year, we'd have

fifteen to twenty setting hens at a time. They'd only get off the nests to eat or drink. After about three weeks, the eggs were done hatching and the hens were put out in the yard with their chicks in separate chicken coops, one for each hen.

The hens would stay with their chicks until the young birds could make it on their own. We fed them oatmeal and cracked corn to supplement the care they received from their mothering hens. At night, we'd close the door to the chicken coops to keep them warm as well as to keep the weasels and skunks out. The numerous skunks and weasels and raccoons in the area caused us to keep a close watch on the poultry. The chicken wire worked pretty well on the raccoons and skunks, but the weasels could go right through.

I remember one skunk, however, that somehow found his way through the wire one night and helped himself to several baby chicks before our old dog, named "Shep" alerted us. Dad killed that skunk with a .22 rifle, but the odor stayed with us for days. And when it rained, the bad smell was intensified.

That old dog, Shep, was one of my boyhood buddies. He was a brown and white collie, quiet and gentle but very intelligent. He'd follow me around from morning 'til night.

Dad had taught him to fetch the cows in at milking time. Dad would say, "fetch the cows" and over the fence he would go, wasting no time. Somehow he knew not to run the cows back, however, and after awhile he'd have them all coming back to the barn, walking ten feet behind the last of them. If one stopped to graze, he'd nip at its hind legs and then duck quickly. The cows would always miss him, but they'd get the message and amble on.

Shep lived with us until he was fourteen years old. Though he moved a bit slower through his later years, he was the same old friend. One morning we found him in his bed where he'd gone to sleep for the last time. I lost a good friend that day. He had protected me when I was little and had been my constant companion in the years of my childhood.

The house on the Palmer place was a two-story, white structure. The barn, implement shed and corn crib were painted dark red and had white trim. The pasture was behind the barn. Scattered about were oak and maple trees and a small stream ran through the grazing area and it was one of my favorite places for trying to catch frogs and minnows.

There were always ground squirrels scurrying about in the pasture in the summertime. Now and then, we would see a ground hog, but because they dug big holes that could break the leg of a cow or horse, dad trapped them or shot them when he could with his .22 rifle and that kept their population to a minimum.

The highlight of living at the Palmer place for me occurred when I was about five. Dad had gone to town with one of our neighbors. Mom kept looking out the window toward the road, while he was gone and so I knew something was up. Whether he had called her from town with the news or whether they had talked it over before he left, I don't know, but she was obviously aware of a big event about to happen. Suddenly, she grabbed me by the hand and we headed out the door to the driveway.

Down the road, at about 10 mph, came dad in a brand new car. He slowed down to half the speed to turn into the driveway and came to a stop in front of us. I can still vividly remember that shiny brass radiator on the front of that "automobile." It was a Model T Ford touring car of 1917. It had four doors and a black canvas top and a spare tire fastened to the running board with a leather strap, if I remember right.

After the three of us looked it over admiringly, dad decided to put it in the alleyway of the barn.

This was before garages. Our implement shed was full of plows, discs, cultivators and other farm equipment. A wide plank ramp lead up to two large sliding doors in the center of the barn, however, and inside on one side was a large room we used as a grain bin. On the other side of the walkway was a tack room about the same size as the grain room. In addition, horse stalls extended along both sides of this alley all the way to the end of the barn. Straight on from the doors and ramp on the other end of the room was a piano box which served as a depository for corn cobs left over in the horses' mangers after they had cleaned the kernals off. Finally a hole in the ceiling led into the haymow where we threw hay down to the horses each morning and night.

I remember dad cranking up that Ford (this was before they had starters) and then driving up the ramp into the barn. As he started up the ramp, though, he needed more power. He had his foot on the low-range pedal and was feeding the gas with the hand throttle. Before you knew it, he was in the barn on level ground with the throttle open and the car was moving pretty fast. He became excited and yelled, "Whoa!" rather loudly.

But when he realized that wasn't going to do the trick with this new critter, he started stomping on the other pedals. Fortunately, I suppose, this action killed the engine and stopped the car before it hit the piano box we had stored at the end of the alleyway.

He said many times after, while reminiscing over the event, that he may just have hit the reverse instead of the brake, but it worked anyway. Even though he had announced his "whoa" with some authority, he'd say, that critter didn't seem to have the respect for his orders that the four-legged ones had.

That automobile was the beginning of a new era for dad. There were three pedals on the floor of that model. The left one, completely depressed, put you in "low." If the pedal was released and came all the way back, you were in "high." If you stopped it in the center, it was in neutral. The middle pedal pushed forward was for reverse and the right pedal was the brake. If your brake failed, you could use the reverse to stop the car, but if you weren't careful, you'd kill the engine like dad did in the barn.

Those were the days when every farmer took care of the roads past his property. We had a wooden plank-angle drag that dad pulled with a team of horses to level out the ruts that resulted from wagons, buggies and other horse-drawn vehicles during the spring or other wet times. We knew nothing of county road graders or snow plows.

When the snow became too deep for the wagons or buggies, we used sleighs and bobsleds to go into town. We did this only about twice a month and always on a Saturday.

It took a lot of time to harness the horses and hitch them to a buggy, wagon or bobsled for the seven miles, so we made the trip for two reasons: one to carry our eggs and cream to sell and the other to buy groceries, mostly staples like flour and sugar and so forth.

Saturdays were the days it seemed all the farmers made their pilgrimages to town. So it was kind of a social time also. They'd meet at the barbershop or at the grocery store to discuss the farming situation, the price of hogs and cattle and that sort of thing.

We had phones then, but they were all on party lines with fifteen to twenty residences sharing the same line. There were no secrets for this reason because most everyone listened in on calls (to get the latest news). If you wanted to tell someone something confidential, you did not do it over the phone. For that you had to go over and see the person face to face in private.

Most of our clothes were homemade, except for the overalls or a set of Sunday-go-to-meeting clothes, which were generally bought from the

7

store.

Whenever we went to town, we'd stop at both my grandparents' houses where the folks would have coffee while my sister and I ate cookies or cake. I always looked forward to these trips because it also meant a nickel for me to buy an ice cream cone or some candy.

And it was fun, too, to go by bobsled in the winter. My folks would put a double-top box on the sled and fill it with loose, clean oat straw. We kids would burrow down into the straw to keep warm, and especially on the way home after a long day or in the evening. Mom and dad would ride on the spring seat in front with a horsehide-lined robe over their laps and feet. Dad also wore a long horse-hide coat that extended almost to the ground.

That coat was distinguished by its round, wooden-peg buttons. They were about three and a half inches long and a half inch in diameter, and inserted into loops of heavy twisted cord rather than button holes.

Besides those trips to town, my folks enjoyed dancing, too. They went to a lot of neighbors' homes, schoolhouses, and "barn-dances." If there wasn't any snow, we'd go in a buggy. Sometimes when there was snow, instead of the bobsled filled with straw, we'd go in a cutter, which was just a buggy on runners—one seaters and two seaters alike were pulled by a team rather than a single horse.

The music for these dances was furnished by anyone who knew how to play an instrument, usually a combination of a piano or an organ with an accompanying fiddle or violin. Once in awhile, we'd be treated to some banjo music. But it seemed to me that almost every other tune was *Red Wing*, a very old, but catchy, fast-paced tune that everyone seemed to enjoy for square dancing.

I loved it when they'd square dance, which they did a lot. I enjoyed most listening to the caller. Those dances were good, clean fun. I don't remember ever seeing a fight or any kind of problem associated with these activities.

As those evenings wore on, my sister and I would get pretty tired. Many a time by ten o'clock, we would find our way into the cloak room where all the coats and blankets were kept and we would crawl into dad's long, warm, horse-hide coat or pull that horse-hide blanket up over ourselves and fall fast asleep until the folks decided to go home. Everyone carried horse blankets to keep their horses warm during the dance.

Our folks usually left around midnight or one o'clock in the morning, but before leaving everyone would have coffee, sandwiches, cake and cookies. Still, on occasion, our journey home was ten or twelve miles or so and when that was the case, we often didn't get home until three or four in the morning, after which we still had to unhitch the horses and put them in the barn. By then, the fire in the kitchen was usually out and when it was cold enough, we'd find a thin film of ice in the bucket beside the Monarch. The same was true of the tea kettle on top of the stove, too.

With my sister Aileen on the porch of the Palmer farm in 1917.

As I've already mentioned, there was no such luxury as a "bathroom" in those days in that part of the country. We called it the "chick sales" and it was in the back yard. You'd sit down with a copy of last year's Sears and Roebuck catalog on the seat beside you. Those old catalogs served a double purpose for everybody then, because that was before anyone had invented rolled toilet paper.

There were, of course, no electric lights either. So my folks carried a kerosene lantern in the buggy. Once it got dark, they would light-up the lantern and hang it in front of the dash board on the buggy or cutter. It was surprising how much light a kerosene lantern put out on a dark night. It was also helpful when we unhitched and put the horses away after arriving home so late from the dances.

My first recollection of lights were of kerosene lamps in the house and kerosene lanterns for outside in the barn or in the "chick sales." On many an early morning, the lantern served as my only light for milking the cows or harnessing the horses.

Then came the aladdin lamps with their mantles. They seemed to be four times as bright as our old lanterns. You always had to be careful about setting a lantern down in the barn with all the dry straw and hay lying around. If one of the livestock knocked it over, it would set off a fire which could get out of control pretty fast.

There were no fire departments around then and the only water available was in the tank so long as it wasn't too far away. We didn't have electric pumps and hoses then. Pumping water by hand from the well took too long to do any good if a fire got out of hand. That meant that if a building caught fire, it generally burned to the ground, usually before any neighbors could be called or brought in to help fight the blaze. For those reasons, we were cautioned very carefully by our folks on the proper handling of lamps and lanterns and schooled on what to do if a fire started.

My folks had leased the Palmer place for three years. When the lease ended in the fall of 1917, we moved back to my grandparent's place. It was just before the end of the year.

Once there, one of my dad's first projects was to build a new double corn crib, since the old one was rotten. He tore it down and burned the old, weathered wood all at once.

His new structure was about fifty feet long and had a ten-foot wide bin on either side of a twelve foot-wide driveway that ran down the center. My recollection is that each side held about two thousand bushels of ear corn when full.

He constructed the crib so that the two lower boards on the outside could be removed for raking or shoveling the corn into the conveyor, which took it up the belt to a corn sheller where the kernels were removed from the cobs and deposited into a wagon for transporting to town where it was sold at the grain elevator. From there it would go by rail to the flour mills or cereal manufacturing plants. Neighbors would help one another haul their grain to town whenever someone decided to sell.

Dad's younger brother, George, worked for him from time to time. Being single, George was inducted into the army in 1917 and ended up serving in World War I.

I liked my uncle George very much and still cherish a lot of fond memories of the times we had together. He would pick my sister and me up in his Model T Ford, which was a roadster, and take us to his sister's house.

My aunt's first name was Emma. She had married Ed Odean and had

My father is on the left in the back row of this picture of my mother's parents, brothers and sisters and their husbands and wives. Mom is holding my sister. I am sitting in the front row — 1916.

four children which they named Chester, Lilian, Vivian and Mildred. I remember the Odean's had four or five mulberry bushes in their barnyard, and that these trees produced a delicious fruit. When the berries were ripe, uncle George would take us over there to pick and eat them.

Uncle George also took us fishing on the Edwards River about three miles on up from Odean's. One day about ten o'clock in the morning, George came to get us in that roadster and because it was warm out, he had taken the side curtains off. We were enjoying the ride along a county dirt road lined with cornfields on both sides, when we turned a corner. We were only going about ten miles an hour when all of a sudden, we were covered with honey bees.

With the window down in front, we had hit a moving swarm square on and our faces, arms, legs and bodies were covered with them and the inside of the car was deluged by the insects.

Very carefully, uncle George brought his roadster to a stop and turned off the ignition. Slowly we opened the doors on both sides and worked our way out of the seats to stand on the ground beside the car.

First, we brushed off my sister because she wasn't more than five. Then, using an old cotton glove and a handkerchief, George and I brushed each other off.

11

Still being very careful, we then removed them from all over the car. They were on the windshield, the dashboard, the floorboards and the seat. We had to remove the seat altogether so we wouldn't get back in and sit on a stray bee.

Yet through the entire episode, not one of us was stung even once. Later, some beekeepers told us it was because they were swarming to move their nest and hadn't gotten riled. But for us, it was an experience to remember!

Uncle George was a very kind and thoughtful person. But during the war he had been a victim of mustard gas and he suffered seriously from complications after coming home. He died at the age of forty-two in 1932. I remember him as the active, healthy young man and it was a shame to have him die so young.

Chapter 2

Life as a Farm Boy

Aside from memories of my uncle and the move back to the family farm, I will not forget the year 1918 for another reason. It is as if it were yesterday. I was standing in the front yard by the gate when a biplane flew directly over the farm about two thousand feet above. That was the first airplane I had ever seen and it was the most exciting and thrilling thing for me. The curiosity and wonder of flight stayed with me from that day on, as did many other memories from that year.

I started my formal education that fall. The school was just over a mile from our home and most of the time I rode my Shetland pony, Bluebell, which I kept in the school's woodshed during the day with ponies and horses belonging to other students.

At other times during good weather, I would walk to school cutting across the fields. It was a half-mile shorter that way but probably took me just as long because there was a creek on that route teeming with minnows, frogs and muskrats. These were pleasant distractions for the

Blue Bell was my first independent mode of transportation as I rode him to the New Pine School daily. That's Shep on the back behind me. Grandfather Samuelson is in front of my pony with two of my cousins and my sister Aileen on the right.

young boy I was, both before and after school.

"New Pine School," as it was called, had one room for all eight grades. It was a white, oblong building dotted with windows down both sides. The door to the room faced the road and just inside the entrance, there were two small rooms for hanging clothes and storing lunch buckets. One was for boys and one was for girls.

Because the school had only one room for teaching, it was common for a student to sit through all eight grades each year. The same was true for most other rural country schools in those days.

When a teacher instructed a specific class, she would have its students sit in the front of the room on benches facing her desk. Some classes had only one student and others had four or five. As I recall, each session lasted only about twenty minutes. It was difficult to tune out those sessions when we were in the back of the room, so there were no excuses for not learning every concept thoroughly.

The teacher's desk was at the opposite end of the building from the door. Across the room there was a large wood stove that resembled a furnace. The teacher kept a metal jacket around it to keep us students from falling against the hot metal or otherwise burning ourselves.

Our desks were set in rows facing the teacher. They were all sizes because they had all sizes of kids sitting in them. We had from twenty to thirty students in the classroom at any one time. The smaller desks were on one side of the room and as the students grew older, they would work their way to the larger desks on the other side.

Beside and behind the teacher's desk, there was a large black board complete with erasers and chalk. At the day's end, one of the older students had the task of cleaning the blackboard and "dusting out" the erasers. They took them outside to pound against the woodshed or a tree in order to get them thoroughly free of

The New Pine School had only one classroom for all eight grades. Our teacher is centered in the back row right behind me.

chalk dust.

Our teacher was a young lady who had completed two years of college where she specialized in teaching elementary school. In those days the teacher boarded with one of the farm families close to school. Since there weren't many automobiles, she stayed with the family closest to the school so she could walk to work.

Once there, her job was made easier with the help of the students. She usually assigned the task of starting the fire to one of the boys in the two higher grades because they were bigger and stronger. The boy assigned brought the wood in from the storage shed about fifty feet behind the schoolhouse. The woodshed was the same building where the students' horses and ponies were kept during session.

Our drinking water was drawn from a deep well in the school yard and kept in a drinking fountain at the front of the classroom during the day. The "chick sales" or "two-holers," on the other hand, were two small outhouses behind the school. One was *His* and the other was *Hers*. If a student needed to use the facilities, he or she would raise a hand with their index finger extended. If one of them wanted a drink of water, they would extend two fingers from the raised hand. The teacher would acknowledge "yes" or "no" by nodding her head accordingly. We called them "chick sales" because of a small, humorous book of several volumes written about the fine art of constructing outhouses. I still have two volumes of this book to this day. They were very popular back then and so the outhouses were called "chick sales."

That was the year, also, of the Great Swine Flu Epidemic which spread all over the nation and the world. Many people died from it. My dad caught the flu during the latter part of January. He was extremely ill for more than a month. For a while my mother would tell me it was "nip and tuck" as to whether he would make it.

Dr. Carlson came from town in his horse and buggy to care for him. He brought a black leather bag filled with pills and other forms of medicine. I remember he had a thermometer in there, too, and a blood pressure device and so on.

He and mom kept dad covered with all the quilts and blankets we owned in an effort to keep him warm. Mom spent a lot of time emptying and refilling hot water bottles until finally they got him to "sweat," as they called it in those days. The belief (and the hope) was that the poison would work its way out of his system through his perspiration.

Several hours passed before his induced fever finally broke. That was considered the turning point. Mom changed dad's nightgown and bedding and soon had him comfortable in dry clothing and bedclothes. By then he had lost a great amount of weight and I remember him looking like skin and bones. He slept ten hours nonstop.

That was a pivotal day in his recovery, but he wore his heavy horsehide coat everywhere he went for a long time after that, trying to stay warm. He was thin and always cold, so he and mom kept the stove filled with wood and "hotter than blazes." It was around the first of July before he was fully recovered.

While he was still in the process of regaining his health, our neighbors came by to help do the chores. I was too young then to be of sufficient help and my folks were very grateful to them and never forgot it. Mom and dad were always the first to jump when anyone else needed help or was in any kind of trouble after that.

The next year another incident happened to dad that was funny to everyone but him. He had purchased about two dozen steel traps for skunk, weasel, possum, muskrat and mink in hopes of supplementing our income. Skunk hides were worth about five dollars each then; muskrat, from one to three dollars; and mink from ten to twenty dollars apiece.

Like our neighbors, we had hedge fences of Osage orange on our farm. Groundhogs would dig holes along these brush fence lines and once they were abandoned, other little animals would use them, so the mouth of one of these holes was a likely place to set a trap.

Dad had a number of such sets and had been pretty successful at catching his share of furbearers. One morning, while making his rounds to check the traps, he came to one that was set in the middle of the hedge row where it was difficult to see. He could tell the trap had been sprung because the chain was down the hole and the trap was out of sight.

Dad got down on his knees in the snow and took the chain in his hands to pull the trap out of the hole. He thought there might be a rabbit in there because there were rabbit tracks in the snow, so he poked his head in between the branches of the hedge to see if he could see what was in the trap.

He could. He was twenty inches from the back end of a skunk. It lunged to get away but was already at the end of the chain so it did what skunks do best. Dad took it square in the face! Leaping backwards, he bumped his head on one of the hedge's stout branches.

The spray was particularly damaging to his eyes and immediately affected his vision. Out of the hedge and back on his feet, he knew he'd have to head home which was a half-mile or so up the road along which the fence ran. When he backed away from the skunk, he knew he was on the road so he tried to guide himself home by its boundaries, floundering from ditch to ditch all the way home.

He knew he was home when Shep got excited and greeted him with loud barks. With the mailbox as a guidepost, he was able to find the small gate to the yard.

My mother saw him coming and couldn't figure out why he was wandering all over trying to get to the house. But once she opened the door, she needed no explanation. She ushered him around to the wash house, got a pan of warm water from the kitchen stove and immediately washed his eyes and face until he could see again. Then she filled the wash tub full of hot water so he could take a bath and change those clothes before she would let him into the house.

She soaked his clothes for three days, but they were still pretty rank. So she hung them in the woodshed until spring. When the nice weather came, she planted the garments in the garden for about a week. Then dug them up and ran them through the washing tubs with lots of soap and hot water. Finally, after all that, they were fit to be worn again.

Whenever the family talked about the incident, dad would say there had been no hint of a skunk at the time but felt some rabbit and the skunk must have been in cahoots to pull a rather effective con on my unsuspecting father. He'd also claim that after he got his eyes washed out, they were stronger than ever. In fact, he claimed he could see in the dark! That might have been, but he never convinced me to try the same method.

I always loved the outdoors and spent much of my time on the creek that ran through the family farm. During the time we lived there, there were no children close by for me to play with, so I became somewhat of a loner.

I enjoyed my time at the creek, which was about a quarter-mile from the house where it flowed through a timbered area located behind the barn. I roamed around watching the birds, ground squirrels, quail and rabbits.

That's me in the shadow fishing for bullheads in Pope Creek. My life long love for stream fishing started on the creeks of my youth.

Once I made a seine out of an old, loose, woven gunnysack. It was perfect for catching minnows which I carried by bucket up the hill to our large cement water tank by the barn. I had so many minnows in that tank that one could hardly see the bottom. I used them for bait whenever dad took me fishing.

In the fall of 1920 when I was seven, I decided that I would like to start trapping muskrat and mink. Dad showed me how and where to set traps for various animals. Then he gave me six steel traps with springs weak enough for me to be able to set them. I set several in the groundhog holes and caught a weasel and a rabbit.

One day I remembered seeing some muskrat slides in the creek where it ran through one of our neighbor's pastures about half-a-mile from our home. I decided it was time to set a couple of traps down there. It was a cold, brisk day and only about ten degrees outside. I loved that kind of weather and was bundled up in my overalls, sweater, heavy jacket, stocking cap and my "four-buckle" over-shoes.

Once down there, I found a muskrat slide on my side of the creek. The stream was about four feet wide at that point and the slide was next to a hole about three feet deep. The muskrats used these water burrows to enter their nests under the bank.

I was going to pound a stake into the ground in the water next to the bank so the muskrat wouldn't see it. Besides, the ground above the waterline was frozen pretty solid, and it was a lot harder to pound a stake in there. After some difficulty I had the stake in place, set the trap and tied the chain to the stake. Then I got down on my knees.

I knew that muskrats liked to slip into the water and that they develop their own personal slides along the banks of streams and lakes. I wanted to place the set trap beneath the surface of the water just at the base of this particular slide where the muskrat might slip right into it. But just as I reached to place it, the bank caved in underneath me and before I knew it I was in the water, completely submerged.

The scene was reminiscent of Jack London's account in the story, "To Build a Fire," where the character gets wet in the sub-zero temperatures of the Yukon Territory. London writes aptly, "It certainly was cold."

The shock of going all the way into extremely cold water was so great, it took me a while to pick myself up. By that time the water had soaked completely through my clothing to my skin. My clothes started freezing immediately, so I started for home at once. The further I went, the more stiff my apparel became. By the time I had gone half the distance home, my overalls were as stiff as boards.

Lucky for me, when I got to the house, mom had the kitchen range in high gear and to paraphrase London, "It certainly was hot." When I took my clothes off standing next to the stove, the overalls stood by themselves until they thawed out. There was never a greater feeling than getting out of those frozen clothes and soaking up the heat of the wood stove. Even though it was a very shocking experience, I never caught a cold.

Shortly after that episode my father and mother bought their first gasoline-powered washing machine. Mom still had to heat the water in the copper boiler, however, and carry it out to the wash shed because we had no piping. When the clothes came out of the washing machine, they were piled into a tub of clean, warm water for rinsing. Next they were squeezed through a hand-cranked wringer and deposited into a second tub of cold water. Finally they went through the wringer a second time and into the clothes basket to be hung on the line in the backyard to dry.

In 1922 or '23, dad made another major purchase by trading in the Model T Ford on a new Hupmobile touring car which came complete with a black canvas top and four doors. Now we traveled in style and it didn't take so long to get to town. The convenience of that car also allowed us to go on longer adventures to bigger towns like Galesburg about twenty-five miles from home.

It was in Galesburg that I saw my first Wild West show inside a big tent. The pavilion was set up on the east end of Main Street next to the Chicago Burlington & Quincy Railroad in an empty lot.

The event was very special, even though I did not realize at the time the magnitude of its stars, Buffalo Bill Cody and Annie Oakley. Buffalo Bill rode into the huge tent on a beautiful white horse. Bill was wearing a black Western hat, buckskin jacket with fringe, buckskin pants and Western boots. An assistant stood in the ring and threw glass balls into the air, while Buffalo Bill rode around in a circle shooting and breaking them with his six-shooter.

Annie Oakley's act was similar, except that she used a rifle and rode a brown horse. I thought it was great shooting, but being a skeet-shooter, I am certain they used self-loaded, fine lead shot in their cartridges rather than bullets.

I remember that Wild West show as if it were yesterday. The showmanship, the talent and the magnificent horses with their shiny silver saddles and bridles made a lasting impression on me.

Chapter 3

The Slawson Place

When I was around nine years old, my folks moved to the Slawson place, a farm they rented just a mile from town. That fall I enrolled in the fourth grade at Woodhull Elementary School. There were about twenty students in my class and we had our own room — quite a change from the one-room school house with all eight grades mixed together. But even though I still walked to school, I didn't have all the interesting distractions to delay my arrival home each afternoon.

By this time, I had started milking cows and performing other chores around home, such as gathering eggs or feeding and watering the chickens. Our new farm had a nice two-story house with a big front yard and a large garden in the back. Just behind the house was the traditional wash shed, and on one side of the house, we had a two-acre apple orchard. A huge, long barn and another outbuilding were located some distance from the house.

Because of our orchard, we had lots of apple picking in the fall. This

This is the farm house on the Slawson place where I developed many pleasant memories from my childhood days.

21

was always followed by the production of apple cider, which usually amounted to about 300 gallons. Mom set a barrel of it in the basement for vinegar and fitted another with a spigot. That one occupied the back porch during corn-picking time.

During the cold weather, the juice would freeze and the alcohol created by the fermentation would settle into the center where it would become pretty potent. Dad and the hired corn-pickers seemed to enjoy it, but I wasn't allowed to touch it once it began to change from apple juice to cider. Mom never touched anything with any alcohol in it and dad was pretty conservative about the brew in those days.

One year during the corn harvest, we had a couple of men who took more than their share of cider. They had no idea how potent it was until it was too late and paid dearly for their over-imbibing.

Since we always had more than enough for ourselves and the hired men, my folks would divide up four of the barrels between the neighbors. Some would use it for vinegar and others kept it for juice.

I always enjoyed the apple-picking activity in the fall because neighbors, friends and relatives all helped pick, grind and press the apples. Everyone enjoyed lunch and dinner at our place on that particular day.

It was in that same year that I first began to experience a puzzling problem. Many times while sitting and reading a newspaper or book, I would get up, take a step and black out. When I hit the floor, I would immediately regain consciousness and be okay.

At first these spells were only occasional, but eventually they became more and more frequent. In addition to these occurrences, I noticed that sometimes when I went to bed, the blankets seemed to turn to lead and my lamp on the dresser seemed to fade away. Needless to say, this was very frightening. The spells lasted just a minute or two, and then I would be all right for the rest of the night.

My folks became very concerned over this after awhile and took me to see Dr. Cowles, our family physician, who checked me over and could find nothing. Afterward they made appointments with several other medical doctors and specialists, but none of them could find any clue to what might be wrong.

By that time, I was blacking-out two or three times a day. The problem seemed to hit the first thing in the morning or during times when I had been reading for at least half an hour. Mom might ask me to go get a bucket of water. I'd stand up and down I'd go.

The problem persisted and became more and more a mystery. My folks became more and more concerned. They exhausted every means they could think of in their attempt to find an answer.

One time many years prior to that, my father was thrown from the spring seat of a wagon pulled by run-away horses. He'd hit the ground with great force and was subsequently treated by medical doctors. But he showed no improvement until he decided to go to a chiropractor by the name of Dr. Barnes, who right away found a hip bone out of place. After just a few treatments, Dr. Barnes had dad back in shape again and my father experienced no further problems from that fall for the rest of his life.

Remembering that success, my parents thought maybe Dr. Barnes could diagnose my affliction. He had a practice twenty-five miles away in Galesburg. After a thorough exam by this man, we learned that I had a broken collar bone from an accident I had while very young. Evidently I had also displaced a vertebra at the base of my neck at the same time and it was pressing against a nerve, causing the problem.

He worked with me under heat lamps for awhile and finally took my head in his hands, gave me a twisting jerk and popped the vertebra back into place. Then he told my folks to bring me back in a week.

After we went home, I had no problems for three days. In fact, I only had one black-out that entire week.

During our next visit, he suggested I not go to school that fall, but that instead I should visit him once a week and spend as much time as I could outdoors.

I thought that was pretty good medicine because it was about that time that I had become interested in a .22 single-shot rifle I'd seen in the hardware store in Woodhull. Known as a "Stevens Crack Shot," the rifle had a falling block action and sold for about twelve dollars. Every trip to town meant another trip to go look at that rifle. I had to make sure it was still there. I was saving my money and had hopes of buying it.

Over a period of four months, I saved about seven dollars and then I

23

heard there had been a fire at the hardware store. All I could think of was that rifle and a day or two after the fire, dad and I went to town. I made a bee-line for the store and was delighted to find the rifle still there. Amazingly, due to the smell of smoke and moderate fire damage, the owner had dropped the price to seven dollars. So I ran back to find dad and dragged him back to look the gun over. The damage was rather minimal upon close inspection—a few water spots on the barrel and a bit of smoke stain on the stock. The inside of the barrel was fine and we both knew we could clean up the water spots and stain with a little elbow grease and some oil.

As soon as we were convinced the proprietor wouldn't sell the gun to anyone else, dad took me home to get my money. I had stored it in a box in my dresser drawer. The whole $7 went for the gun and dad loaned me 15¢ more, enough to buy a box of fifty .22 short shells. The long cartridges were 25¢ at the time but he wouldn't loan me that much.

I wasted no time putting that Crack Shot to work. Dad paid me two cents a head for every ground squirrel I killed and I used that money to buy more shells.

There was a big grove of maples on one side of our orchard and a few walnut trees, too. There were a lot of red squirrels that made their homes there. They were delicious when fried like chicken, and our family really liked them. So I soon added them to my hunting plans and that kept us in meat from time to time. During the year off from school, I hunted and fished and wandered along the creeks and throughout the timbered areas around home.

Hickory Barrens was my most favorite spot. It was full of red squirrels, rabbits, bobwhite quail and ground hogs. I hunted the ground hogs in the spring and summer months because I could get twenty-five cents apiece for their scalps or a pair of their ears. They had a bounty because of their tendency to dig too many holes in farmers' pastures. The holes were pretty dangerous for horses and sometimes even the slower moving cows because they could step into the hole and break a leg.

In short, the Stevens Crack Shot was my constant companion. I could be found spending most of my waking hours seeing that the rifle was worth its price many times over.

Anyway, I followed my doctor's orders and as the treatments

progressed, the frequency of my black-outs decreased more and more. Finally they stopped completely. What a relief! At the end of the forty treatments, I had no more symptoms and was ready to start the fifth grade.

We surmised the problem probably had its inception when I had fallen off a grade cellar door to the hard steps below. I was only two or three at the time. I had hit my head and shoulder and shed plenty of tears. But since we lived seven miles from town and had only a horse and buggy for transportation my parents didn't take me to see a doctor.

Mom said I cried considerably for a couple of days but she and dad didn't think the injury was anything too serious. I had broken my collarbone, evidently, but it had healed itself in my young body.

Following my treatments, the only time my neck ever bothered me was when I worked really hard or became extremely exhausted. Unfortunately, that remains true to this day.

My life went back to normal after my year-long therapy vacation. I remember once in the fifth grade looking through an Idaho history book. It left lasting impressions on me, the greatest of which were the pictures of the mining area around Wallace and Kellogg. I wondered at the time if I would ever have the opportunity to travel to that beautiful and fascinating Western state. I was a young boy, mind you, who had never been out of Henry or Knox counties in Illinois and that was a big dream for me then.

That summer when school was out, I went to work in the fields cultivating corn. I ran the horse-drawn binder whenever we cut oats and barley. Dad bought a lot of mules in those days and had broken them to drive and work. We used them in the fields until he sold them to the "hard-road" contractors. Those were days before bulldozers or any of the large dirt-moving equipment we have today. It seems incredible to have lived through such technological advances as we have seen between those early days of the twentieth century and now near the close of it.

The dirt roads and hard roads were built by hand labor and animal-powered "fresnows" and "dirt skips," as they were called. The contractors generally preferred mules because the animals could stand the heat and hard work better than horses.

The Trigg farm was located about half way between our farm and

Woodhull. There was a big white house on it. Earlier, before there was such a place as Woodhull and before any of the other farms were established in that part of Illinois, there had been a dirt road running cross-country from Peoria to Moline and Rock Island (also in Illinois). The road stretched-out following the course of the Mississippi River.

On the same spot where the Trigg house sat, there had been a stage station with an overnight house where travelers could get supper, a bed for the night and breakfast the next morning. Legend has it that many a wealthy traveler had been murdered there and their bodies dumped into a deep well underneath the house. When the way station burned down—so the story goes— they found a number of skeletons in the well.

As a boy, I was never afraid of the dark and I never spent much time worrying about ghosts. I walked past the Trigg house many times after dark and had never been bothered by it until one night when I stayed in town to play basketball and watch a game. I started home about 9:30, after dark. There was no moon that night, but the stars gave me enough light to see the road and keep out of the ditches. I remember a gusty wind was blowing as I made my way home.

Suddenly, about the time I was almost in front of the Trigg house, I made out something white, about five feet tall, moving in front of me maybe a hundred feet away. It raised up and moved back from the road. Then it stopped and stood there.

I froze and my heart all but stopped. For what seemed like an hour (it was probably just seconds) I stood there unable to move, facing my adversary. But, as suddenly as it rose up, the white image crumpled to the ground. As soon as I could get my legs to move, I walked cautiously toward it to see what it was.

The object of my momentary paralysis, as it turned out, was a sheet of white wrapping paper that had probably fallen from a buggy or wagon passing by. I imagine it laid on the ground until a gust of wind lifted it vertically and placed it neatly against the fence. I've never quite forgotten the thrill of that particular incident and can imagine how ghost stories get started.

It must be obvious by now how much I loved the outdoors.

We had a neighbor by the name of John Wilcox who shared that love.

He lived about three-quarters of a mile from our place and he hunted raccoons with his dogs. My folks would let me go with him on Friday and Saturday nights on occasion because I didn't have to go to school the next day.

John would pick me up about seven o'clock in the evening during the fall and winter months. There were many instances when we didn't get home until six or seven the next morning.

He had two good dogs we would turn loose in one of the big creek bottoms, generally near the cornfields. We carried a kerosene lantern as we walked and we used a three- or five-cell flashlight to find the "coons" in the trees after the dogs had done their job.

I usually carried my Stevens Crack Shot to shoot them. Racoons were worth anywhere from twenty to thirty dollars each then, so we had to tree only one a night to make the hunt worthwhile. In those days, that was big money. The farmers in the area always welcomed John and his dogs because the coons had the bad habit of getting into chicken houses where they would kill too many chickens.

We'd bag an occasional skunk, too. A day's wages back then was three dollars. A skunk hide was worth five to seven dollars and the farmers were happy to have us rid their area of these chicken killers, too, so that made the risk worthwhile.

We had a way of catching them so we wouldn't have to put up with the smell. John had a small brown and white rat terrier that would corner a skunk and then bark incessantly until we caught up. One of us would shine a flashlight into the skunk's eyes and the other would work around beside it.

A cornered skunk always holds its tail straight up its back ready to spray when it has to. With the skunk blinded by the flashlight, the other guy could reach down from the side, get a good hold of the tail and quickly jerk the skunk up off the ground. Held up and dangling by its tail, it couldn't use its notorious defense system. So we'd carry the animal by its tail down to the creek where we would stick its head underwater and drown it without wasting a bullet. Holding it by the tail, we didn't have to put up with the smell.

These experiences were always a thrill on any kind of night — rain, snow or whatever didn't matter. I loved hearing the hounds on the trail

27

of a raccoon and then their incessant barking when the animal took to the tree. I have many pleasant memories of coon and duck hunting along the Mississippi and the Edwards river bottoms close to home with our neighbor, John Wilcox.

One Saturday night a barber by the name of "Bun" Wycal from Galesburg came out and hunted with us. Bun also had two good dogs.

It had been raining for several days, so the cornfields were extremely muddy. It was still raining that night, when the dogs treed a raccoon on the other side of Edwards River. The river was running brown with all the muddy water from the fields. We were all looking for a place to cross.

Bun was about twenty feet ahead of me walking along the bank when he yelled, "Here's a good place. It's a sandbar!"

Just as I reached where he was standing, he jumped and disappeared completely. What he thought was a sandbar turned out to be nothing more than dirty foam that had built up ahead of a limb stretching out into the creek. Bun came back up sputtering and spitting water. He then made his way across the creek, figuring he might as well, I suppose.

Though he was carrying the flashlight when he went for his unplanned dip, his batteries had weakened considerably because it was about 1:00 in the morning. The weak batteries, of course, caused his outlook on things to appear pretty dim. He was so anxious to get across the creek and join the dogs that he hadn't taken a very thorough look at his so called sandbar. But he was alright — the water was only five or six feet deep where he had fallen in. Besides, the incident gave John and me quite a few laughs that night at Bun's expense.

Prior to the threshing season, dad bought a cart and harness for my pony so I could haul drinking water to the men in the fields. The water containers were glass or crock gallon jugs with several thicknesses of burlap wrapped around them and sewed together.

After filling the jugs at the pump, I'd soak the burlap to keep the water cold by evaporation while I made my rounds. It took about an hour to make the whole trip from the pump to the field, serve all the field crew, then go on to the steam engine and the threshing machine.

I also hauled water for other farmers with my pony cart and harness. They were farmers we sometimes exchanged farm hands with when there wasn't enough help to go around. My responsibilities meant eight to ten trips like that in a given day for which I earned three dollars for the full day's efforts.

My earnings from this job coupled with money I made from selling furs and rabbits went toward purchasing clothes as well as for buying more .22 shells to replenish my supply. I hunted rabbits in the winter and dressed them out so I could take them to town where I went door to door selling them for twenty-five cents apiece—about the price of a box of fifty .22 "longs" in those days.

I enjoyed being an entrepreneur, though I didn't call it that, and particularly enjoyed the independence my small earnings gave me.

I'll never forget the shock when the stock market broke, though. Dad and I were plowing corn and we had just reached the end of a field close to home. A salesman was waiting for us at the edge of the field. He explained what happened.

That day marked the start of *The Great Depression* which broke thousands of people over the following five to ten year period. Those who lived through those times can imagine what the Soviet people must be going through since Russia fell. With grain, cattle and hog prices dropping, farming was, at best, a break-even venture until 1932 when all the banks for fifty miles in any direction closed and almost everyone around us lost everything they had.

I started high school in Woodhull, while we still lived on the Slawson place. Adventuresome and full of energy, I went out for all the sports.

The footballs and basketballs of that period were made out of leather with a rubber bladder inside. We had very little of the protective gear that modern high school athletes are accustomed to strapping on before a game. In fact, our helmets were made of nothing more than leather.

That same year when I began high school, our landlord asked dad to move so his own son could take over the farm. Dad rented a farm close to Ontario, a small community about twelve miles south of the Slawson Place and about four miles from Oneida—halfway between Woodhull and Galesburg.

That meant I had to change schools and start my sophomore year at Oneida, where I graduated from high school.

I recall one other event that happened at the Slawson place, that influenced my life enough to tell about here. It was my first close look at an airplane on the ground.

We had a stubble field along the road just opposite the Trigg place. My folks had gone to Galesburg with the neighbors that day and I was home alone.

By this time, they had traded the Hupmobile for a new Model T four-door sedan. It was parked in the barnyard near where I was working. I heard an unusual sound and looked up just in time to see a double-winged airplane landing in the stubble field.

I threw caution to the wind immediately and climbed into dad's new Ford. As soon as I had it started, I drove out the gate and down the road toward the Trigg house. Sure enough, there the plane sat, just a ways off the road. The pilot was out and standing next to it, talking to a dozen or so people who had climbed our fence to observe the sight. As quickly as I could, I stopped the car and joined the spectators.

The pilot was a so-called, "barnstormer." He was there to take anyone up for a ride who could afford the five dollar fare and was willing to pay for it. It was a two-seater bi-plane with an open cockpit, one seat for the pilot, the other for a passenger.

I didn't take the flight, but considered that moment to be a pretty dramatic experience considering all the commotion and excitement it caused—along with the fact that I had so impulsively driven dad's car out onto the open road without his permission. I soon decided I'd better get the car home before the folks beat me there and discovered it missing.

My only previous experience driving had been under dad's supervision in the barnyard. I was, however, able to get the automobile turned around and headed back home without a mishap.

When the folks came, I told them about the airplane and what I had done with the car. I got the scolding I probably deserved, but on that particular occasion escaped dad's razor strap, which he held in reserve for my "attitude adjustments."

I have vivid memories of our first real radio in those years of my early teens. It was a Philco with a single tube and ran on a six-volt battery. There was no speaker for it, though. Instead, it had four ear phones that you plugged in. We were close enough to Chicago to get several good stations, but our favorite was WOC (they only used three letters of identification back then) from the Palmer School of Chiropractic in Davenport, Iowa. I can still see my dad after dinner in the evening, sound asleep with a set of earphones on, sitting in his favorite chair.

Considering what we have nowadays, another feature of prominence those years was our crank-type telephone which hung on the wall. It had two large 1.5-volt batteries and operated on a party line. All lines in those days were party lines.

For me, the Slawson place represented the true beginning of the twentieth century because it was there I first began to see the developments that were starting to come out of the industrial age—as they began to appear in and around our household. Yet life there was still simple and uncomplicated.

The unfortunate events associated with the stock market crash and the period of the Great Depression still lay ahead. They were to test all of us in ways we never dreamed possible.

Chapter 4

Two Kinds of Education

Ontario, Illinois, was about twenty miles south of Woodhull. When we moved there, it meant new neighbors, new friends and a completely new school system.

The new farm had two hundred forty acres of rolling land with a nice creek and a pasture on the south side of the road. Another eighty acres of flat land lay on the north side of the road where the house, garage and chicken house were located. The barn, corn crib, hog shed and milking shed were all on the south side.

It was excellent farm land, owned by a businessman who lived in Galesburg fifteen miles to the south.

Ontario wasn't a big town. It consisted of a country church, a parsonage and a farm house or two. It was about four miles due west of Oneida where I attended my last three years of high school. Oneida was a little larger as a farming community with two grocery stores, two drug stores, a theater, some other businesses and several restaurants.

Oneida was cut right in two by the main line of the CB & Q Railroad which ran between Galesburg and Chicago along Highway 34. Because the town was divided by the track, there were two separate business districts with the railroad and highway going down the middle of them. Each of these districts had its own restaurants, grocery store and drug store even though they were less than one hundred and fifty yards apart. But I am happy to say that the geographical split was the only division the town had. There were about six hundred people in Oneida. It was a very unified town and gave me many fond memories.

The house on our new farm was rather old. It had three bedrooms (two of which were upstairs) and a living room and kitchen in the back downstairs. We could walk out the door of the living room to a screened-in porch which served as the main entrance to the house.

We had a fairly large chicken house on this place, located west of the house. We raised Rhode Island Reds as a preference and our flock

32

produced twenty-four dozen eggs each week. We took them to town every Saturday along with the cream from the cows we milked morning and night.

Raw milk was run through a hand-cranked De La Valve cream separator. The thick cream would pour out the spout into either a five- or ten-gallon can which we used for hauling the cream to town.

The money we made from selling the cream and eggs bought our groceries for the week following. My allowance, which by that time had risen from a nickel to a quarter, also came out of that weekly check.

We had a pretty large red barn with a cattle shed on one side. The double corn crib and hog house were also painted red.

The hogs provided some humorous moments from time to time. Since dad kept about twenty-five brood sows each year, we always had to put rings in the noses of the little pigs so they wouldn't root the pasture. We used a special copper ring for this which had two sharp points and was bent in order to fit a pair of hog-ring pliers. One person set the ring in the pliers while the other caught the pig and held it between his legs. The person holding the pliers would then grab the animal's snout with his spare hand and set the ring in the pig's nose. Then we'd lift the pig over the fence and turn him loose.

We generally had a hundred or more pigs to ring in this manner, so by the time a fellow had caught a hundred pigs, wrestled with them to put the ring in their noses and lifted them over the fence nearly four feet high, he knew he had done a piece of work. The fact that the pigs were confined in a pen helped, but the wiggling and squirming gave man and boy ample challenge.

We had ten cows in our milking shed, which we milked every twelve hours at five thirty, morning and night, seven days a week. Dad and I each took five cows apiece most of the time. When he was busy in the fields, however, I would milk all ten. He did the same for me whenever I didn't make it home on time from basketball practice.

I'll never forget one evening when I came home after school and had to go back that evening for play practice. When I arrived home, dad had gone to help the neighbors. He had left word through mom for me to do all the chores and the milking because he knew he'd be late.

I rushed around feeding the horses, cattle and hogs. Then I went into the cattle yard and began herding the dairy cows into their milking shed. Our big bull happened to be in the same yard with the milk cows.

I was in the middle of the yard when the bull appeared from around the corner of the barn. He dropped his head and proceeded to paw the ground as if he were getting ready to charge me. I knew if he did, I wouldn't make it to the fence. At that point, I happened to notice a brick bat lying on the ground in front of me. The pigs had chewed off the corners so that it was about the shape and size of a baseball.

The bull began snorting and shaking his head up and down, which convinced me even more that he intended to charge.

I picked up the brick bat and let fly — low and behold — I hit him right between the eyes! I'm sure his eyes crossed as his tongue came out. His knees buckled, and down he went.

A gun couldn't have done a better job of putting him down. I was sure I had killed him.

Needless to say, I was pretty nervous as I herded the cows to the shed and locked them in their stanchions. The bull lay so still that I was convinced he was dead. Many thoughts rushed through my mind—none of them good. How would I explain this one to my dad?

As I stood in the milking shed door in a state of frenzy, the bull finally moved his head and staggered to his feet. His first few steps reminded me of someone who had drunk too much.

Relieved that fate had gone my way, I milked the cows and carried the milk across the road to the house making two trips. Then I changed my clothes as quickly as I could, jumped into my Model T Ford and made it to the school play practice with five minutes to spare.

It was several days afterward that I finally told dad. I waited until I was absolutely sure the bull was going to live and that it was perfectly okay. Dad just laughed at the story and informed me that, on another occasion, he had also witnessed the bull acting that way, but that dad had been closer to the fence and was able to get away.

Interestingly, my experience with the bull was the last time it ever acted that way toward anyone. I suppose my fate with the bull could have been worse, had I not been so accurate in throwing the brick bat. That was a close call, but it didn't compare to many other experiences in my life that have since convinced me that the Good Lord had his hand on my shoulder. When I think of some of those events, and what perils I have faced, I know He has been there to help me.

One such experience happened one evening after school. We had track practice where I threw the discus, put the shot, and occasionally ran the hundred yard dash and the 220 and 440 relays.

We were going to compete in the Knox County track meet the following Saturday. I was driving my Model T Ford Touring Car and had started for home as soon as the coach dismissed us. I knew there were lots of chores to do, so I wasted no time getting home. Since the high school athletic field was on the other side of the railroad, I had to cross the tracks in the center of town to get home.

This was taken of me one day while I trained for a track meet the following day.

It was late in the day in the early fall and the sun was just above the horizon. The tracks ran east and west, so the sun was setting directly on the tracks. I stopped just short of the crossing but couldn't see the *Zephar*, a fast train with its engine painted bright yellow with a bright red band running around the top. It blended in so well with the brightness and color of the sun that it was virtually invisible to me.

So I stepped on the "low" pedal as I normally would and gave the car gas with the hand throttle. Just as my front wheels reached the track, the engineer saw what I was doing and gave me a blast with his horn. I quickly let the clutch come back to neutral and hit the reverse pedal. In less than a second, I had backed off the track. And just in the nick of time, because something from the train hit the tip of my front fender and left a mark there. That train was traveling about sixty miles an hour and that moment was about as close as I ever want to come with disaster. I can still hear the "tick" of the train on my fender whenever I think about the incident.

I first started trapping muskrat, mink and other furbearers to earn spending money for clothes. With the Depression underway, my folks were having a hard time making ends meet. They both worked hard and

35

put in very long hours, but there was a real need for me to earn money too.

During the trapping season in the fall, I would get up at four in the morning to walk my five- or six-mile trap line before milking and doing other chores I had to do before going off to school.

My friend, John Wilcox, lived too far away for me to go coon hunting with him at this time, so I saved my money and bought two coon dogs of my own. One was a Blue Tic and the other, a Redbone.

With all the school activities I was involved in along with my daily responsibilities on the farm, I could only take the dogs out on Friday and Saturday nights or other evenings when I didn't have to go to school the next day.

There were a lot of rabbits and quail on our farm. So I was able to keep the family in this table fare whenever the season for hunting was open. I used my .22 rifle and hunted with my dad and neighbors from time to time. They used twelve gauge shotguns and number six shot. So I felt pretty good to know that I could shoot as many animals "on the run" with my rifle as they did with their shotguns.

One morning in the spring of 1931, I picked up the neighbor children who rode with me in my Model T Ford Touring Car to school in Oneida. The roads were in pretty good shape except for one area where there was a soft spot in the road bed. Previous traffic had created two ruts about a foot deep through this area and these ruts were a bit wet. As I drove through, a car wheel with a tire on it passed by and went rolling on down the road in front of us.

Instantly I looked about to see if there was another car behind us. There wasn't! And just as quickly as I realized this, my car came to a stop. One of my rear wheels had come off, jumped out of the rut and passed us by. I hadn't felt the sensation because the ruts were so deep that the car had slid along on its under carriage for twenty-five feet or so before coming to a stop.

Fortunately we weren't far from a neighbor's house, so we walked over there and called dad who came and took us on to school in his car. On his way home, he put the wheel back on my car, then pulled it out of the rut and took it to town. There he traded it in on a nice '28 Chevrolet coupe.

36

That Chevrolet looked like a brand new car to me with its green body and black top. It was a beautiful car and I appreciated dad's good sense.

At that time, gasoline cost from ten to fifteen cents a gallon. As I remember I got about thirty miles to the gallon from that Chevrolet, so a buck's worth of gas went a long way.

The Depression hit harder and harder each year as cattle, hog and grain prices continued to drop. Dad couldn't afford anymore outside help by then, so he and I did all the farming. We worked from four in the morning until dark every day. But I was young and in good condition so the work didn't really bother me.

That fall after we had finished the task of threshing at home two neighbor boys, both good friends of mine, and I headed north-northwest in the Chevrolet. We paid our way by following the harvest season and made it all the way to Canada, all of us sharing in the expenses. We lacked the necessary money to stay in hotels, so we just pulled off to the side of the road and slept on blankets and quilts we laid out on the ground. We bought our food in grocery stores along the way and occasionally ate in restaurants we found in some of the farm towns. Fifty to seventy-five cents would buy you a pretty good meal in those days.

We would work one farm until we finished the job and then we'd drive north until we came to another farm that needed our help and could pay us for it. We did that all the way through North Dakota until we came to the Canadian border at which point we turned around and headed home.

We worked our way back through North Dakota during their threshing season. We worked ten-hour days pitching bundles in the fields for three dollars and three meals a day, when we could. Breakfast was generally served about five-thirty in the morning. We'd get a big lunch at noon and then a huge dinner when we came in from the field about six. And where we could, we slept in the hay mow of some barn.

I turned as brown as an Indian that summer because all I wore each day were jeans and a pair of shoes. My hair was light naturally and it turned almost white as it bleached beneath the daily sun. I am quite certain the amount of exposure to the sun I received that summer contributed to the skin cancers on my chin. I had them removed in 1987.

This photo was taken on a ranch in North Dakota after we completed harvest for the farmer who lived there. I wore nothing but a pair of shoes and pants that whole summer. My two "pardners" who traveled with me that summer are the fellow on the left and the one with my arm around his shoulder. The farmer is the third from the left and the other two were his neighbor's eighteen year-old girls who also worked with us on that particular farm.

On our last job in North Dakota, before returning home, we worked with two other young men named Tom and Jim from Detroit Lakes, Minnesota. They asked if they could ride back to their homes with us in the open trunk of the Chevrolet and promised us some good fishing in return for the ride. That sounded pretty interesting to us, so we made them a deal and they rode in the back end with the lid propped open. All went well and soon enough we arrived at their homes where they said "hello" and picked up their fishing gear.

We left Detroit Lakes about eight that evening and drove north probably fifty miles on nothing but dirt roads. Finally we pulled into an area at one end of a lake where several boats were tied up along the shore. The Indians used them for harvesting wild rice, they told us.

It was too late to fish by then, so all five of us slept on the ground. Early in the morning one of the fellows tapped me on the shoulder to awaken me and whispered, "Let's go catch some walleyed pike for breakfast!"

Since we slept in our clothes, it didn't take us long to get into a boat and push off. Tom took the oars and gave me the pole and reel, armed with a small spoon. We hadn't gone a hundred feet from shore when I had a terrific strike. I fought the fish and got it along side the boat. Tom reached over and grabbed it just back of the head and brought it aboard. It was a Northern Pike about two feet long and weighed about seven pounds. But before I knew what was happening he had unhooked it and thrown it back into the lake with the disgusted comment, "G— D— Snake!"

That was the biggest fish I had caught in my entire life up to that point so when Tom threw it back, I was tempted to break one of the oars over his head. I had read stories about Great Northern Pike in *Sports Afield* and *Field and Stream*. The articles had always indicated Pike were prize game fish. I guess Tom saw the look of disappointment or shock on my face when I asked, "What did you do that for?"

He explained that Northern Pike were much too boney and not all that good to eat and added, "We want walleyes for breakfast."

Then he resumed rowing and I started fishing again. The lake was absolutely beautiful. There were no buildings and no sign of man anywhere you could see. We had driven down a very narrow road through large plots of timber to get to it and in most places around the lake the trees extended right up to the shore line, though the area where the Indians kept their boats was somewhat of a shallow bay with a channel opening to the lake through the wild rice.

The water was clear blue with small stringlets of vapor rising off the surface into the early morning light. It was so quiet and beautiful that I'll never forget it.

After that pike incident, I caught six nice walleye weighing two to three pounds apiece. Tom figured by then we had enough for breakfast so we headed back across the lake with my catch.

The rest of the crew was up and had a good fire going as we landed the boat on the shore. Tom and I cleaned and filleted the fish. As he and Jim had brought along flour and the other necessary ingredients as well as the tools for frying, they cooked them over an open campfire, which they knew how to do very well. We had "nearly raw" fried potatoes, bread and breaded fish. What a great breakfast it was!

After eating, Tom and Jim took my two buddies out fishing for an hour or so. They caught another half-dozen nice walleyes for our friends from

Detroit Lakes to take back to their families. Having had a great experience, we loaded up, drove them back home and headed out for Illinois.

We got home about a week before it was time to start my senior year of high school. By this time in my high school career, I had become deeply involved in basketball, track and softball. We didn't have enough boys in our school for football.

Our basketball court was in an old church and was so narrow that the sidelines were less than a foot from the walls. On one end the basket sat right up against the end of the building, while it was on a frame in front of the stage at the other end. The only seating for spectators was on the stage, while the coach and substitutes used a small alcove in the middle of the east side. In spite of our facility, Oneida won the Knox County Championship in 1931 and placed second in 1932. I played on the team all three years of my high school experience.

One night we had a game with our neighboring town of Altona. I was six feet tall, weighed 180 pounds and didn't have one ounce of fat. My height was an obvious advantage because I could jump pretty high, rebound well and tip the ball into the basket. That particular evening we were in the last quarter of the game when someone shot for a basket. I came down the floor pretty fast and leaped as high as I could to pick the ball off the board. In the same moment, while I was stretched-out in mid-air, one of the Altona players managed to get his shoulder into a deadly position for my descent.

I lit straddling his shoulder with all my weight on a part of the male anatomy that is not in anyway immune to such an impact. The pain was so great I passed out. They carried me off the floor, put in a substitute and resumed the game.

Altona had the advantage by one point. Finally, when the pain had diminished somewhat, I was able to get up. With just a minute left in the game, the coach asked if I was ready to go back in.

"Yes," I responded, painfully, and in I went. The action was intense in that last minute. Both teams missed several shots. With only two seconds to go, someone passed me the ball. I set my feet, made a jump shot and won the game!

My glory did not last as long as the pain, though. I was in bed for the next two days and remained pretty sore for about a week. The coach never sent me to a doctor nor even suggested that I see one. Times were different then.

Aside from basketball I played catcher on the softball team. We had a pretty good team one year and won the county championship. But next to basketball, my favorite sport was track. I could run the 100-yard dash

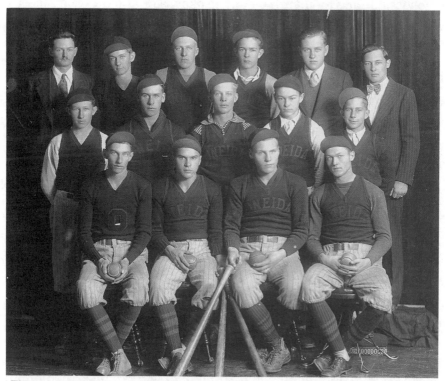

Though I enjoyed some of the other sports more than baseball, we still won the District Championship in 1931. This photo gives a pretty good idea of the height advantage I had in basketball.

in ten seconds flat. I liked to pole vault, too, and could go more than eleven feet, but the coach wouldn't let me participate because he was afraid I would damage my shoulders for the shot and the discus. I was not necessarily graceful in the pole vault. In those days, they used wood shavings and sawdust in the pole vault and high jump pits and sometimes the bedding got rather thin and my lack of grace caused my landings to be a bit uncomfortable.

During my senior year, I won our district championship in both the shot and the discus, so I guess my coach's wisdom played out. The victory qualified me to compete in the state meet in Champaign, Illinois. But there was one problem: the school had only four dollars and sixty-five cents in its athletic fund so they could not pay my way.

I wanted to go so badly however, that I decided to hitchhike to Champaign-Urbana — a distance of some one hundred and fifty miles. My folks said they thought it would be okay, so I asked Coach Moser and he agreed that it would be alright if it meant a chance for me to participate.

"We'll give you all the money we have," he said and handed me the $4.65. But the coach was also a member of the Tau Kappa Epsilon fraternity at the University of Illinois in Champaign, so he called to see if they had an extra bed and whether they might put me up during the track meet, which they did. They were great, fed me a couple of meals on top of that and made me feel right at home.

To launch the trip, I started out early and traveled all day. I walked some and caught a lot of short rides. After finally finding the fraternity house and eating a good meal, I welcomed my bunk in hopes of being in good shape for the next day which was Saturday, the day of the meet.

I got up, had breakfast with the guys, grabbed my track shoes and uniform and walked eagerly over to the athletic field to sign up for my two events. You might imagine that was quite an experience for a country boy. I did not win or even place, but I did surpass my previous bests in both the discus and shot put. It was a great experience just participating.

Can you imagine any coach today giving one of his students less than five dollars and sending him off hitchhiking to a track meet one hundred and fifty miles away? But those were the days of the Depression after all, and you had to work around problems like the lack of money in any way you could.

Also during my senior year, I worked in a Standard Oil service station which was located across the tracks and on the other side of the highway from our school.

My folks decided to move back to the Woodhull area in the fall of that year. This time they rented the Shetler place. It was two miles north of Woodhull. They moved just before the first of the year.

Because of my involvement in basketball, track and other senior class activities, I didn't want to move. So I found a rather spacious room over the post office, which I rented for six dollars a month until school was out. It even had its own bathroom!

My mother fixed me up with the necessary dishes, pots, pans and bedding and let me use a three-burner kerosene stove to cook on. I slept on a steel cot and was a full-fledged bachelor until I graduated in May.

Since there were no chores to do, I had the opportunity to work in the station both before and after school. I jumped at this chance to make enough money to pay the rent and buy something to eat. I loved fried egg sandwiches with ketchup, so that seemed to be what I ate most of the time. My folks also furnished me with home-canned meat, vegetables, and fruit, so my menu did have a little variety.

The owner of the oil station was also the Standard Oil distributor. Everyone called him "Boot" because along with the fuel he hauled to the local farmers, he carried distilled liquor as well — in other words, he was a bootlegger.

He openly carried one-gallon cans of alcohol on his delivery truck during the entire time I knew him, and no one ever bothered him about it. He was a nice, pleasant fellow who was born and raised in Oneida and who knew everyone.

All the while I lived in town above the post office, I opened his station in the morning and ran it until eight-thirty at which point a man relieved me and kept it open until five in the afternoon. Then I would return from school and work until closing, usually around seven.

One morning, however, my replacement didn't show up until around five minutes to nine. School started at nine, but the school house was only about a hundred and fifty yards away on the other side of the highway and tracks. Running as fast as I could, I thought I could make it without being late.

The highway gave me no problem, but the tracks were another thing. This was the main line and there were lots of trains passing through carrying cattle, hogs and grain on toward Chicago. In addition, there were always passenger trains passing through town and you never knew when one might be coming.

As I traversed the first rail of the track, I slipped or caught my foot somehow and went head first into the opposite rail and knocked myself out cold. I must have laid there between the rails for ten minutes, because when I finally came to and made my way on to school, I was fifteen minutes late. It seemed once again that someone had His hand on my shoulder because the trains ran through there at that time of the year less than thirty minutes apart and no one had noticed me lying there.

The first person to see me with a bump on the side of my head was our principal, Mr. Ekstrand, who suggested I lie down for a while before going into class. It was nice to have that kind of attention when you needed it. Clarence Ekstrand was a very fine principal who oversaw all twelve grades in Oneida. We called him "Mr. Clarence Ekstrand." His brother, Fred, was one of our coaches and equally respected. We also had very nice and extremely capable teachers. There was no hanky panky: honesty, integrity and patriotism were the order of the day, every day.

As I look back and reflect on those hard times when money was scarce, it seems that hard work was the only solution to our problems, regardless of the situation. Those who experienced the Depression now recognize for the most part what an education it was. It certainly left an impression on me.

As a result, I have always vowed never to go into debt with anyone. Whenever I bought a house or something else on payments, I had a job and knew what my payments would be. I knew how much we would have to have in order to purchase clothes and food or anything else before I ever put my name on the dotted line. I also made payments in advance, whenever possible, so that the extra payments would tide us over if something happened to my job or if a major illness struck our family. I have always felt, throughout my life since then, that making it through the Depression was an education every bit as valuable as the one I received in school.

Chapter 5

What Once Was Lost

Living alone in an apartment during the last half of my senior year was far from boring. Because of the Depression, my folks could not help me pay for my apartment and that's why I spent so much time working at the Standard Oil station. The job paid for my rent, clothes and any food I wished to buy, though as I've mentioned the folks supplied me with goods from home.

Besides working before and after school at the station, I did my own cooking and housework, so my only available study time was just before bed each night. I also devoted many hours to practice for track and basketball. Yet with all these extra responsibilities, I still managed to graduate from high school with a B+ average.

Right after graduation I packed everything I owned into my '28 Chevrolet coupe and headed north to join my parents and sister in Woodhull.

Once back at the farm, I worked long, hard hours with dad in the fields all summer and into the fall. We toiled many days until dark, especially during the oat and wheat harvest. Many times we would return to the fields after dinner to shock the grain by moonlight.

Being in excellent health, I could work all day until dark, change clothes and go to a dance until the wee hours of the morning. I remember several times driving into the barnyard only to find dad coming out of the house with milk pails. But he would only shake his head and smile. I don't remember him ever saying anything negative about my all night escapades. I guess

Upon graduation in 1932, I hoped for adventure, but I had no idea of the many good things ahead.

he knew how hard I worked from daylight to dark seven days a week, so as long as I did my share, he never said a thing about how I used my own time on the side.

Soon after graduation, I received word that I had won an athletic scholarship to Knox College in Galesburg. I started college there that fall. My parents were somewhat ambivalent though. My mother wanted me to go and my father wanted me to stay home and help with the farm. Finally they agreed to let me try it for a year and see if I couldn't finance it myself as there wasn't enough money at home to pay for my attending college.

I had a monetary advantage in that my mother's sister Myrtle lived with her husband in Galesburg and the two of them offered to let me stay there during the school year.

My uncle, Glen Tribler, worked as a district manager for Standard Oil Company. He had an office on the southside of Galesburg and knew of a gas station that needed extra help. It wasn't long before the owner had worked out a schedule that would allow me to attend classes, work part time during the week and full time on the weekends.

In those days we had to hand pump the gas up into a ten-gallon glass tank by using a lever on the side of the pump. The tank had marks cut into the glass by which we measured the amount. Once I did that I could feed the gas into the automobile tanks by gravity, allowing the gas to flow down a rubber hose and through a hand-held nozzle.

We offered three grades of gasoline: ethyl, regular and economy. A customer could buy the blue economy gas for just 10 cents a gallon or "ten gallons for a buck!" as they would say.

I can't say my first year of college was all work and no play. Within the first week, I had been rushed by Tau Kappa Epsilon, the same fraternity I had stayed at to attend the state high school track meet the year before. I liked them so I signed the pledge.

Aunt Myrtle and her husband were pretty upset with me for that. They didn't feel I could afford it. I suppose they were correct because every dime I had or earned, it seemed, went for some necessity required by the fraternity.

I enjoyed college and seemed to be doing really well until tragedy struck. I turned out for the freshman football team and was assigned to play right end. During the very last game of the season, I caught a forward pass and ran into what seemed like the whole opposing team.

After being tackled by the initial barrage, they piled up on me as they often did in those days. When everyone finally got up, I couldn't.

Someone had forced his knee hard into my groin and I was in severe pain. They had to carry me off the field and I lay in bed for two weeks. The consequence was more severe than just the pain, as the injury forced me to drop out of college and return home to live with my parents the rest of the winter. I was no help to dad either because the doctor told me to refrain from lifting. I could do only light work.

That spring I started a job running a country service station about fifteen miles from home, near Ophiem, Illinois. I pumped gas, sold candy and ice cream and watched over two nickel slot machines that had been set up in the station.

My boss was Perry Stevens who is still a friend after all these years. He was single and slept in a room near the back of the building. He gave me another single bed in his room and that's where I slept when I was there. Aside from being my boss, Perry was a contract painter and paper hanger. He usually left for work around seven-thirty in the morning and returned somewhere between five or six in the late afternoon.

I had the responsibility of running the station while he worked his trade. When he took over station duties in the evening, I was free to spend the evening anyway I wanted and would go out with my friends whenever I had the opportunity.

Despite having a job, there was never much money and so going out once a week was about all any of us could afford. Three or four other fellows my age liked to attend the Saturday night dances. I did, too, and would go with them. Our two favorite places were the Roof Garden, about twenty miles east of us in Galesburg, and the Armory, thirty miles to the west in Davenport, Iowa.

Those were the days of the big band sound, so we most often danced to the music of Glen Miller, Jan Garber, Lawrence Welk, Artie Shaw and Sammy Kaye as well as other top names from the big band era.

One Saturday night I went into Galesburg with my friends to dance at the Roof Garden. We danced all evening long and then they dropped me off in front of the station, about 2:00 in the morning. It had been a beautiful night with a full moon, and I remember walking up the steps, putting the key in the door and pushing it open quietly.

Perry's bed was on the left, just inside the door. When I opened it to go in, the full moon made the place almost as light as day. Perry was up on the edge of his bed in an instant pointing a .38 caliber revolver directly at my stomach. He was no more than a foot away from me. My heart stopped. He was cocking the hammer and appeared as if he were actually going to shoot. His eyes were glassy and he must have just come out of a deep sleep. Then, with my heart pounding, I uttered the words, "Perry, it's me — Don!"

To my relief, he lowered the gun. Sweat immediately broke out all over his face. We kept quite a bit of money around the station and Perry had made a habit of sleeping with the loaded pistol beneath his pillow. Whenever he and I get together we reminisce over that close shave. He tells me how grateful he is that I spoke so calmly in telling him who I was. I am always reminded by these conversations that someone indeed had His hand on my shoulder that night.

By late summer I had recuperated enough from my football injury to go back to work. At that time, Gus Johnson, a construction company owner who lived next door to Grandmother Johnson's, offered me a job building "hard road."

He had a contract to widen a paved road north of Cambridge, Illinois, about twenty-five miles northwest of Woodhull. My first assignment was to help clean the edge of the old pavement while they graded the road to prepare it for the concrete.

That lasted about a week, when one afternoon the boss came over to me and asked me to take his Model A Ford roadster on a run to town to pick up several items for him.

"Make it as fast as you can," he added.

I proceeded to do just that — over some pretty rough roads that featured numerous king-sized bumps and holes you had to pass over. The car had, at one time, sported a rumble seat in the back with a lid. He had removed both of them to allow it to be used like a pickup.

I thought he would be pleased that I had gotten back so fast, but when I drove up after returning, I saw his face take on a ghostly appearance. He had forgotten to take out half a case of dynamite that he'd left sitting in the middle of an assortment of loose, heavy tools. By itself the dynamite wouldn't have been much to worry about, but he forgot to remove the fuse caps too, which adorned the dynamite sticks. If one of the loose tools had bounced into the box of dynamite and hit on those sensitive caps, that would have been the last of Don Samuelson's memoirs. The Almighty hand was nudging my shoulder that day too, it seems.

The following day the boss assigned me to a different job. I joined two other workers unloading sand and gravel from the rail cars for use in a concrete mixer located near the railroad tracks.

We used what they called the "tripod and skip" method to unload the sand and gravel from the rail cars. The tripod consisted of two 4x4s about five feet long bolted together at the top to form an A-frame. Another 4x4 was fastened to the top of the A-frame and extended across the rail car where it was clamped to the top of the far side. The A-frame was clamped to the top of the side of the rail car that had the unloading chute which guided the sand and gravel into piles close to the big cement mixer.

A pulley hung from the underside of the point of the tripod. A half-inch steel cable ran through the pulley and the end in the rail car was fastened to a dirt skip that we used to unload the sand and gravel. The skip had two wooden handles about three feet long and a body shaped similar to a scoop shovel that would hold about a half a ton of sand or gravel.

The other end of the cable was fastened to a winch powered by an automobile motor fastened to a heavy skid anchored to the ground out past the sand and gravel piles.

The man operating the winch had two levers, a brake and a clutch to control the cable. My partner and I handled the skip in the rail car. Finished, we would drag the empty skip to the end of the rail car, signal the winch operator who would then engage the clutch and that started the winch pulling in the cable. When this happened, we pointed the skip into the sand or gravel to fill it and then guided it up to the tripod where we dumped it on the chute to empty it.

Two of us could unload as much as two hundred fifty tons of sand and gravel in an eight hour period, as well as change the tripod and move the cars into position for the next load with a couple of rail jacks.

As luck would have it, I had another close call on that job too. The train crew came to pick up our empty rail cars and leave us with loaded

49

ones. The engineer, thinking the coupling was locked, started the train back toward us very quickly. He soon realized the problem. When he tried to stop, the uncoupled cars kept on racing toward us.

My partner noticed what was happening, yelled and then took off over the side of the car we were unloading. From my vantage point, I could see the other man below shoveling sand into the mixers. He was in between the cable and another piece of machinery and had no way to escape.

Instinctively, I jumped on the edge of our rail car and unhooked the pulley that extended from a hook on the top of the tripod. The cable dropped quickly and the man was able to get out of the way. But just as I did this, the loaded gravel cars collided with the car I was standing on and sent me flying. Luckily I bounced off the tripod and landed in the sand. If I had been deflected in the other direction, I would have been thrown into the retaining wall which kept the sand and gravel from getting onto the tracks. If that had happened, I would have fallen onto the tracks beneath the moving gravel cars. That alternate fall would have been about twelve feet besides, and there were plenty of braces and posts there for me to hit my head against, had I gone that way.

The cement mixer operator witnessed the whole incident and related the story to my boss, Mr. Johnson, when he came in from the highway construction project in the afternoon to see how things were going. He came over and personally thanked me for saving the other man's life.

Since the wooden gravel chute was bolted to the railroad car we were working, it did not survive the collision. As the car moved suddenly down the track, it took the chute with it and slammed it into several of the posts which extruded above the retaining wall shattering it to pieces. About all that was left of that chute were pieces equivalent to kindling. The next day I was assigned the pleasant duty of building a new chute because, after all, we could not continue without one.

Late that summer after we had finished the highway construction job, I moved back to my folk's place and helped dad with the fall projects such as plowing and picking corn.

The Depression was getting worse day by day. Money was scarce and many of the folks around the countryside were worried. Grain and livestock prices continued to decline as they had for months. Most of the farms in that area were rented or leased on a crop-share basis. The renters would furnish the labor, seed, fertilizer and equipment and generally got to keep 60% of the grain they raised. The landowners would take the remaining 40% at harvest time as rent for their land.

The farmer usually stored his share in his bin or corn crib where it was used to feed his livestock and the land owner generally had his sent off to the elevator to be sold. If the farmer had the storage room however, as some did, he would keep all the grain stored, hoping to get a better price at a later date.

In the fall we always faced the task of hauling and spreading the fertilizer generated on the farm. We would clean out the cattle and horse barns, the chicken coops and hog houses and spread the manure out over the farmland with an old horse-drawn manure spreader. After that we would plow the fields.

That particular fall, after we'd picked our corn, I helped another farmer about ten miles away, south of Alpha, pick his corn. As I remember it, dad had talked to him in town and mentioned that we had just finished our picking. I was happy to have the job.

His name was Dick Howell and besides me, he had three hired hands picking corn that year. Two of them were migrant workers from Kentucky. They were following the corn harvest north.

Mr. Howell owned several teams of draft horses and one team of small spirited mules. He was aware of our experience with our own mules in that dad used to break them to work. Because Howell had this knowledge, he asked my dad if I would consider helping with his corn harvest — with the understanding that I would use the team of mules.

The pay was five cents a bushel and he thought I would be able to pick a hundred to a hundred and twenty bushels per day. That would add up to five or six dollars a day, so with that in mind, I accepted. The mules were well matched. They were dark brown and weighed nine hundred to a thousand pounds apiece.

Mr. Howell gave me a bedroom in his house so I could stay on his farm during the harvest. Every morning at four o'clock we were up feeding and harnessing the teams. Then we'd go back into the house for a big breakfast of bacon and eggs, fried potatoes, bread with butter and jam, and coffee. As soon as we were done, we would go out to hitch up the wagons and head for the fields.

I met the two migrant workers that first morning. One said to me, "I understand you are going to drive that little team of mules."

"You bet," I replied.

"I'm glad," he commented with relief, "because I wouldn't get close to them for anything in the world."

Apparently the mules had these two guys buffaloed! Granted, they were high-spirited and they liked to play. In fact they would put their heads down and kick their hind feet into the air just for fun. But I always made a point of talking to them whenever I harnessed them and they never made any attempt to kick me during the entire three weeks that I worked them. In addition they knew how to work!

It was rather wet that fall and the fields had become pretty muddy. Nonetheless, that little team could pull a full wagon of corn through the mud holes more efficiently and with more ease than the draft horses that weighed twice as much. Because the corn crop wasn't the best that year, we had to work really hard to get more than a hundred bushels a day. With the wet, nasty weather, we worked long hours trying to get it out of the field.

I never could pick as fast as my dad, who in his prime could bring in three sixty-bushel loads a day. Besides, with this quality of corn, we had to cover a lot more territory before we had a full load. During that harvest I averaged two fifty-five to sixty bushel loads a day.

I swear those mules could tell time. If I tried to make an extra trip around the field before noon or quitting time, they would put up a fuss. If I went in the direction away from home across the field, they would dally and stall. I would end up yelling at them to move along as I picked.

They were regular clowns whose antics clearly showed their feelings. They liked to stick their heads down and kick almost as high as the wagon box. But I believe they were always careful to look around and check out my location and to make sure they didn't hit anything solid like the double tree or the wagon.

I really enjoyed working with them when I curried them early in the morning before harnessing. They loved to have me scratch their heads, especially around the ears. They actually got to be like a couple of pets for me. Meanwhile, the two migrants from Kentucky and everyone else remained in fear of even walking behind them — something I did all the time. Everyone else always gave them a wide berth.

I had worked fourteen hours a day, six days a week for the entire three week period and my check at the end of the job was about one hundred dollars plus room and board.

Much of our entertainment in those days centered around family picnics or fishing trips to local lakes and rivers. Alpha Lake was about four miles straight west of our farm. The railroad company had dammed up a small stream about half a mile from the little town of Alpha to form the lake.

The village of Alpha was located on the main rail line between Moline, Rock Island and Galesburg, Illinois. These were the days of coal-fired steam engines. Water was pumped from the lake to large wooden storage tanks located along the tracks. Every train traveling through would stop for refilling its water tanks. It took a lot of water to keep those old steamers going.

Alpha Lake was about a mile long, four hundred feet wide and thirty feet deep near the dam. After the dam had been constructed and the lake filled-up, a group of people from the area built a clubhouse and two bath houses, one for men and one for women and formed a corporation named the *Crescent Lake Club*. They also hauled in truckloads of sand and made a swimming area complete with a nice sandy beach. The entire project was financed by selling yearly family memberships for twenty dollars each.

Aside from serving as a nice swimming area, the lake featured sunfish, crappie, black bass and catfish which provided good fishing. About six hundred families, including almost everyone within a twenty-mile radius, bought memberships.

Crescent Lake Club, of course, was named for the shape the water made as it filled in around the shoreline. It wrapped itself around a small hill which was developed into a picnic area with well made tables, benches and fire pits for small campfires. The total picnic area covered about five acres of nice grass which was kept mowed all summer. It became so popular that most folks called it Crescent Lake rather than Alpha Lake after that.

Another unusual aspect of the Crescent Lake Club was that for about ten weeks during the summer, the organization hosted free movies for members. A large movie screen was erected at the bottom of a naturally sloping basin on the side of the hill across from the clubhouse. The organizers built plank benches into the side of the hill in a slight curve facing the screen. As I remember it, about fifteen rows of seats extended up the hillside. The movie projector was above the seats. The black and white silent movies began just after dark every Tuesday night.

The movies would draw a crowd of families every week. They came early, for the most part, to enjoy a picnic during the last daylight hours before the movie. When all the seats were full, the rest of the audience sat on blankets placed on the ground or on the grass to watch. Several hundred people of all ages attended the shows each week.

During Depression times, this kind of set-up was great for the entire family. For twenty dollars, they could swim, fish, go boating, enjoy a picnic and see ten moving picture shows a year. This setting enabled me to learn to swim and fly fish. Little did I dream at the time that in a few years I would be the manager and caretaker of the club and that I would run it for two years—but that's another story.

One event in my life that I've never forgotten occurred after an evening swim following a movie at the Crescent Lake Club. We lived at the Shetler Place at the time and I was home helping my folks. I was about twenty years old and drove my '28 Chevrolet coupe with a heavy foot on the gas pedal. Whenever there was a clear, straight road ahead, I'd have my foot pressing the pedal to the floor or close to it.

On this particular evening, it was a Tuesday I believe, we had finished the chores, eaten supper and were ready to go to the show at the lake. My folks and my sister, Aileen, drove out of the barnyard as I was getting into my car. They took the straight route to the lake, just four miles away.

I drove into town, a distance of an extra mile, to pick up a package at one of the stores. Then I headed out the highway for three miles and cut back another mile to the road my folks had taken. By the time I hit that road, I was just one mile from the entrance to the lake grounds.

There was a narrow, arched steel bridge in that stretch that sat on a road fill in such a way that it had a twenty foot drop-off on both sides. But since there was no traffic ahead of me, I really cruised through there — so to speak. As it was, everything went great and I beat my folks to the lake. I pulled into the parking lot across from the club house, grabbed my swimming suit and headed for the men's dressing room.

Several of my friends were already in the water. As soon as I could, I joined them and we swam and dove off the high dive until it was almost dark enough to start to the movie. We then watched the show from eight o'clock until about ten. Afterward, Edward Carlson, one of my friends, asked for a ride home. I said I would enjoy his company.

As we walked toward my car, we could see that the departing traffic was bumper to bumper, so we stood for a while and admired the light of the full moon rippling in the water. It was beautiful and it was a nice warm night, too.

"Let's go swimming until the traffic clears out," Ed said.

I agreed and it took just long enough for us to change back into our suits before we were back in the lake. We talked and swam and talked some more. For a time, we sat on the diving platform raft in the center of the lake. It was midnight when we decided to get dressed and head for home.

The scene was dramatically different by then from what it had been two hours before. My car was the lone vehicle in the lot, as we were the last people to leave the lake.

When we climbed in, I turned the key and stepped on the starter. When the motor fired up, I put the car in reverse and proceeded to back out of the parking spot. As I took hold of the steering wheel to turn the back end of the vehicle to the left, it spun in my hand like a top and the car did not turn to the right as I had intended. There was no clue that anything had broken when I turned the wheel.

We got out, checked thoroughly and decided that something had broken within the steering mechanism. But we couldn't determine what it was.

Fortunately the clubhouse had a crank telephone, so I called my dad and got him out of bed. He came to pick us up and took us both home. The next morning, we took a chain and pulled my car into the Chevrolet garage in Woodhull. Since we could not steer the vehicle, we fastened down the tie rods so the front wheels would remain straight. Whenever we came to a corner, we had to work it around by hand or slide the front end. Although the trip to the garage was a slow, tedious process, we finally made it and had no serious problems.

The mechanic in the shop discovered that the steering shaft had broken in two inside a worm gear which meshed with other gears to control the direction of the front wheels. The two pieces of broken shaft were worn and black, which indicated that it had been broken for some time. The only thing holding them together was a small half moon key which locked the worm gear to the shaft. Apparently when I parked the car or tried to back out the evening before, the key snapped off.

How lucky can one be? I often think of what would have happened if the key had snapped just before I flew over the bridge that afternoon. Or what would have happened if it had snapped while I met a car or passed over a deep ravine or ditch. I shudder to think about it! But again—the hand was on my shoulder.

During the fall and winter months of 1933 and 1934, I ran a ten mile trap line. Walking it, I wore out a new pair of hip boot each year. We still lived on the Shetler place and by that time, I had about sixty traps which included Victor #1's, #2's and about a dozen jump traps.

Every morning about four I would get up, leave the house and follow a series of hedge fences for about a mile until I reached a small creek. It was west for about four miles where I hit a fork of another creek extending southeast to about a mile from our house on the south. The traps were set for muskrats in the creek and for mink in several drainage tiles that ran into the creek. During each season I caught more than a hundred muskrat which brought me from $1.00 to $3.75 apiece. In addition, I caught about a dozen skunks a year and an equal number of weasel. Mink, however, were

Part of my trapline catch. The bigger hide was a racoon; the thinner one, a mink; the rest were muskrat.

a real prize because they brought fifteen to twenty dollars each. One year a raccoon happened on to one of my traps, so I had it tanned and made into a small rug which I still have to this day.

Trapping gave me several hundred dollars to buy gas, clothes, boots, and other necessities. Whenever I walked the line, I carried a Harrington and Richards .22 caliber pistol in the holster on my hip. It came in handy for shooting cottontail rabbits which I would find resting in holes in the snow or in the grass along the creek.

I usually dressed the rabbits right away and hung them on a clothesline in the wash shed when I returned. Later I'd take them to town where I'd go door-to-door and sell them for a quarter each. Though we used some of them for our own food, the profit from the rabbits bought new .22 shells which was important because during that time my folks had a hard time buying even basic staples such as flour and sugar.

Those were the two last years my family lived on the Shetler farm. By the end of 1934, grain and livestock prices had hit rock bottom and there was no money. What hurt my folks the worst about the Depression was that they had purchased eighty acres of good farm land for three hundred dollars an acre when they first started farming and had maintained their payments faithfully every year until the financial disaster caused the banks to close. They had bought the land on a contract for twenty-four thousand dollars and had paid all but five thousand of it. Unable to pay the balance, they lost it.

At that time, corn was selling for fifteen cents a bushel and oats went for five cents a bushel. A young five-hundred pound steer sold for about ten dollars—if you could find someone who had ten dollars!

The only good memory I have about those two years was that I never went hungry. Dad butchered a beef and several nice hogs, which mom canned. Our large garden helped supplement the meat supply and the cellar was full of canned fruit, beef, pork and vegetables. We worked hard and long hours for next to nothing, but we never went to bed hungry.

Another problem encountered by my folks and thousands just like them was the difficulty marketing agricultural products. To sell grain, you had to make an appointment with the manager of the grain elevator two or three weeks in advance. It didn't matter that you might be selling just one load of corn or oats. The appointment was necessary if the farmer expected to get paid.

The ultimate low came one day when the sheriff, who had been a boyhood chum of my dad's drove into our yard. With tears in his eyes, he served my father with foreclosure papers. It wasn't the sheriff's fault; the courts had instructed him to serve the papers on my dad and most of the neighbors for miles around. "Sheriff sales" occurred at farm after farm around us until finally it was our turn. Most all the banks had closed within 50 miles in every direction from our home.

My folks were allowed to keep their personal items and the household furniture, stoves, washing machine and so forth. Lumped together, these items were valued at five hundred dollars. The officials allowed dad to keep the team of black horses, too, which he had owned from the first day he started farming. Midget and Queen were their names and they had given me many pleasant hours after I graduated from riding my pony. I had ridden them all over the countryside and they were the team I had started plowing corn with when I was only eleven years old. They were gentle and they always came running when they were called. We kept them through the winter because Mr. Shetler, who owned the farm, allowed us to stay on. In the spring, dad sold them and we moved to town.

Adding insult to injury was the blow both my folks and my grandmother received when the banks closed. Grain prices dropped so low, we also lost the 160 acre farm where I was born. The county sold it for the twelve hundred dollars in deliquent taxes. Dad was having a tough time, himself, and couldn't help his mother when she needed it. He had tried desperately to find someone who would help him pay enough of the taxes to keep the county from selling the farm, but to no avail. He had no luck. A bank in Chicago bought my father's notes on earlier loans. They kept the notes renewed each year, so the folks couldn't own any property.

Many years later in 1947, right after World War II, I went back to Illinois on my vacation. I took the opportunity to contact the man who still held dad's notes and asked if he would have lunch with my dad and me. His name was Hitchner.

He agreed to meet us. I had settled in Sandpoint, Idaho, by then and it just so happened that this fellow Hitchner had a brother who also lived in Sandpoint. The two brothers owned Hitchner and Hitchner Cedar Pole Company in Sandpoint. One served as a Chicago banker while the other ran the pole yard.

After meeting the banker at his office, we took him to a nice restaurant. Mr. Hitchner was a pleasant man and as soon as he learned that I knew his big brother in Sandpoint, the conversation became very congenial. I then told him of my dad's circumstance of not being allowed to own land. He confessed he knew nothing of the situation. I suspected the bank had bought the notes back in the '30's for mere pennies on the dollar when the balance was at five thousand, so I asked Hitchner if he would sell the note back to me for five hundred — ten cents on the dollar. Then I laid five one-hundred dollar bills on the table to assure him it would be a cash deal.

He didn't hesitate for a second and said he would accept the offer.

"As soon as we finish lunch," he said, "we'll go back to the bank and turn the note over to you marked PAID IN FULL."

That day in Chicago turned out to be a beautiful day — much better than we had ever hoped when we left home that morning. Needless to say, Mr. Hitchner's gesture took a big load off my mother and father and they were much happier after that.

Chapter 6

Days Around Crescent Lake

When my folks were forced to move to Woodhull in 1933, they rented a really nice, modern bungalow at the edge of town for $25 a month. It was a one-story house with two bedrooms, a full basement and a floored attic, where I slept. My sister had one bedroom and my folks, the other. The house was located right next to a new high school that had been built five or six years before the Depression hit the hardest.

Since my dad had worked as a carpenter before he started farming, he was able to get small carpentry jobs around town. He also helped many of his friends who had been fortunate enough to stay on their farms. Having worked so hard all his life and then losing everything, my dad went through some difficult emotional adjustments.

One of his boyhood friends owned a hardware store in Woodhull. His name was Claude Weaver. The Depression had brought him much suffering too. He was a really nice man with a wonderful family. Unfortunately after we had moved to town, my dad and Claude started drinking. Since this was during Prohibition, they bought the alcohol from some bootlegger. They cut it with water and drank alcohol whenever either one of them could get fifty cents or a dollar. I guess this went on in the back room of the hardware store, so very few people knew what was happening.

I lived at home at the time and didn't realize that my dad was drinking that much. This was probably because I was so involved with my own job working for the local veterinarian. He had several large incubators in which he hatched chicken eggs so that he could sell the chicks, which brought more than the eggs. It was my responsibility to work from six at night until six in the morning handling eggs and turning the ones in the incubator which I did by using a lever on the incubator. I generally worked twelve hours a day, seven days a week straight at that job — for only $6 a week. Three dollars of my weekly salary went to my mother for room and board. With the rest I bought my own cloths. I usually had about a dollar left over that I could consider my own spending money. I generally used it to go to a dance once a month with several friends. But to do so, I had to talk my boss into staying at the hatchery until I came home.

Occupied with my own busy schedule, I was not aware of the serious nature of my father's problem. He told me several years later that for two years he hadn't drawn a sober breath. What finally brought him to his senses was watching his friend, Claude, lose his mind. At that time, the condition was known as "getting the snakes." When dad saw Claude in this condition, he quit drinking "cold turkey" and never took another drink of any alcoholic beverage the rest of his life. He died of a heart attack just a week or so short of his eighty-fourth birthday.

During the fall and winter of 1933, I worked at the hatchery all night then went home and slept for a couple of hours. I'd get up early as I could though, to go hunting rabbits, squirrels, ducks and red fox during the rest of the day. I usually got home just in time to eat a bit of supper and return to the hatchery by six in the afternoon.

My hunting brought us enough rabbits and squirrels to keep meat on the table the year around. Both were good eating, and we all liked them. I used a Model 24 Remington automatic rifle with .22 long rifle shells.

During those days I hunted from time to time with my old neighbor and friend John Wilcox whose rifle was a Winchester pump action .22 special. John was an exceptional shot and a good hunter. The two of us could usually get close enough, undetected, to put an end to a red fox when we found one. But because John still lived on his farm and I lived in Woodhull, I hunted alone a lot. We killed around thirty red fox each winter and sold their furs for about $5 apiece.

Two interesting events happened to me one particular day in the spring of 1934, when I went squirrel hunting along a creek bottom about three miles south of Woodhull. This area was known as the "Pope Creek Bottoms." Pope Creek was about ten feet wide in most places but varied in depth. It had dirt banks about seven feet high. I had been walking about fifty feet from the creek through the pasture, ambling very slowly, searching for squirrels among the oak and occasional walnut trees which filled the landscape. Squirrels love walnuts and acorns so this was a likely place to find them.

61

Strolling along in this manner, I suddenly heard a splash in the creek and a few seconds later, another. I stopped to listen but was unable to see over the bank from where I stood. There were four or five more splashes in sequence, all separated by about the same time frame. I decided to move in closer to investigate. Carefully, quietly, I moved up to the edge of the bank. What I saw was amazing....

Perched on a forked tree trunk lying in the water was a mother muskrat. Lined up on the main trunk of the log were five or six baby muskrats about a quarter of the size of their mother. When the little fellows moved up the log next to their mother, she would push them off with her nose. Then the babies would swim down the side of the log to the end of the line, crawl back up out of the water and wait in line for their next turn.

As soon as she knew one was safely out of the way, she nudged another off the log and then she repeated the procedure. I watched this family of muskrats for about fifteen minutes with only the top of my head visible to them. They were unaware of my presence and seemed fully engrossed in what they were doing. Apparently this was some kind of game she was using to teach them to swim. I've never had the privilege to see anything like it since.

After I left the muskrats, I moved away from the creek and into some small hills where there were more trees. Just after coming over one of the knolls, I saw something move. It was a tiny baby red fox peeking out at me from the mouth of a groundhog hole. As soon as I spied it, it ducked back down into the hole.

I decided I would attempt to catch it. I looked around and found a stick about ten feet long, with a fork at one end. I broke the limbs back to where they would fit over his neck without allowing him to slip through. Then I crawled up behind the hole and set the forked end at the edge in such a way that if he stuck his head out again, I could pin him against the other side and hold him there until I could get to him.

Remaining quiet, I patiently waited for about fifteen minutes when suddenly, up came his little head. I made a quick jab, but he was much quicker and I missed. Throwing the stick down, I was disgusted with myself for missing him. I picked up my gun and walked past the hole, fully intending to go on with my squirrel hunting. Low and behold, the hole was just two feet deep and there the little fellow sat at the bottom of it, all by himself.

I reached down to get him and discovered that he was barely more than a handful of fluff. Then I noticed that his left eye had been cut and was swollen and festered shut. Feeling sympathetic, I carried him back to the car and headed for town and the veterinarian's office. My former boss, "Doc," cleaned his eye out with boric acid powder mixed in warm water. We found that although the eyelid had been injured, there was no damage to the eye itself. So Doc gave me some boric acid tablets and instructions to dissolve them in warm water and clean the animal's eye in this same way twice a day.

I fed my new little pet cow's milk through a doll baby bottle which had a small nipple every day until I could teach him how to drink out of a dish. Every time I washed his eye out, he would purr like a kitten and push his head against the cotton swab I was using. I played with him every day

whenever I had the time. I made a pen with chicken wire, got a collar and chain for him and named him Rusty. His color was a gorgeous red and he had a nice white tip on his tail. I stirred an egg into his food once or twice a week to keep his fur shiny.

By this time I had traded my Chevrolet coupe for a '29 Ford coupe with a ledge back of the seat by the rear window. That's where my fox would ride watching everything that went on. If I stopped the car and someone walked up, Rusty would come over and lay his head on my shoulder

Rusty, my pet red fox which I raised from a tiny ball of fur to a full grown beautiful fox.

against my neck and watch them with his pointed black ears and alert eyes. If people didn't reach in to pet him right away, he kept an eye on them for about fifteen minutes and then would move toward them. Then it was okay to pet him — as long as there were no swift moves.

I lost Rusty in the winter when he was two and fully grown. It was during mating season and he became restless. We lived on the edge of town and one morning when I came home from my night job, I went out to feed him but he was gone. Though I still kept him in a cage, he had worked until he broke a hole in it through which he slipped out.

Since there was about two inches of snow on the ground and the temperature was right at zero, I decided I'd try tracking him. I took my Model 97 Winchester shotgun from the closet, put on all the warm clothes I had and began the pursuit. I certainly had no intention of shooting him because I knew he would come to me if I could catch up to him, but I thought I might run across a rabbit or two on the way back. I also carried his collar and a light chain about ten feet long. My search proved fruitless, however. I finally gave up and headed for home so I could eat supper as I had to be to work by six that evening.

It was almost dark when I got back home. I was very cold and my hands were numb. The shotgun was loaded and my hands were so cold I decided to step into the basement through a grade cellar door and unload the gun where it was warmer.

At the bottom of the steps I pointed the 12 gage model 97 Winchester shotgun toward the wood wall of the fruit room and proceeded to unload. For some reason it went off. The pellets bored a hole into the wood wall, behind which was a gallon crock half full of cream. I "centered" it as if I had taken aim.

In retrospect, I think my fingers were so cold my thumb slipped off the hammer as I took it off safety. I had no feeling in my fingers and can't think of anything else that could have happened. You had to hold the hammer back on that shotgun in order to pump the shells out which I was attempting to do, onto the cellar floor.

Of course it had to be at a time when mom was entertaining a couple of neighbor ladies with coffee. They were sitting at the table directly above me. I remember all was quiet for a bit — no one could speak, including me!

As soon as I recovered from the shock (the sound of the explosion inside that basement was tremendous) I ran upstairs to assure my mother and her friends that I was alright and explain to them what happened.

As for my pet fox Rusty, I left the door to his cage open and left food for him. He came back on several nights and ate the food. I knew it was him because I found his tracks on occasional mornings, but he never stayed and I never saw him again. He probably found a mate that helped him regain his wild and natural instincts.

In the spring of 1934, one of the painting contractors in Woodhull, Bob Nelson, offered me a job as his helper at forty cents an hour. He had just taken the job of painting the town's water tower, which supported a sixty-eight thousand gallon tank. The only requirement was that I provide my own brush which cost about six dollars.

The top of the tank was one hundred and ten feet above the ground. The tank was made of redwood and had a wood cover. Its four corner supports were made of heavy angle iron which were bolted together with spacers between them. There were also horizontal beams, every ten feet on all four sides, extending from the ground up to the bottom of the tank. One-inch thick steel rods crisscrossed beneath the tank between each section of the beams in the same way from top to bottom. Turn buckles in the center of each rod kept them secure.

We were to paint the whole thing, including the metal structure that supported it. Before we could begin the painting, we had to clean the rust off the metal using steel brushes. In order to accomplish this, we worked from twelve-inch planks we laid across the girders. We moved them from one level to the next all the way to the top of the tank, where I'm sure my finger prints can still be found etched into the steel I held onto during the first couple of days on the job.

After that however, the height didn't seem to bother me. Eventually I got so I could hang out over the edge of the corner posts 60, 70 and 80 feet above the ground, clinging to a cross rod with one hand while working the brush with the other.

There was a walkway around the bottom of the tank which had a railing on the outside. I painted up the side of the tank as far as I could reach from the walkway, while Bob used a rope and boatswain's chair to paint the top half down to my paint line.

After we had cleaned and painted the tank, we went to work on the structure that held it. Bob attached an air hose 125 feet long to a large air compressor on the ground. That allowed us to use a paint sprayer on the metal structure that supported the tank. It was the only way we could get the paint in between the angle irons that made up the four legs.

Using aluminum paint, I worked on one of the corner posts about eighty feet from the ground. Standing on the stepladder on a couple of planks near a corner, I had the paint gun in my right hand and hung on to a cross rod with my left. At one point while leaning out spraying the outside edge of the leg, I decided I needed to get back inside the structure. I couldn't see behind me, so I reached back with my right hand (still holding the paint gun) and tried to find the other cross rod so I could pull myself back inside. When I found the rod, I wrapped my hand over it as best I could without losing my grip on the paint gun. But the trigger was between my hand and the rod, so the gun started spraying. Once I got it stopped, I turned around and climbed back on the ladder. When I glanced over at my boss, I saw a man whose face resembled the Tin Man from the original *Wizard of Oz* — only there was fire shooting out of his eyes! His face was covered with aluminum paint.

He had walked over and was standing on one of the planks near my ladder when the mishap occurred. I couldn't have done a better job of painting his face if I had been looking at him! My silver artistry covered him from the top of his head to the top of his painter's bib overalls.

Despite the fact, Bob never said a word. He just turned around, walked over to the ladder, descended to the ground and washed the aluminum paint from his face with paint thinner. In a little while, he returned with a smile on his face. We had a few good laughs about the incident every time we got together after that.

While we were working on the water tower, I became acquainted with an elderly gentleman who had started the Standard Oil station across the street from the water tower. He asked me if I would be interested in running the station for him when we were done painting. I mentioned this to a friend of mine, Keith Kirkland, and we decided we would take the gentleman up on his offer. We ran it 24 hours a day, Keith working it in the day time and I, at night. This suited me just fine, because we had a cot in the station on which I could catch a few winks on most nights and that allowed me to hunt fox and rabbits, fish or do whatever I wanted to do during the day.

After we started the operation, I found that Saturday and Sunday nights were the only times I ever had anyone stop between the hours of one and five in the morning.

But Keith didn't care to work at night so the situation worked out great for me. While operating the station, the Mayor and City Council gave me permission to shoot the barn pigeons that liked to roost on the edge of the water tank roof. They were considered a nuisance because of their droppings. The water tower was directly across the street from the station and, as it was during the time I had Rusty, my pet fox, I was able to keep him in pretty good shape with the pigeons I bagged. So they went to good use.

About the same time we took over the service station, the ladies from the Women's Christian Temperance Union (WCTU) asked me if I would be a scoutmaster and start a Boy Scout troop in Woodhull. Their request stemmed from the fact that the school children had been stealing candy bars and other small items around town. The ladies theothorized that Boy Scout activities might give the boys something positive to do. I agreed to take on the job and they agreed to put $100 into a Boy Scout fund to help get things started.

A troop is generally limited to thirty-two boys but I had forty-seven. There were no other adults helping me that first year, either. Needless to say, taking forty-seven boys on a hike or weekend camping trip in the woods keeps a person on his toes! I enjoyed the experience though. After the first year, a fellow by the name of Bernard Cox came to help. When I started another job and left Woodhull, he took over and did great work with the boys.

I had been a Boy Scout when I was eleven and twelve years old. The Presbyterian minister served as our scout master. He was transferred after two years however, and that meant the end of the Woodhull Boy Scouts until I started it again in 1934.

Sometime during the winter of that year, the elderly gentleman who was caretaker of the Crescent Lake grounds passed away, leaving the job open. I thought that would be a good job to have and contacted the board of directors to apply for the position.

They hired me and I started work on April 1, cleaning up the grounds, clubhouse and bath houses, including the whole area around the lake. My ability to swim and my lifeguard training allowed me to fill in when the regular lifeguard was ill as well as before and after the heaviest swimming period. I lived in my swimming suit most of the time that summer.

Since the membership consisted of a few more than six hundred families, one of my responsibilities was to ensure that all who came to use the lake facilities were paid up members or guests of members. I also had the responsibility of mowing the lawn. With the picnic area covering four acres and the parking area another acre, I had a pretty sizeable mowing job with my reel-type push mower. Whenever I got too hot mowing however, I'd just run down by the clubhouse, dive into the lake and swim across. Then I'd come back, get out and continue mowing.

One particularly interesting job greeted me every Wednesday morning. Following the Tuesday night movie, I had the task of cleaning up the peanut shells around the show area. I would generally rake up about five bushels of them after each show.

The concessions stand, run by Mr. Cedeberg, was very close to the show area and he would bring the peanuts into his stand in one-hundred pound burlap sacks. Then he would transfer the peanuts into small paper sacks that sold for five cents apiece. Considering the amount of work I faced every Wednesday morning, everyone apparently loved peanuts.

There was a storeroom at one end of the clubhouse where we stored the brooms and other yard and cleanup equipment. I found a leather davenport in there which opened up into a bed, plus a couple of chairs and an old dresser. With these basic items, I was able to fix up a place so I could stay at the club.

This was great in the fall when duck hunting opened. I could get up before daylight, take my shotgun, board the boat with my decoys already in it and row around the corner to the far side of the lake where my friend Jay Griggs and I had built a duck blind. It was nothing more than a pit we had dug into the ground on a point of land that stuck out into the lake. We had constructed a roof for it earlier in the year and covered it with sod so that by fall, grass and weeds were growing out of it.

It was such a good blind that once a red-tailed chicken hawk landed on it and sat there for about five minutes with the two of us inside. He was only about a foot above our heads when we finally stoodup. Some friends who had been hunting in another blind told us about the hawk landing on our blind. They didn't think we were in it until some ducks landed among our decoys and we stood up to shoot at them.

My duck hunting friend at Crescent Lake was Jay Griggs who holds one of our many limits of ducks. Our favorite hunting water was called Alpha Lake but it became popularly known as Crescent Lake after the club was developed.

I loved duck hunting — not so much for the killing of the birds as for the pleasure of watching them. We never shot teal, wood ducks or redheads but enjoyed calling them in to our decoys. Actually about the only ones we ever shot were drake Mallard "green-heads." The drakes, of course, were the males and they were used for food for our families.

One morning I had an interesting experience at the duck blind. I had gotten up before daylight as usual during hunting season. I was out on the lake, had placed the decoys and was just crawling into the blind as the first light of morning peeped over the horizon. A flock of six or seven green-winged teal flew overhead, circled the lake and came around to land among my decoys—all of them but one, that is. It hit the water, bounced into the air, made another short circle and came in to try another landing. Again just as it hit the water, it bounced back into the air.

Then I noticed why. It was a blue and white barn pigeon!

Somehow he'd taken to the flock of teal, thinking evidently they were his own kind. He'd joined them, probably, somewhere in flight. The sensation of his feet penetrating the cold water must have been quite a shock for him, however, because after two attempts at landing, he flew off toward town a little more than half-a-mile away.

Our duck blind was very comfortable because it was out of the wind. We had constructed a nice seat across the back and had installed a round kerosene stove that sat between us to keep us warm, heat-up the coffee and toast our sandwiches when we hunted all day long, which we did on weekends.

I have a lot of pleasant memories from my two years at Crescent Lake and those early morning hours spent in the duck blind before going to work each day in the fall.

The lake had a large population of black bass, crappies and bluegill, all of which provided great sport for a fly fisherman. One of the club members by the name of Dude Grand lived in Alpha. He was an electrician by trade, about fifty years old, and an excellent fly fisherman. Before long he convinced me to buy a split-bamboo fly rod complete with reel and line and join him in this fine sport. He then proceeded to teach me the finer points of how to fly fish. I learned how to handle the back cast and make the fly hit the water before the line. I also learned how to tie flies from him and later, bass bugs.

Like the duck hunting, I did most of my fly fishing in the early morning but also enjoyed the hour before dark in the evening on many a day. I would stay on the water until it was too dark to see the fly or bass bug and then would go back to my residence at the Clubhouse.

Fly fishing was great sport for me. I released the fish ninety-nine percent of the time, only keeping one or two on special occasions. I enjoyed the challenge of tying my own creations and catching fish on them and still do. It remains my favorite sport. Now, instead of fishing for bass, crappie and bluegill, I cover the mountain streams of Idaho for trout.

In late October, 1935, I put away all the benches and other equipment and closed up the lake facilities for the last time. My job there spanned the time from April 1 to November 1 of those two years. After closing up, I looked for something to take me through the winter until the following spring.

My uncle Carl "Coolie" Johnson lived with his wife Charlie Ruth in Auborndale, Florida. He was a contract painter and paper hanger. I wrote him and asked if there was any chance I could work for him in Florida.

Coolie wrote back that he had just taken a pretty good-sized job in which he was to paint and do the finish work on a number of pre-fab houses in a housing development. If I wanted to come down and help him, he said, I could stay with him and Charlie Ruth. He said he would also pay me twenty-five cents an hour.

I could find nothing else around Woodhull that winter, so I decided to go down to Florida and work with Coolie. I left home shortly after the first of November. Driving southeast in my '29 Ford coupe, I had no idea of the major changes that were coming in my life.

Ruby and I with Steve and Donna on a return visit to Auburndale where my uncle Carl "Coolie" Johnson and his wife, Charlie Ruth, lived when I first went to Florida. It was to this house that one of their neighbors, Mr. McKillup, brought Ruby and her mother over for a visit — an event that changed our lives. Ruby and I fell instantly in love and were married after a very brief courtship.

Chapter 7

Ruby and I

The distance from Woodhull, Illinois, to Auburndale, Florida, was about a thousand miles. It took three days to make the trip, which was in itself uneventful. Motels averaged three to five dollars a night with meals ranging from fifty cents to a dollar. I arrived at my aunt and uncle's the first part of November and went to work with him the next day. Going to work in November and December in short sleeves was a new experience for me. It was nice and warm most of the time with a few rain showers in between.

My uncle had six houses to paint, inside and out, so we had plenty to do. My aunt, Charlie Ruth Johnson, packed fruit for one of the large citrus plants between Auburndale and Winter Haven.

The Johnson's owned a nice, modern two bedroom home on a hill about a block from Lake Arieanna, about two miles from Auburndale. Lake Arieanna teemed with large mouth and small mouth bass that grew to record size. Crappies, or as they call them in Florida *speckled trout*, were also numerous and excellent to catch as well as eat. Charlie Ruth's brother, "Blacksmith," was a dyed-in-the-wool fisherman who took me with him a time or two. The winter months were not the best for bass fishing however, so I never tangled with a record-size bass during the several occasions he and I fished together.

My uncle's place had a number of orange and grapefruit trees surrounding the house, so needless to say, we had fresh orange juice in the refrigerator all the time. I helped my aunt squeeze a bucket of oranges every day. This went on until Christmas that year. I spent most of my time right around their place and seldom went anywhere else unless I needed something.

That was to change though when, around Christmas one Sunday, a beautiful young woman named Ruby entered the picture. One of my aunt and uncle's neighbors was a nice old gentleman in his early eighties by the name of Mr. McKillup. That afternoon he brought a lady, Mrs. Lillian

Mayo, and her daughter over to my Uncle's for a visit. They had come to Florida with one of their neighbors and his son and upon arriving had rented a house about a block from Mr. McKillup's for the winter.

Apparently the impression I left with Ruby Mayo that first day wasn't the best, as sources told me later. She had said I reminded her of Ichabod Crane! When she first laid eyes on me, I had just donned a pair of pants with narrow legs ending about three inches above my ankles and my white shirt sleeves stopped about halfway between my wrist and my elbow. But those were the best clothes I owned at the time, as it was still

Ruby with her mother and three of her brothers. Cecil Page, one of her half-brothers, is on the left. Bob and Art Mayo, her true brothers, are on the right.

the height of the Depression. You didn't buy new pants or shirts in those days until your others were so worn out it was difficult to tell which hole to put your arm or leg in when you dressed in the morning. I recall lots of people wearing short-sleeved shirts and high-water pants. What really counted back then was whether or not your clothes were clean.

For two weeks after meeting Ruby, I kept my nose to the grindstone,

73

working as much as I could. One Saturday when we had the day off, I mowed the lawn, helped clean up the yard and performed several other jobs around the place. When I finished around eleven-thirty in the morning, I noticed Mr. McKillup working in the driveway alongside his house and decided to walk over to visit with him. We had been talking for almost fifteen minutes when Ruby Mayo came around the corner of Mr. McKillup's garage — probably for the same reason I was there. The three of us chatted for a short time when I finally worked up the courage to ask Ruby if she liked to fish.

"I sure do!" she replied.

Encouraged by her response, I commented, "I think we can use Blacksmith's boat this evening, so I'll pick you up about five o'clock."

Since I had something to do that afternoon I never got around to contacting Blacksmith about using his boat. When I returned home late in the afternoon, I went over, picked up Ruby and drove her down to where the boat was tied. But the boat was not there. Blacksmith, I figured, had decided the night was good for bass fishing and had probably taken it out on the lake.

Making the best of it, we decided to take a ride through the orange and grapefruit groves in my '29 Ford Coupe. It was a beautiful evening and we did a lot of riding, talking, and getting acquainted. I learned that Ruby's father, John Henry Mayo, was a painter and interior decorator by trade. Tragically, he had come down with lead poisoning. The doctors had told him to quit painting and that the best place for him would be on a farm. Until then Ruby's family had lived in Meridan, Connecticut, where she was born. Ruby and her two brothers, Robert and Arthur, were born in Meridan. Her family moved to Springfield, Vermont when Ruby was four. Two years later they bought a 14-room house in Goulds Mills, a suburb of Springfield. Her father continued painting but was told by his doctor that he should stop because he had lead poisoning. The family then moved to a small farm near Amsdan, Vermont about nine miles from Springfield. Ruby's father died of a stroke April 14, 1931, so I never had the opportunity to meet him.

Aside from her two older brothers, Robert and Arthur, Ruby had three half-brothers, Kenneth Mayo, Cecil Page and Wilmer Page. Both of Ruby's parents had lost their first spouses through early deaths and had married each other later. Her mother was very nice, and a hard-working lady. I thought the world of Ruby's mother.

Ruby and I enjoyed each other's company very much, so every night after dinner we'd go for a ride. We soon discovered we both loved to dance. I found her to be an excellent dance partner right away. So dancing became an additional entertainment in those days aside from riding together in my car. There were several night spots in the area where we could get a table, buy a couple bottles of beer and listen to music or dance as long as we wanted.

Beer was legal at the time, although no hard liquor could be sold. If I remember correctly, a bottle of beer sold for fifty cents. Most of the clubs had a small orchestra, and one of the most popular songs was "The Music Goes Round and Round and Comes Out Here." We danced many a time to that tune each evening.

Our drives and dancing had gone on for only three weeks or so when we decided to get married. My version of our decision to "tie the knot" goes as follows: It was a leap year, 1936. Ruby asked *me* to marry *her* while we were parked in one of the many Florida grapefruit groves. Hearing the question, I took off running but stumbled over a grapefruit in the orchard where she caught me! Ruby tells the story differently, but that's how romance is.

Rain the following Monday kept us from work, so Ruby and I drove to Polk City, the county seat, to buy our marriage license. Three weeks later we were married in the rented home near Mr. McKillup where Ruby's mother and her friends lived that winter.

The morning of the day we were married, we built an arch out of palm fronds, orange blossoms, and flame vine at one end of the living room. The flame vine in full bloom was beautiful against the palm fronds. The orange blossoms filled the room with a very pleasant aroma, adding their special touch.

Ruby wore a pale-aqua wedding dress and had made her own coronet out of fresh orange blossoms. Ruby was certainly a pretty gal and it was a beautiful wedding. I was definitely a lucky guy and I knew it! We were married by a Presbyterian minister, Irwin Wherry, on February 22, 1936.

My uncle Carl Johnson and aunt Charlie Ruth stood up with us.

Our wedding party, February 22, 1936. Our minister is kneeling with his hand on his chin. Ruby's mother is on my right; Mr. McKillup, is on Ruby's left.

I know that many of our relatives and friends thought our courtship was too short and believed the marriage would never last. Indeed, we faced some tough years together with very little money. Aside from learning how to live on a very tight budget, we learned how to live with each other and remain committed through the years. But we made it through those years without ever going into debt. Ruby and I always lived within our income and tried to save a few dollars wherever we could. At the time of this writing, having celebrated fifty-six years of marriage, we feel we've proven the skeptics wrong and plan to stay together through whatever faces us ahead.

Our honeymoon lasted just two days. We went to Bartow, a short distance south of Winter Haven, in Florida. We had to head back to Auburndale on Sunday afternoon though, because of my job. I continued to work until about the first of March when we filled the back end of the Ford Coupe with grapefruit and headed for Illinois.

Ruby's mother had given her forty dollars. I probably had about the same amount. In just three days, we drove through to Woodhull where my folks lived. My parents had moved again from the Craycraft place to the Burgess place while I was gone during the winter.

They welcomed us when we came to town and we stayed with them for about a month. Then I contacted the board members at the Crescent Lake Club where I had worked the summer before. Upon learning that I had gotten married and that Ruby and I didn't want to live in the one room in the clubhouse, they met and decided to build a one-bedroom cabin on the hill above the lake.

That was our first real home together. My folks gave us a double bed and we bought a new washing machine from the power company for $35, making payments of five dollars a month. We also needed a refrigerator, so we went to the Sears Roebuck store in Galesburg where we found a new one for $100. We also made arrangements to pay for it at a rate of five dollars per month. I don't believe there were any monthly interest charges on either appliance.

My dad had the contract to build the cabin, so I donated my help. We finished the structure around the first of April just about the time my job started. All that remained was to paint and finish the outside of the cabin, which I did myself. It was the first time that I almost ended our marriage. One day I was painting from a ladder, using a flat black sash paint over the trim around the windows of our cabin. Ruby started teasing me. I told her to quit or I'd paint her nose black. Sticking her nose out, she said, "I dare you!"

Her invitation was all that was necessary. Reaching over with the sash brush, I caught her nose right at the bridge and painted it coal black. If I had used instruments, I couldn't have done a better job. The fire in her eyes was instant. She was pretty upset to say the least! She marched into the house promptly to clean the paint off and then went over to the movie bleachers where she sat for a couple of hours. Later she informed me of her serious consideration that day to "go back to Mother in Vermont." She finally got over the shock. Since then we've laughed about that incident many times over the years.

So, though many of our relatives and friends thought a marriage preceded by such a short relationship would never last, we've proven

77

them wrong. Granted, we haven't always agreed on everything as neither one of us is the least bit shy about letting the other know of our opinion on something, but neither of us ever harbored grudges toward the other. Once we discussed something and decided which way to go, that was the end of it and that remains true today. There is no complaining or turning back. We make the best of it together and that has always been our way.

One policy that we have always followed is to lay everything on the table and discuss the alternatives. Then we proceed with a plan wherein we are working together. I'm sure this is is one reason our marriage has been so strong and has lasted all these years.

In addition, Ruby has always known every detail of our finances. There were never any secrets or one-party bank accounts. Moreover, Ruby's name is listed on every piece of property or other asset that we own. Our life agreement has been fifty-fifty from the start, and continues to be so today.

On April Fool's Day that year, I went to work painting and putting out the benches in the Crescent Lake picnic area. I raked the lawn, cleaned the clubhouse and bath houses and, in general, spruced up the entire area for the season. My job, as it had been before, was to to serve as park manager and grounds maintenance person as well as be the early season lifeguard before the regular summer-time lifeguard arrived on the first of June, then to act as lifeguard again after he left in August. During the three months of summer, I also watched over the area before he came on duty and after he left each day. Sometimes when he was ill or couldn't work I would fill in for him during the day, too.

During the two years I spent at Crescent Lake, I was called upon to rescue six persons, all of whom had either gotten in over their heads, couldn't swim or had health problems — people who would have drowned without help.

But another serious problem of a very different nature occurred that last year at Crescent Lake. Late one afternoon during the summer, Ruby had decided to go swimming. She had purchased a latex swimming suit which happened to be the rage at the time. They fit like the skin on one's body. Because they fit so well and were so smooth, the sensation was just like swimming in the nude or (so they claimed).

Shortly after entering the water, Ruby started swimming out toward a raft in the center of the lake. Disaster struck, however, when she felt the back of her new suit split. She turned around immediately and headed back to shore to a point where she could stand in relatively shallow water. Unfortunately the dying bathing suit refused her the opportunity to get out and to make matters worse, the water was pretty chilly.

Ruby was cold and shivering when I finally appeared, and her voice was trembling as she called to me and then quietly told me her problem. She had been standing in water up to her chin waiting for me to come near the bathing area. Upon learning about her predicament, I went to get a bath towel so she could wrap it around herself and get to the bath house for her clothes. That particular incident ended Ruby's enthusiasm for the latex rubber rage in fashion swim wear.

We had a great summer that year at Crescent Lake in spite of the long hours and the hard work. The only real concern we had was that my job ended on November 1st. What was I going to do to put food on the table through the winter?

One of the three members of the board of directors at Crescent Lake Club was a man nicknamed "Whitey." He was also superintendent of the Alpha Coal Mine which was owned by the Shuler Coal Company. It was located about a mile south of Alpha in Illinois.

One of the owners of the coal mine, Charles Shuler, had mentioned

This photo of our dear friends, Charlie and Suzie Shuler, was taken later at their home in Scottsdale, Arizona. Ruby and I lived with them for four years in Davenport, Iowa while I worked for them as their chauffer.

he was looking for a young fellow to work for him and his family as a chauffeur. They lived in Davenport, Iowa. Knowing my job would terminate for the winter on November 1, Whitey recommended me.

One day shortly after that, Mr. Shuler came out to the lake to meet Ruby and me. Apparently he liked what he saw because he offered me the job for sixty dollars a month and said there was a five-room apartment over the garage where we could live. In addition, he said, I could keep my own car in the back corner of the garage.

As soon as I had all of the Crescent Lake equipment stored away at the end of November, Ruby and I moved to Davenport. We ended up staying there and worked for Charles and Susie Shuler for the next four years.

The Shulers were the greatest people in the world to work for. My job was to keep their three cars clean and polished as well as drive Mrs. Shuler wherever she wanted to go in her daily rounds. I didn't have to wear a uniform and they always treated us like members of their family. In short, they were such fine people to work for because they were so nice to Ruby and me.

Up to that point, Ruby and I had spent our lives in rural areas and had not been exposed to business opportunities or Civil Service jobs. Living in Davenport, a city of eighty thousand people at the time, brought us both a new perspective. Meeting and working with Mr. and Mrs. Shuler's relatives and friends opened up our thoughts and expanded our minds to the many opportunities available all around us if we just had the courage and ambition to seize them.

This fine couple set a wonderful example for us to follow. Because they were so nice and provided such excellent role models, we came out of our working relationship with them inspired to go on to bigger and greater challenges in our lives.

One morning in 1940, Mrs. Shuler informed me that she had an appointment with her hair dresser in Rock Island. When I picked her up at the designated time, her two young children, Davie and Susie, came out of the house with her. She asked me to drop her off at the hair dresser's and then take the children to the park for an hour while waiting to pick her up again.

After we dropped her off, we drove to the park as she had suggested, where I left the car in the parking lot just above the swing and other playground equipment. As soon as I stopped, Davie and Susie took off like a couple of quail headed for the playground. I followed walking slowly down a dirt path to the park. Noticing a sparkle in the dirt, I reached down and tipped it out with my fingernail. It looked like a diamond, so I put it in my jean pocket and went on to watch over the children. Sometime later, I rediscovered the stone in my pocket, so I took it out and put it in one of the drawers of my old oak roll-top desk.

Several years later after I was on the Davenport Fire Department, I asked a jeweler friend to check the stone. He informed me that it was a half-carat diamond. After having it set into a ring, I gave it to Ruby for her birthday. She still has it, but it is set in the third ring casing now because the first two wore out or had broken prongs.

Another interesting experience with the Shuler family occurred in either 1937 or '38, when Mrs. Shuler's sister, Mrs. Stibolt, lost her husband. The Stibolts lived in Rock Island, Illinois, across the river from Davenport. Mrs. Stibolt had three boys, Tom, Dick and Victor; and the Shulers had three adopted children, Davie, Barry and Susie. That year the two sisters decided to spend the summer at Spring Lake, New Jersey. They rented a beautiful home across the street from the tennis club just a block from the ocean beach. They also asked Ruby and me to go along. Mrs. Shuler drove one of their Buick sedans. I drove a station wagon.

On the trip east to Spring Lake, I experienced another very close call. Mrs. Shuler led the way with Mrs. Stibolt and some of the children in her car. I followed in the station wagon with Ruby, Jennie Hookie (Mrs. Stibolt's cook) and Lucille Anderson who was the Shuler children's nursemaid. Our route took us over a paved cross-country highway through Pennsylvania. We came suddenly to a short steep hill. A railroad track ran close to the hill right at the bottom. Oak trees and brush grew on both sides of the road.

The regular railroad cross-arms were located on the right side of the road next to the tracks. Mrs. Shuler drove across and kept going so I followed her about fifty to seventy-five feet behind. Just as we cleared the tracks, a freight train went across the road right behind us. I would judge that Mrs. Shuler and I were traveling about forty to forty-five miles an hour when we made that crossing. I don't think our station wagon had passed more than twenty feet beyond the tracks when the train crossed the road.

This experience occurred before there were ever signal lights or automatic traffic arms that come down to keep people from crossing when a train was coming. Everyone in my station wagon could have been in serious trouble had we been only a couple seconds later in making the crossing. Considering all conditions, we were very lucky indeed, to say the least. Fortunately we arrived at Spring Lake with no more close shaves.

The home that Mrs. Shuler and Mrs. Stibolt had rented for the summer was a magnificent white house surrounded by beautiful flower beds and a manicured lawn. In addition, there were quarters for the help in the back of the house. Jenny, Lucille, Ruby and I had a nice living space there and we thoroughly enjoyed the summer.

My job was to act as lifeguard for the six children. The families had a membership at an ocean beach as well as a large olympic-size swimming pool back away from the beach. I spent lots of hours that summer with the children. For example, I took them sightseeing in the station wagon. One trip was to Lakehurst, New Jersey, to see the airfield where the Hindenberg had caught fire and blown-up.

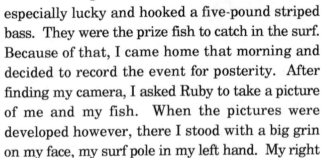

I often arose at daybreak and walked down to the beach to fish in the surf, where I

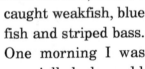

caught weakfish, blue fish and striped bass. One morning I was especially lucky and hooked a five-pound striped bass. They were the prize fish to catch in the surf. Because of that, I came home that morning and decided to record the event for posterity. After finding my camera, I asked Ruby to take a picture of me and my fish. When the pictures were developed however, there I stood with a big grin on my face, my surf pole in my left hand. My right hand had been photographically cut off at the wrist, and there was not a sign of my beautiful striped bass to be seen. Ruby had a hard time living that one down. Nevertheless that summer was one of the most interesting and beautiful times Ruby and I enjoyed during the early years of our marriage.

One day Mrs. Shuler and Mrs. Stibolt gave the four of us who worked for them three days off to go to New York City. I drove the station wagon with the four of us to Sandy Hook, where we left the car and took the Sandy Hook Ferry into New York via the intercoastal waterway.

It was quite a thrill to see and pass the Statue of Liberty on the way into New York Harbor where our ferry docked. These moments brought forth thoughts of my grandparents coming into the New York Harbor aboard the vessels which brought them from Sweden to the United States past the Statue of Liberty where they had to go through customs on Ellis Island.

The entire experience was pretty exciting for us four country kids. We stayed in a nice hotel in downtown Manhattan. Ruby and I walked to Jack Dempsey's tavern one afternoon and Jack happened to be there. We did not talk to him because he was with a group of what seemed to be old friends, and I didn't want to intrude. I was somewhat bashful in those days, so we just sat at the bar, drank a glass of beer and watched the movies of some of Jack's prize fights.

The four of us spent part of one afternoon and evening at Coney Island riding the Ferris Wheel, the famous roller coaster and several other rides. We had a great time, and then we boarded the subway and returned to our hotel. That evening we went to a show at Rockefeller Center where we saw the Rockettes. It was, indeed, the highlight of our first trip to the East Coast. We all thought Mrs. Shuler and Mrs. Stibolt were very considerate to provide us with that opportunity.

The first of September came fast so we had to start packing for our return to Rock Island and Davenport. The trip home was pleasant and uneventful.

Ruby and I continued to have many wonderful experiences during our years with the Shulers. Mrs. Shuler was from the Weyerhauser family, her mother, Mrs. T. B. Davis, was one of the Weyerhauser daughters. She was a wonderful lady, too. It was my pleasure to drive Mrs. Davis also, on several occasions. I always looked forward to such opportunities.

Because of this association, Ruby and I were privileged to have another interesting experience in the fall of 1939. The Weyerhauser Company owned a sixty-foot paddle wheel boat on the Mississippi River. The Shulers had invited Mr. Shuler's brother John and his wife as guests

We were seventy-seven stories high on top of the Rockefeller Center in New York City the day this photo was taken back in 1939.

on the week-long September cruise up the river. Ruby and I went along too. I was the general flunky and deckhand while Ruby did all the cooking. I also helped take the boat through the various locks on the way up and back.

The captain (who was also the pilot) took care of the boat full-time. On the return trip, he asked me to take the helm while he went below to check the diesel motor and turn down the grease cups on the bearings of the paddle wheel shaft. I knew how to steer the boat and which side of the buoys to stay on in order to keep within the channel. All went well going down stream and we were making good time. The channel cut over to the right side of the river alongside some high rock cliffs that went straight up one hundred feet from the water.

We were just coming alongside the cliffs a hundred and fifty feet offshore when the boat turned and headed for the rocks. I did everything I could to turn it away but to no avail. Just then, and just in time, the captain came through the door and saw what was happening. He quickly cut the throttle and threw the paddle wheel in reverse. Luckily we stopped short of hitting the rocks.

According to the captain, we had picked up a water-soaked log which had become wedged in the rudder, locking it into one position. Right then and there I received instructions on how to stop and reverse the paddle wheel, but I never had another opportunity to use the lesson the rest of the way to Davenport.

The vessel was a magnificent one. It had a beautiful kitchen with mostly copper pots and pans and other utensils. Everyone enjoyed the nice sleeping quarters. There was a large room at the front of the boat with glass on the front and the sides for viewing. The boat could travel in eighteen inches of water, so we explored some of the bayous (slack water areas on the sides of the river). We also did a bit of duck hunting from time to time. Finally, late one afternoon, we arrived at the docks in Davenport. Transferring our personal gear into the cars, we all regretted the end of a beautiful week on the Mississippi River.

Mr. Shuler had a lot of business meetings in Chicago. So the plan was for him to catch a train at Clinton, Iowa, about sixty miles north of Davenport. Unfortunately he also had a habit of cutting corners when it came to travel. On several occasions I had only sixty minutes to get him to a train that was sixty miles away on roads where the speed limit was sixty miles-per-hour. Several times we'd drive up and he would step onto the train just as it started to move. I don't remember him ever missing a train, but it was often very close. On days when the weather was nice, Mr. Shuler liked to ride in his bright red Buick convertible, the same car I usually used to get him to the trains.

By 1938 I had two weeks' vacation coming so Ruby and I decided to drive back to Vermont. I had never met Ruby's brothers or their families. We also wanted to see her mother and bring her back to Davenport to visit us for a couple of weeks. We took off in our '29 Model A Ford coupe with boots in all four tires because they were so worn out. Boots were corded patches you put inside a torn or punctured tire between the inner tube and the casing to reinforce it. The trip took us about four days and we thought ourselves fortunate not to have any problems with the tires. We drove two thousand miles that trip. Today as I look back on it, I wouldn't drive ten miles on tires like that.

We really enjoyed bringing Ruby's mother back with us and having her meet all of my family. She took the train back to Vermont following her stay.

One morning in 1938 on one of our trips to the train, I explained to Mr. Shuler that even though I loved working for his family, I just couldn't see any future in it. Serving as chauffeur for them had been a wonderful experience for Ruby and me, but we needed to set out on our own. Therefore I asked his and Susie's permission to take the exams necessary to become a member of the Davenport Fire Department. Charlie agreed with me and told me to go ahead and apply for the exam which I did in the days following.

Davenport was a city of 80,000 people and the fire department was one of the most modern in the United States according to what I heard at the time. It consisted of a central station downtown with four substations situated in strategic locations around the city.

Sixty-five men took the three-part test in 1938. The first segment was a two-hour written examination. The second included a series of tests on one's physical condition. We had to chin ourselves twenty-five times, do twenty-five pushups, hang with our back against a ladder and raise our legs out straight twenty-five times, and then climb a rope to the ceiling of the gym in ten seconds. If we could do this, we received a perfect score.

The final portion of the exam consisted of three parts. First, they set a hundred-foot extension ladder up against the sixty-foot hose tower. Then the officials timed us with a stopwatch, starting when our feet left the pavement and stopping when we had climbed the ladder to the top of the tower, walked around the top on a narrow ledge and descended down the ladder again to the pavement.

Next they had a fifty-foot section of two-and-a-half-inch fire hose complete with brass couplings and held together in a contraption with shoulder straps. The section of hose called a *doughnut* rode on a man's back like a packboard and weighed about seventy-five pounds. Everyone taking the exam had to put the doughnut on his back and climb a vertical fire escape ladder five stories straight up, step off onto the roof, return to the ladder and climb down again to the pavement — still carrying the doughnut! For this we were also timed, start to finish.

The last challenge involved a *pompier ladder*, an oak strip of wood with a strap of iron on both sides. It was about twelve feet long with a three-foot steel hook on the top set out at a forty-five degree angle from the shaft. Steel steps protruded from each side of the shaft for use as rungs. We had to use this device to climb to the roof of the training tower, which was five stories high, and back to the ground.

How did the ladder work? When we took the test, we had to pick the pompier ladder up from the ground and lay the hook end through the second story window. Then, we had to climb up to that spot and throw our left leg over the window ledge. Hanging out the window in that position, we then had to manuever the ladder out of that window and run it up so that it hooked to the window above. The procedure continued until we reached the top of the tower. Upon reaching the roof, we had to get off and reverse the procedure on our way back to the pavement. Again we were at the mercy of the stopwatch to determine our final score.

After we had completed the test, a fellow named Les Schick ended up the number one man, but he had taken the test several times. Though I finished second, there was only one vacancy that year, and so my friend Les got the job. I learned years later that he'd become chief of the Davenport Fire Department. I came back again the next year and competed with sixty-five other men. This time I made the top of the list. Early in 1940 I was appointed to the Davenport Fire Department.

Having been notified of the appointment about a month before I was to start work, we had time to find a house and move. One of the hardest things I had to do was tell Mr. and Mrs. Shuler that I had received the appointment. Both were very helpful however, in our transition and that helped everything fall into place nicely. The Shulers continued to be our friends through the years. Mr. Shuler passed away several years ago, but we still visit with his wife when we go to Arizona each winter.

We bought a home on Eighteenth Street in Davenport. It was a two-story stucco house across from a new grade school in a very nice part of town. I was ready to begin a new adventure.

I'm standing with Barry Shuler in front of the Shuler's garage above which our apartment was located. We lived there the whole time I worked for the Shuler's.

Chapter 8

While I Was a Fireman

In the spring of 1940, I started my new job on the Davenport Fire Department. One of the side benefits was that I could ride the city buses to and from work for free. In addition, I could ride on my days off. Our house was about three miles from the Central Station, but the city bus stopped about a block from the house and dropped me off about a block from the station.

I should also mention that the Duck Creek Golf Course was two blocks behind our house. Later several of my fireman friends and I played golf there once or twice a week. The golf course was within the city limits, which was nice, because we couldn't leave town except on our days off for reasons that I shall explain later.

This was still the Depression so Ruby and I lived on a tight budget. Many a month we had problems setting aside even twenty-five cents each for us to go to the movies. We carefully planned for food, clothes, gasoline, entertainment and anything else that cost money.

During the first two years on the fire department, I was assigned to be relief driver. In other words, my responsibility was to replace regular drivers when they went on vacation or took sick leave which meant living out of a suitcase. The experience of acting as relief driver was the best training I could have received, however. I had to know how to operate all the fire trucks in the department and the equipment on them as well as how and when to use it. Each fire station was assigned a district to protect. That meant I had to know every street and alley in town as well as the location of businesses that worked with hazardous material and how to handle it in a fire situation.

For much of the time those first two years, I studied and walked each district to learn the city streets. Sixty-five fire alarm boxes, numbered accordingly, were scattered all around Davenport. Their purpose was to give people who didn't have a telephone a way to notify the department of a fire in their area. All firemen were required to know the location of each box according to its number. For instance, if someone broke the glass and pulled down the hook in box No. 15, we would know that the fire was in the vicinity of Tenth and Brady, thus making our arrival to the scene much speedier.

About this same time I started running ads in newspapers expressing interest in antiques, guns, coins, music boxes and anything else of value. On my days off, I was all over town running down addresses of people who had contacted me about something they wanted to sell. This enabled me to learn the city street system much faster.

Our schedule involved twenty-four hours on duty and twenty-four hours off. Although we were required to stay in town on our day off, we could take three days in a row every seventeen days and go anywhere we wished. We usually visited my family in Illinois, about twenty-five miles from Davenport. We also took advantage of three-day breaks to go hunting, fishing or do whatever else was our pleasure.

Back to my first day on the job....

I reported to the chief at the Central Station that day. He was an Irishman named Richard Kelley — "Dick" to his friends and "Chief" to the members of the fire department. He assigned me a regular bed and locker in the large bedroom right over the fire trucks. That morning the back-end driver of the 100-foot ladder truck reported in ill, so I was assigned to drive in his place. The captain and driver on the front end explained how to steer the back end and then decided we should take the truck out and run it around the block to allow me an opportunity to get a feel for it.

They drove the vehicle out of the station, around the block and then returned to its original slot. I had a steering wheel that controlled the direction of the back two wheels on the truck. It was necessary to steer the back end in the opposite direction when we turned a corner, which I did until my end came to the corner and I could straighten it out again. There were no brakes or any other means of control on the back end except for the steering wheel, called a *tiller* was just behind the ladder along with the back seat.

We had just backed the truck into position when the bells rang, signalling a fire in our area. The chief's car led the way, followed by the number one pumper and then the ladder truck. Fortunately I had no problems doing my job, and we made it to the fire and back without my wiping out any cars or running over a sidewalk.

The next day when the regular driver came back, I was assigned to

This portrait shows the cap I wore after being assigned to the number one pumper truck at the Central Station.

the number one pumper at the Central Station. Lieutenant Fred Swenson was my boss, and Leonard Golden was the driver. I stood on the end of our fire truck, an American La France one-thousand-gallon pumper, complete with hose, fire extinguishers and all the latest equipment of that time. For the next two years I continued to be a relief driver moving from station to station and truck to truck.

Then I received a promotion. My new position was a permanent job driving the one-hundred-foot ladder truck. In addition, I had been trained to operate the ladder which was controlled by hydraulics. It was a bit tricky to operate, and at first there were no safety stops on the ladder. A little carelessness could easily result in a wreck. But I had a very good instructor named Red Tressler who taught me how to operate the ladder and keep everything in top shape. He became one of my very best friends. Ruby and I stayed in contact with Red and his wife Bess until they both passed away. I worked in the shop with Red during the day. That in itself was a great experience because I learned all about the motors and fire pumps from the inside out.

I was involved with many fires and interesting situations during my years with the fire department, but two in particular left indelible marks in my mind.

Just a short time after being assigned to the number one pumper at the Central Station, there was a two-alarm fire at the Vale Apartments housed in a structure four stories high and about a block long. The building had a heavy slate roof and had gone through considerable remodeling which included false ceilings and walls throughout. The fire was discovered around two o'clock in the morning. It was already out of hand when the first trucks arrived, so the chief called a second alarm, which meant everyone with that station had to come in.

I was off duty, so I drove to the station, donned my boots, helmet and fire gear and headed to the blaze. When I arrived, the slate roof had caved in and the rubble from the roof was lying about on the top floor of the building. Some of the bathrooms had dropped out of the top floor and flames were shooting through the holes. I climbed the fire escape on the west end of the building and joined Lieutenant Swenson and the driver, Leonard Golden.

They were standing on the fire escape with a two-and-one-half inch hose and nozzle playing the water on one of the hot spots. Fred told me to take the hose into the building and try to knock down the inferno that was shooting out a hole in the floor about seventy-five feet from the wall and fire escape. As I worked my way toward the fire, Fred and Leonard pulled up the hose and fed it to me. When I finally got into a position where I could hit the flames, I opened the nozzle and proceeded to spray. I was standing in water and debris up to my knees when the floor started to collapse at the far end of the building. It was impossible for me to run, so I shut off the nozzle and wrapped myself around the hose, intending to ride it back to the wall and fire escape and hopefullly down to the next level.

The floor collapsed to about twenty feet from me and stopped, enabling me to work my way back to the fire escape where Fred and Leonard were. We wasted no time in getting off the fire escape before the wall collapsed into the building. We finally succeeded in getting the fire out, but the building was a total loss. When I saw that floor start to crumble, I could envision myself going right down the middle of it — definitely a memory I've never forgotten.

The other incident took place about three o'clock on a beautiful Sunday afternoon when we responded to a fire at the Wallgreen Drug Store at Second and Main, two blocks from the Central Station. When we arrived, smoke was pouring out of holes in a manhole cover in the center of the sidewalk on the west side of the building.

The pumper crew laid a two-and-one-half inch line from a hydrant on the corner. We installed a fog nozzle and opened the hydrant. When we pulled off the manhole cover, the smoke really filled the air. By hitting the fire with a fog nozzle, we were able to cut the heat and fire sufficiently to go down the hole. We dropped a ladder through the opening and I took the hose and fog nozzle down to the basement under the sidewalk. With Fred and Leonard feeding me the hose, I worked on the hot spots until they were out.

When all the flames were doused and the smoke and steam had cleared away, we discovered that Wallgreens had been using the room under the sidewalk for storage. In fact they had stored a lot of excelsior, a packing item, within the room. They had also kept three fifty-gallon steel barrels of wood alcohol in the same spot with the excelsior packed around the barrels. When the manhole cover was new, it had a number of heavy glass inserts in it to let light into the basement. Over the years however, several of those inserts had been broken. We surmised that someone had dropped a cigarette on the sidewalk which probably rolled down into the hole, landed in the excelsior and started the fire.

With flames all around the alcohol barrels, the intense heat expanded the alcohol so that the containers were as round as balls. The crimp on the top and bottom started to straighten out. It is truly amazing that the barrels didn't spring a leak and blow up. If this had happened when I went into the area, I would surely have been cremated. My colleagues probably wouldn't have fared so well either.

These two situations were not typical for me, but they illustrate that one never knew what danger might be lurking when the alarm sounded. Some experiences were routine, while others were life-and-death in their potential danger. Along with the hazards, we had some fun too during the time we spent in the fire house.

Everyone slept in the large bedroom over the fire trucks. We all went to bed wearing our shirts and underwear while on duty. Our pants were lightweight black canvas with a pair of heavy duty suspenders , called *speeders.*

The speeder pant legs were pulled over a pair of knee-length rubber boots that sat waiting alongside each man's bed. When the alarm sounded, we jumped out of bed, into our boots and pulled up our pants. This operation took only three or four seconds. Next we headed for the famed brass pole, threw our arms and legs around it and slid to the lower floor where the trucks were parked. We placed our heavy raincoats over a chair on the lower floor so we could slip into them, put on the helmets, jump into the truck seat and start the motor just as soon as the dispatcher called out the location of the fire. This whole procedure, from the time the bells rang until the chief's car and the fire trucks left the station, took about thirty seconds.

One night when the alarm sounded, one of my colleagues got up automatically, dressed and slid down the pole in his sleep. But being asleep, he forgot to get away from the pole when his feet hit the floor. The fellow that followed landed on his head and almost knocked him out. Needless to say, that woke him up quickly.

On another occasion in winter, a call came about two o'clock in the morning. Our higher echelon consisted of Chief Richard Kelley and his two assistant chiefs, one of whom was Henry Uken. Sometime during the day Henry had decided to change the speeders located with his boots by his bed. So he took the pants off the boots and took them to his locker so he could take them home and wash them. He had another pair of clean speeders in his locker, which he intended to put back over his boots, but something evidently occurred which caused him to forget to do that. The lights were out in the bedroom when he went to bed and he failed to notice his oversight.

When the bells rang out around two that morning, Henry jumped out of bed, slipped on his boots and slid down the pole. Then he grabbed his raincoat and helmet, climbed into the chief's car and was off with the rest of the crew. The fire was in the second story of a house. Henry had to climb a ladder to direct the action on the inside. There was Henry on the ladder, decked out in rubber boots and long johns with his "trap door" visible in the back. It was quite a sight for everyone who braved the cold to come and see the fire. Everyone got a big kick out of the assistant chief fighting fire in his underwear.

For approximately eighteen months, I was the regular driver on one shift assigned to the one-hundred-foot aerial ladder truck. This was the second hundred-foot ladder truck of its kind in the United States. New York City had the first one. The driver's seat was open, as were those on all our fire trucks. Davenport Fire Department had two ladder trucks. The original was kept in operating order in Station No. 2 on the westside of town. It was built by the White Motor Company and its tires were hard rubber. Its wooden ladder could extend to sixty-five feet.

I had the opportunity to drive the original truck to a couple of fires while Red Tressler, our mechanic, put safety stops on the ladder of the new one-hundred-foot Pirsh ladder truck. The newer model would really get out and go when we had a fire, so it always pulled into a fire right behind the chief and the pumpers. The White was different, however. Its top speed was about twenty-five miles per hour, so generally the fire would be out by the time we arrived. Besides the slow speed, its relic qualities seemed to amuse onlookers as we passed by. All in all though, I enjoyed my experiences with the crews while operating the ladder trucks.

Early in 1942, besides being promoted to regular driver of the newer truck, a very important event occurred which was to affect my life. I had signed up for an examination at the YMCA to maintain my certification as lifeguard. I had an appointment at eight o'clock in the evening on the eighth of May to take my tests, so I took the bus down to the YMCA.

The expected birth of our first child had kept me pretty close to home for several months and when I arrived home, I found that Ruby had started labor pains and that our good friends, Jim and Evelyn Breinich, had taken her to the hospital. I wasted no time getting there and stayed with her for a while. The doctor thought I should go home however and get some sleep. He assured me they would call me when the time came. Following his orders, I received a call about four o'clock in the morning, but it wasn't the hospital. It was the fire department summoning me to a two-alarm fire at the Vale Apartments, which I discussed earlier. My shift went on duty at seven o'clock in the morning of May 9, but I returned to the station from the fire about 7:30, took a shower there and put on some clean clothes before heading to the hospital. The chief had given me a couple of hours off.

Upon my arrival, I learned that Ruby had delivered a bouncing baby girl shortly after seven that morning. After visiting Ruby and our new daughter and seeing that both seemed to be doing fine, I had to return to the station. I did get a little time off later that day to visit them again. We named our daughter Donna Jeanne. She was a healthy, beautiful baby — a little person who was to make quite a difference in our lives.

From the time she was a little girl, Donna loved the outdoors. In later years our family was to spend many a weekend camping and fishing in the mountain streams and some of the valley lakes for sunfish and perch. When Donna was about five years old we took our fourteen foot aluminum boat with a 7.5 hp motor. We spent three days on it following the shoreline around Pend Oreille Lake.

We stopped on shore and fixed lunch each day. At night we looked for a good sandy beach where we could pull the boat ashore and set up camp. At that time we had a cocker spaniel named Twink registered as "Twinkle Starlite." She was white with rust brown markings. She was Donna's dog and constant companion.

We built a campfire on the beach for cooking supper and breakfast and used the lake water for drinking, doing dishes and washing hands. Each night we lay in our sleeping bags out under the stars and slept comfortably. The weather was perfect all three days and nights. The only problem we had was when Donna became thirsty during the night and decided to get a drink. We had washed dishes that evening but hadn't emptied the bucket containing the dishwater. When Donna found a cup, she dipped from the wrong bucket. We had used quite a bit of soap that night, so one swig gave our five year-old the right impression. She knew immediately that she was washing her own mouth out with soap. We have laughed about the episode on many occasions.

Another special memory I have of Donna involved a hike she had taken while visiting Farragut State Park with a group of her fellow seniors. She and a young man decided to walk up to a fire tower on the side of the mountain. She eventually left her companion behind. The following Monday morning she was proud to tell us about the hike and how she had easily out-walked the young man. Then she turned to me and with a confident grin said, "I can walk the socks off of you, Dad."

"That's a deal," I responded. One Saturday in July we set out to hike to Chimney Rock, a land mark in the Selkirk Mountains north of Sandpoint, Idaho, which can be readily seen from Priest Lake. Rising early we drove up Pack River to the West Branch Road. There we left our four-wheel-drive jeep. Donna, Twink and I started up the mountain toward the towering rock slab named for its resemblance of a chimney. It rises three hundred and seventy-five feet above the ridge between Pack River and Priest Lake which lies to the west.

All went well, for it was a beautiful day. We followed a ridge and a few game trails on the way up as there was no trail. About noon I noticed that Donna had been stopping to tie her shoe strings quite frequently although she hadn't complained. After lunch we took a game trail around the north side of the rock so we could see Priest Lake and the other side of Chimney Rock. About two o'clock we decided to leave this beautiful area and head downhill toward our Jeep. Strangely enough Donna's shoestrings kept coming untied at pretty even intervals and of course, we had to stop while she tied them. We arrived at the Jeep about five

Shown here with a prize Dolly Varden I caught from Lake Pend Oreille, our little yellow Jeep contributed to many a fine outdoor adventure.

o'clock — one tired dog and one very tired girl, both mighty glad to see that old yellow Jeep.

After graduating from high school, Donna went into nurse's training at Deaconess Hospital in Spokane, Washington. Upon receiving her R.N., she served on the open heart surgery team for three years.

In the meantime, she had married Doug Foth, and they had two lovely daughters, Debbie and Dianne. At the time of this writing, Debbie had graduated from college and was teaching in the Yakima area of Washington and Dianne was still in college.

Donna quit nursing until her girls were in high school. Then she started a job as coordinator of open heart surgery at the Yakima Hospital. She earned her Master's Degree in Nursing during that time, went through a divorce, and moved to Bellevue, Washington, where she became the Director of Emergency, Prenatal & Surgical Services at the Overlake Hospital. There, she married Charles Collins who worked for Boeing Aircraft Company.

That bouncing baby girl has come a long way since she joined us in Davenport, Iowa, and we are very proud of her. She continues to enjoy the mountains and the great outdoors by backpacking in the summer and cross country skiing in the winter. She has accomplished some wonderful goals during her lifetime.

Back at the fire station, until about May, 1943, my responsibilities included taking care of the fire truck and its equipment as well as driving it routinely. I worked with Red Tressler in the fire department shop during the days.

One morning the chief came over to me and said, "Don, I have a new job for you, but it will be temporary." The chief worked and rode in his car to fires from eight in the morning until about four in the afternoon every day. During the rest of the time on each shift every other day, one of the assistant chiefs rode in the chief's car to fires. We had two assistant chiefs so one could take each shift. There were also two chief car drivers that were rated lieutenants whose responsibilities included driving the chief's car during their respective twenty-four-hour duties.

One of these drivers, Lieutenant Elmer Weise, had been diagnosed with cancer and this caused him to take an extended leave. Consequently, the chief appointed me acting lieutenant and assigned me to the chief's car until Elmer returned. I am sure that my knowledge of all aspects of the department plus my experience as fill-in driver and my background with the equipment helped me gain the appointment. By that time I knew every street and fire alarm box in that city of 80,000 people. I knew Davenport so well that I could almost identify the color of the house when an alarm came in.

This new duty required me to drive the chief to the fire before anyone else arrived. I really enjoyed working directly for him because he was so supportive. His car was a red Buick four-door sedan. I sometimes drove it through the streets of Davenport at eighty miles per hour with sirens screaming and red lights flashing. The chief sat beside me prodding me on while he operated the siren.

When we arrived at a blaze, the chief directed the firemen and equipment on the outside of the building while the chief's driver took the inside of the structure. Our chief covered all the fires in the city. If we went to a fire in one of the other districts, the assistant chief on duty stayed in the Central Station and rode in the seat of the No. 1 pumper if there was a fire downtown.

We carried a resuscitator, oxygen tanks and first aid equipment in the chief's car. As I was his driver, I was required to operate all these items. We also carried a two-quart pyrene fire extinguisher, because we dealt with a lot of restaurant fires. The pyrene gun was very effective at extinguishing a grease fire on stoves or in air chutes overhead.

During the first four years with the department, we were assigned to doing fire inspections on businesses in Davenport. Since I was located in the Central Station, I was asked to inspect various downtown blocks from time to time. Our job was to seek out hazardous conditions and make a report on the problems we found, after which a copy was given to or sent to the building's owner or manager. They were usually given a time limit to correct the problem in relation to the severity of the situation. The safety of the people was, of course, one of our main concerns. Some examples included storage of gasoline, paint, paint rags, electrical problems or grease build-up in restaurant kitchens, et cetera. During some of these inspections, I had a few rather embarrassing moments.

Peterson-Harned-VonMar was a large department store located on one of my inspection blocks downtown. One time while performing my duties, I had gone through the top floors and storerooms working my way down a floor at a time. When I reached the second floor, I came to a restaurant located along one side. We were to always check the grease chutes and stoves. At the time I was in full dress uniform, complete with cap and badge. I noticed a door that certainly must lead to the kitchen so I opened it and walked in. At that instant, women started screaming. I quickly discovered I was in the ladies' restroom. My hasty retreat required going through the dining area where a group of ladies were

eating lunch. I know my face was beet red. I did not have the nerve to cast a glance at anyone as I escaped the embarrassment.

Several days passed before I mustered up the courage to go back to check the kitchen; this time my first priority was to find someone to lead me through the correct area. What had contributed to my demise was the fact that there was no sign on the bathroom because that particular dining area was for ladies only.

Another red-faced moment came when I was inspecting a large warehouse on the fourth floor of a building. We always made a point of checking out the closet where the paints and oil mops were stored. On that afternoon I went all around

This is the formal uniform I always wore to and from work each day or when I was out on inspections.

the room. Next to the exit door was a small room with a plain wooden door. As I opened it, I spied a gal sitting on the john. She let out a fairly respectable scream too. I shut the door quickly! But this time fortunately, I was spared the spectators so I continued with my inspection.

All in all, the hazards associated with being a fireman and the personal satisfaction that came from surviving them, along with the laughs we had, made my years with the fire department some of the more interesting times of my life. Coincident to this experience however, was my ever-increasing concern with the progress of World War II. Like most Americans alive at the time, I shall never forget the Sunday morning on December 7, 1942. It was about 11 A.M. and I was reading the Sunday paper at our home on 2218 East 18th and listening to the radio.

Suddenly the radio announcer broke in with a special report: "The Japanese have just bombed Pearl Harbor and they are still attacking our ships and naval installations." I can remember the shock as if it were yesterday. The concern grew as the war escalated in both Europe and the Pacific. Finally in December of 1943, I decided to enlist in the Navy and that signaled the end of my fascinating career as a fireman with the city of Davenport.

Chapter 9

In the Navy at Farragut

From the time the Japanese bombed Pearl Harbor through the following year of 1943, I became more and more concerned about the war. It just didn't seem that we Americans were gaining in any way. Ruby and I talked the situation over many times during 1943. I was thirty years old, married and had one child. On top of that I was a member of one of the largest fire departments in our country and fire personnel were considered essential to the protection of our citizenry. That meant I would not be obligated to go. But that December, a year after Pearl Harbor, I enlisted in the U.S. Navy anyway and was sworn in. I continued to work on the fire department until I was called to duty.

Ruby and I didn't have much money at the time, so I started selling some of the antique guns, music boxes and other valuables that I had collected. The funds derived were put in the bank for Ruby and Donna.

We lived next door to Jim and Evelyn Breinich. He decided to enlist in the Army when I chose to go into the Navy. Since money was so scarce, we decided that Evelyn and her two girls, Marilyn and Barbara, would move in with Ruby and Donna while Jim and I were away. The two families split expenses and the Breinichs rented their house.

Jim's orders came a few days ahead of mine, so he left for training at the Georgia Army Base. Mine required that I report on March 27, 1944, to the Courthouse in Davenport. There were about thirty Navy recruits in my group. We boarded a train and assumed we would be sent to the Great Lakes Naval Training Center just outside Chicago. Instead we rode for three days heading west through the Dakotas, Montana, Glacier Park and into North Idaho. When the train stopped to let us off, we were in Athol, Idaho. It was midnight. We were then loaded onto wooden buses called *cattle cars* by the Navy men and hauled about six miles east to Farragut Naval Training Station, located at the south end of Lake Pend Oreille.

Our cattle car pulled up in front of a barracks at Camp Hill. Farragut

Training Station was made up of six training camps with about ten thousand recruits in each. At the time Farragut was the largest city in Idaho. With Ship Company personnel included, it was a city of more than sixty thousand people.

When we left the buses, we first met a chief petty officer who informed us that he would be in charge of our training unit. He assigned us beds and lockers. Then we had a chance to sleep for about three hours before muster. Upon awakening early the next morning, we dressed, showered and marched to the mess hall for breakfast. Out next assignment was to march to the Ship's Company barbershop for haircuts. From there we went in formation to another large warehouse where each recruit was issued Navy clothes. The ensembles included work clothes, a set of blues and a set of whites. We also received both dress blues and dress whites, complete with shoes, navy hats and a heavy blue wool winter overcoat or *Pee Coat* as it was called.

This portrait of me in my dress blues was taken when I went home on leave from boot camp in 1944.

Our basic training lasted five weeks and we learned a variety of skills. For example, we spent a lot of time marching and rowing the big life boats on the lake out of the boat docks at Bayview. Everyone had to learn to swim in the huge drill hall swimming pools. We ran our share of turns through the obstacle course and we all had instruction on the use of firearms in the indoor rifle range. Following the lectures we fired ten shots with both a .22 rifle and a Hi Standard .22 automatic pistol on the indoor rifle and pistol range. Then one day we were assigned to the outdoor rifle range where we fired 30-06 bolt action rifles at targets on the 100-yard rifle

103

range. Each man fired ten shots slow-fire at one hundred yards and then ten shots rapid-fire at the same distance. On both the indoor and outdoor ranges I shot almost perfect scores.

One of the officers in Ordinance noticed my scores and asked me if I would like to come into Ships Company Ordinance as an instructor at the end of my basic training. I agreed to take him up on the offer so he told me to contact him as soon as I had completed basic.

When my unit finished training, we received two weeks' leave as well as tickets to go home before being assigned regular duty aboard a ship or a Navy base somewhere in the world. The train ride home took three days and that gave me about a week with my family. It went by very quickly and then I had to return.

Back at Farragut, I and the others were assigned beds in OGU (out-going unit) where we were to await our assignment orders. I volunteered to do carpentry work around OGU while waiting. While waiting I contacted the officer who had talked to me earlier about becoming an instructor. He put in a request that I be transferred to Base Ordinance. The response took ten days. In the meantime all my buddies received their orders and left. Finally mine came through too and I

Maybe there really is something about a navy uniform that inspires romance. This was taken of Ruby and me when I arrived home on my first leave just after boot camp.

reported to the indoor rifle range at Camp Benion. I felt very fortunate that these events fell into place the way they did. My Navy induction papers showed my background with the Davenport Fire Department. Apparently the Navy Fire Department officials had noticed this and had requested that I be assigned to Navy Fire Control, though they were somewhat late issuing their request.

If I had become a member of this group, I would have been an instructor, probably at Farragut. These instructors spent each day putting out oil fires in a concrete structure resembling the compartments in a ship. The teacher had to lead a group of recruits into these burning compartments which had floors and walls covered with ignited oil. Even though everyone had heavy fire resistant clothing and wore masks, the frequency of such drills led to severe effects on their bodies giving them all health problems eventually. I discovered through the years that every man who had been an instructor in Navy Fire Control at Farragut had died of cancer or lung disease. I sincerely believe that a certain Someone was again watching over me and controlling my destiny.

I worked at the indoor rifle range at Camp Benion for the next five months. My job was to lecture to a company of one hundred and twenty men several times a day explaining the range procedure. This covered both rifle and pistol rules. Five or six other men shared duties with me. The rest of my time was spent coaching about ten men on the firing line with their .22 pistols and rifles.

In the fall I was transferred to the outdoor 100-yard rifle range where there were a hundred firing stations. We had from sixty to seventy men on the line at one time, using Springfield bolt-action 30-06 rifles. The men first fired ten rounds of slow-fire, then ten rounds in a sitting position and another ten rounds rapid-fire at this distance. Coaches were assigned to work with five men each.

Many times we worked with men who had never even *handled* a gun in their lives, let alone fired one. We had to watch them every second so they didn't inadvertently point a loaded and cocked gun at other men on the firing line. I coached in this area for about two weeks.

Our gunsmith was Roy Drabble from Ogden, Utah. I worked with him from time to time until he suddenly had an attack of appendicitis and was sent to the hospital for two weeks followed by a trip home for two more weeks to recover. As a result I took over all gunsmithing duties during his absence. When he returned, he was given orders to transfer to the Sand Point Naval Air Station on Lake Washington in Seattle. Roy had been stationed at Farragut for two years and it was Navy policy to transfer everyone after two years on one base or ship.

From that time on through the rest of my time in the Navy, gunsmithing was my duty. I repaired all the rifles, shotguns and pistols used on the outdoor rifle range and the six indoor ranges. I also re-barreled and headspaced all the Springfield rifles that were used on the outdoor range. This was always standard policy after 60,000 rounds had been fired through each weapon. Guns become dangerous to shoot when the headspace exceeds certain tolerances. One of my jobs was to check this area on all guns that were used on the firing line each week. This was very important because we were dealing with pressures that could exceed 60,000 pounds per square inch. A rifle with excessive headspace could blow up and injure the shooter badly. His eyes, hands and face were in the most danger of injury.

When I was transferred to the outdoor range, my bunk was in the main range office with two other men, one from each shift. Each shift stood watch every third day. In all, nine sailors had been permanently assigned to the outdoor range. The other six lived in a bunkhouse with a kitchen and dining area. We did our own cooking and could draw our supplies from the commissary selecting any food we wanted. We could eat steak three times a day if we desired. We had access to all the ice cream and to whatever fruit was in season. Each shift had one man who cooked and selected food for balanced meals. Since I am not a cook, I washed the dishes.

Our boss was Chief Boatson Craig, a full time Navy man who had

I'm second from the left standing with the crew that worked the Outdoor Rifle and Pistol Range at Farragut in 1945. That's Chief Bos'n Craig seated in the center.

retired but was called back during the war. He was a fine officer and a good boss. He and I got along really well. Even though we didn't always agree on every issue, he would listen and we could openly argue our points without any fear of his holding a grudge. Most of the regular Navy men would click their heels, salute and say, "Yes, Sir!" whenever he gave them an order. If he told me something that I didn't think was correct or if I thought there was a better way to do it I would suggest so and we would discuss the situation. Craig hated "yes men." Several times I heard him mutter, "G– D– yes men!" after a sailor clicked his heels, saluted and said "Yes Sir!" and then walked away.

When I wasn't repairing guns or sighting them in, I coached on the firing line. We had wheelbarrows sitting behind the line between and in the center of each twenty-five firing positions. The men picked up their spent shell casings and deposited them in the wheelbarrows. Next, the range personnel put them in fifteen-hundred-round wooden ammunition boxes, after which they were stored in a warehouse until we had gathered enough to fill a railroad boxcar. They were then shipped back to St. Louis, Missouri, to be reloaded.

During one particular week, several events occurred at the changing of the watch for the base administration building. As I mentioned before, men were named as chiefs and lieutenants by the mere fact that they had a college education, even though they may not have had one minute of military training. For example, one of these men might be a shoe clerk in New York or Chicago who had never laid a hand on a gun in his life.

Officers on the base took turns standing watch in the administration building. They wore a holster complete with a loaded .45 Colt automatic pistol. When one officer relieved another on duty, the latter was to remove his automatic pistol, take out the loaded clip, open the action and lock it open. Making sure the gun was unloaded, he then handed it to the relief officer, who in turn, made sure the gun was empty, closed the action, pointed the gun at the floor and let the hammer down. Next he would insert the loaded clip. By so doing, there wasn't a cartridge in the barrel but the clip was full.

You loaded the gun by pulling the receiver back and letting it go.

That action picked up a cartridge where upon the gun was ready to shoot. Twice during one week, two different officers accepted the gun and inserted the loaded clip with the action open. When they closed the action, it picked up a loaded round of ammunition out of the clip. Upon pointing the gun toward the floor and pulling the trigger, one officer shot a hole in the floor and another put a hole in the steam radiator and added insult to injury by shooting a hole in the window shade right after the first shot. An automatic weapon reloads itself when you shoot it. All that is necessary is to pull the trigger.

When Captain Kelley heard about these two incidents, he called my boss, Chief Boatson Craig, and ordered him to build a pistol range at the base. He then ordered all the officers on the base to qualify with the .45 Colt automatic pistol. The crew built a twelve-position pistol range with both twenty-five and fifty-yard firing lines.

The Navy's pistol course consisted of fourteen shots slow-fire at fifty yards, fourteen shots timed-fire at fifty yards. Then again: fourteen shots timed-fire at twenty-five yards and fourteen shots rapid-fire at twenty-five yards. When the pistol range was completed, our boss asked for volunteer instructors. I didn't say a word about my experience in pistol shooting, so he picked several of the old regular Navy men to help him coach. Craig himself was a good shot. He had a Match Model .45 Colt pistol that he had used in matches after retiring from the Navy the first time. The training operation went on for about a month.

One afternoon after the last company of men left the outdoor range, I went out and brought the wheel barrows in and transferred the empty brass into the ammunition boxes. When I came back to the range house with the last load, Craig had a target set up at twenty-five yards and was practicing with his competition pistol. I stopped the wheelbarrow and watched him shoot a couple of rounds. He turned around, saw me standing there and asked if I had ever shot a forty-five. I replied, "A few times."

"Would you like to try a shot or two with my gun?" he asked.

"Sure," I accepted.

I drew down on the target and my first shot was the center of the ten ring. He looked at me with a funny expression and asked, "Can you do that again?"

"Probably a lucky shot," I responded.

"Try it again," he urged.

This time my bullet cut the first hole I'd put in the ten ring.

Then he asked, "Where did you learn to shoot like that? Why didn't you tell me you could shoot one of these thing when I asked for volunteers at the pistol range?"

"I learned a long time ago not to volunteer for anything," I said.

He laughed upon hearing that and told me from then on, I was to help him on the pistol firing range.

I shot the expert course in 1945 and for two days in a row my scores were the highest ever recorded at the Farragut Naval Base. As a result I qualified for and received my ribbons as an expert pistol shot. After that, my responsibility was to demonstrate rapid fire to every class that we instructed. I shot seven shots in fourteen seconds at a distance of twenty-five yards. All seven shots could be covered with a silver dollar.

We built a 300-yard firing line and a 500-yard firing line so we could qualify expert riflemen with the Springfield 30-06 rifles. I subsequently qualified as expert rifleman and received my ribbons for that also.

One important aspect of both the pistol and rifle ranges was safety. Even though its importance was stressed constantly, it seemed to go in one ear and out the other as far as some men were concerned. I don't remember any specific problems that occurred at the rifle line, but the pistol range was different. It wasn't uncommon for a man to turn around with a loaded gun in his hand to ask a question and point the gun right at the supervisor or at others along the firing line. No matter how many times the danger of pointing the gun was explained, one had to watch the men every second. On two different occasions I had men with loaded pistols in their hand and their finger on the trigger turn around and point the weapon right at my face or body. I'm partially deaf in my left ear because one recruit, with his gun pointed in the air, pulled the trigger about a foot from my left ear — while talking to me. I've never undestood why we were not required to wear ear plugs on the rifle or pistol ranges. There was never a mention of using them for protection.

In the fall of 1945, all nine men who had been assigned to the outdoor range, including me, received orders to transfer to the naval base at Shoemaker, California, where we would then transfer outside of the continental United States. Nine other sailors who had been aboard ship for the past two years were sent to relieve us. When they arrived, Craig lined us all up in front of the range house and asked each of us to brief the new men on past experience and duties after which he assigned each of them to our jobs. As he went down the list, he assigned all my colleagues' jobs to the new men, but he didn't assign anyone to take my place.

Not one of the new men had any experience in small arms repair, re-barreling or headspacing high-powered rifles. Craig asked each new man individually if they could perform my responsibilities, but he came up blank. Then he dismissed us all. The next morning he called me into his office and asked, "Don, do you want to go to sea or do you want to stay here?"

"Sir," I responded, "I haven't had any say as to where I was going or what I was going to do up to this point so I don't see any reason for me to start now. I will do whatever the Navy wants me to do wherever I can do the most good."

Upon hearing my comment, the officer smiled and excused me.

For two weeks I kept my bags packed and ready to ship out. Every night I washed my handkerchiefs, socks, and whatever clothes I had dirtied. I wanted to be ready to leave when my call came. One day however, I happened to be in the administration building when I ran into one of the yeoman who handled transfers. Having been asked the status of my orders, he was surprised that no one had told me. My orders had been cancelled. It seems that my boss Craig and Commodore Kelley had called Washington and asked that my orders be cancelled when no one could be found to assume the base weapon repair.

During my assignment with the outdoor range, I worked long hours but not without some fun. Every evening several of us did a lot of pistol shooting. Sometimes we threw small condensed milk cans in the air and shot at them. On other occasions we set playing cards on edge and attempted to cut them in two with both .22 and .45 bullets. The .45 was easier than the .22 because of the bullet's larger diameter.

We enjoyed doing all sorts of trick shooting. Another benefit of working at the outdoor rifle range was that we could check out a 30-06 rifle and go big game hunting. Jim Lutz was one of my colleagues. He also happened to be an old elk and deer hunter from Harve, Montana. Jim was responsible for taking me hunting when I bagged my first whitetail deer.

The night before the season opened on the first of November, we checked out rifles and left Bayview by way of the north gate. Armed with weapons and a few sandwiches, we hiked up to the old lookout foundation of Cape Horn. It was approximately three miles from Bayview. The ground was covered with about six inches of new snow. Although we didn't have a tent, we discovered an old root cellar which had been used by the lookout personnel for storing food. We had taken two Navy blankets with us so we cut pine boughs and made a bed. Wrapping up in the blankets, we slept on top of the mountain that night during which two more inches of snow fell giving the next morning's scene a clean and beautiful appearance. We knew any tracks we spotted would be fresh. Arising at daybreak, we ate a cold sandwich and started hunting.

When we split-up, Jim walked around to the southeast while I dropped off to the north and worked my way west and back toward him. I made a circle and came back to my own tracks in the snow. Low and behold! Something had been walking in my tracks following me. It looked like cat tracks except each was four to five inches wide.

After following my tracks and those of the invader for about fifty yards, I saw Jim coming around the side of the mountain.

He took one look at the strange tracks and said, "That's a cougar!" He assured me however, that these cats were not generally dangerous to human beings and that this one was probably more curious than anything.

After talking for a few minutes, we split-up again to hunt some more. I hadn't gone very far when I ran into some very fresh deer tracks so I decided to follow them a little way. After going slightly more than a couple hundred yards, I saw that the deer trail went over a little bump on the side of the mountain. Slowly I worked my way up to where I could just peek over the top very carefully and quietly. There he stood, about fifty yards away, looking back in my direction. Quickly but quietly, I slipped the saftey off my rifle and zeroed in just back of his front legs and pulled the trigger. He took off as though I hadn't even touched him. In two jumps he was in the brush and gone.

111

I walked over to where he had been standing and found no blood. Following his tracks, I discovered red blotches in the snow near what was probably his fifth jump. I followed his trail another hundred yards before I found him piled up in the snow, stone dead.

This was my first deer hunt and my first deer. It was quite a thrill for an old farm boy who had never shot game any larger than a cottontail rabbit. Dressing out an animal that size on the steep side of a mountain was a new experience for me but I finally got the job done. It may not have been too professional, but my mission was accomplished.

Jim heard me shoot and started working his way around the mountain toward my location. He showed up just as I was trying to clean the blood off my hands and arms with the snow. I put my metal deer tag on the animal and marked my license with the date. Then I started dragging the animal out.

Meanwhile Jim resumed hunting and said he would meet me at the Old Depot in Bayview that evening at which point we would return to the rifle range together.

Dragging the deer downhill on a Forest Service trail with six inches of snow or better was a breeze, but then I ran out of snow about a mile from the bottom. This was my first deer and I didn't want to spoil the hide, so when I hit the dirt and rocks, I decided to put the animal on my shoulders with its front legs forward to my right and the hind legs dangling behind on my left. He rode like a fur collar.

When I reached the Old Depot in Bayview and dumped my deer off on the porch outside, I was bloody from head to foot. Though I couldn't see the whole picutre, I'm sure I must have been quite a sight. After I laid the deer down, I realized I had another problem: we were not allowed to take deer onto the base. At that time Ruby and Donna were living in a room we had rented from some friends of ours in Sandpoint named Jack and Eva Knaggs. I called them and asked if they would like the deer. "You bet!" they said, and drove out to pick it up.

Jim came off the mountain about dark, and we caught a ride back to the rifle range. That hunt turned out to be one of the most memorable times of my life. Jim was a good friend, an excellent hunting guide and a really nice guy — all that made it a treat. I am reminded of that hunt every time I see Cape Horn Mountain and I will never forget the excitement and drama of bagging my first deer up there. Since that day, November 1, 1945, I have been successful on many other hunting excursions, but none of them ever matched that day in my memory.

Besides bagging a whitetail, the added thrill was in seeing the cougar tracks. It was the first of two experiences I had with the big cats while stationed at Farragut. The second came during a hike up Bernard Peak, almost directly south of the base. The north side of Bernard Peak drops almost straight down into Pend Oreille Lake. Another shipmate named Keegstra and I had decided to climb the west side. This particular climb took place in early fall. The northwest side was too steep, having a series of benches on the lower segment. The trail there follows a steeper grade before leveling off somewhat at the top.

We were enjoying the woods and the scenery when we hit a rock outcropping that gave us a spectacular view. We could not only see Buttonhook Bay below us on the lake but also the valley extending toward Athol to the west and Sandpoint to the north. It was a very nice day and we weren't paying much attention to anything but the scenery. Consequently we had climbed much higher on the mountain than we had intended. As neither of us had brought a flashlight, we concluded it might be wise to get down to lower levels of the mountain before it got too dark. We reached the jack pine flats at the bottom just as darkness set in but still had two miles to go.

Before we had gone another mile, it was pitch black in the trees with no moon. Only a few stars gave us the wee bit of light we had. I have always had good eyesight and can see really well in the dark so I led the way. We were about half a mile from the base. Everything was totally quiet. There was hardly a sound except when one of us stepped on a dry stick which would then crack loudly. Suddenly, something let out the most terrifying scream I have ever heard. And it was very close — not more than a hundred feet away! My blood turned cold, and I'm sure every hair on my head stood straight up. We both froze in our tracks. Not a sound followed, though it is possible our hearts were pounding so hard we couldn't hear anything else. We stood still for some time before electing to move on cautiously.

I had no idea at the time that the sound had come from a cougar. Later though, when I described it to my friend, Jim Lutz, and several

113

other old-time hunters, they concurred that it definitely was a mountain lion. They speculated we might have intruded into the territory of a female with cubs and that she might have been admonishing us to get out of her area. Another friend suggested it might have been a male cougar on the hunt.

Writing about Bernard Peak reminds me of a true story that has to do with the building of the first fire lookout on the mountain. The cement abutments are still there where the Civilian Conservation Corps, known as the CCC, built the structure during the Depression.

The story goes that there were fifty CCC men camped on a flat right next to where they were building the lookout tower. The crew had a cook who got up at five a.m. every morning to prepare breakfast. The camp was set right in the middle of a huge huckleberry patch. When the cook looked out of his tent flap this one particular morning, he spotted a black bear cub feasting on the huckleberries. Deciding to have some fun, he picked up a big dishpan and spoon and ran toward the bear, beating on the pan. The racket roused the entire camp. The small bear quickly ran up a dead tree snag.

One of the other fellows thought it might be fun to catch the cub so he found a piece of half-inch pipe about eight feet long. He used a length of soft wire which he doubled and ran through the length of the pipe so that it formed a loop at one end. His plan was to climb the snag where the bear had stationed itself, slip the loop over its head and then bring him down. By this time the cub was twenty feet up the tree watching as the crowd gathered below.

The fellow who thought up the way to catch the cub put on a pair of pole climbers and hooked the climbing belt around the trunk of the tree. With the pipe snare in one hand, he began climbing up toward the young bear. About twelve feet off the ground, he started moving the pipe snare into position to drop the wire over the bear's head. The cub had been eating huckleberries for some time before the cook discovered him, so his little tummy was full. As the pipe and wire snare came close, the bear became very nervous and turned the huckleberries loose. His stalker saw what was coming and tried to duck, but the goods hit him square in the face. Suddenly one of his climbing spikes came loose, and that caused him to turn upside down where he hung by the pole belt. The bear came down the other side of the tree at the same time and made his retreat.

Everyone laughed so hard they let the cub get away. According to sources, it was ten minutes before the men could get a ladder to rescue the tangled-up climber.

During my years in North Idaho, I have listened to my share of bear stories. One tells of a cook at Hughes Meadows, north of Priest Lake, who had baked several pies for the logging crew and set them on the window sill to cool. A bear decided they would make good dessert and stole them.

At another logging camp a couple of guys rigged up a snare over the hole in the garbage pit and tied a small cable to one end. Then they ran the cable through a knothole near the floor at one end of the bunkhouse. They tied the other end of it to a man's bed. That night a bear got caught in the snare and took off. The fellow in the attached bed was sound asleep. Needless to say there was a bit of commotion and shock when the bed with its victim came out of line and started down the center of the bunkhouse. The mobile sleeping unit came to a halt when it crashed into the end of the building. According to witnesses, it had been thoughtful of the culprits to tie the cable to the foot of the bed and spare their victim of a sure headache when his new mode of transportation hit the wall. That ought to be enough North Idaho bear stories!

Early in 1945, while still in the Navy, I bought a 1928 Pontiac four-door sedan for sixty dollars. I purchased it from a sailor who had been transferred from Farragut. This turned out to be my hunting and fishing car until January 1946, when I sold it to another sailor who left the car at the base after being discharged.

Les Brown from the Brown Lumber Company of Sandpoint later purchased the car and restored it. The sailor that I had sold it to had not changed the title to his name, so I had to sign it over to Les who incidently later became the mayor of Sandpoint. When I was governor, I appointed Les to the Idaho Horse Racing Commission and over the years we became good friends.

Somehow about this same time, a nurse at the Farragut Hospital was transferred. She had purchased a 1931 Chevrolet coupe a month or so before. It had no anti-freeze in the radiator and ice had pushed the frost plugs out of the side of the motor. I took a chance and bought it from her for sixty dollars. Afterwards, I rode with a friend into Coeur d'Alene and bought a used head for the motor at the Forest Brothers wrecking yard, for about $12. I installed it on the motor and hammered the frost plugs back in the next evening. Then I filled it with plain water, to check the radiator to see if it was okay. It didn't leak so I drained the water out and filled it with anti-freeze. The car then ran beautifully and since it had new tires, I drove it the rest of January, February and March until my discharge from the Navy.

Chief Petty Officer O'brien and Chief Bos'n Craig catch the flag as I, 2nd Class Gunner's Mate Samuelson, lower it while closing the Rifle Range at Farragut after the end of World War II.

Chapter 10

From the Door of a Sporting Goods Store

When the war ended in the fall of 1945, men throughout the armed services faced the transition to civilian life and the adjustment to living with their families after being away for extended periods of time. With this in mind, the War Department set up a procedure based on points to determine the order in which men and women in all branches of the service would be discharged and sent home.

Because I served in Ship's Company, I was able to rent an apartment in Farragut Village for the last four months of my Navy assignment. Ruby and Donna stayed there with me while we awaited orders for my discharge in Bremerton. We lived only a block from the Ship Service Commissary. It was great to have my family with me those last four months in the Navy. We celebrated Christmas in our small home. Donna was three and a half years old at that time.

The point system caught up with me in January 1946 when I received my orders to report to the Bremerton Naval Base in Washington state for Honorable Discharge from the United States Navy as a Gunner's Mate Second Class. When I applied for the discharge, I was offered an advancement to Gunner's Mate First Class if I would stay in the Navy for four more years. Since I had enlisted in order to do my part to win the war and the war was now over, I decided I was ready to go back to civilian life.

My final discharge came on January 25. It was signed by Admiral Harold Bye who later moved to the Sandpoint area and spent the rest of his life at his home on the Dover Highway along the Pend Oreille River. Admiral Bye was a fine gentleman who loved the outdoors and the beauty of North Idaho.

As soon as I returned from Bremerton, we loaded our personal belongings and my Navy gear into our '31 Chevrolet coupe and directed it east toward our home in Iowa.

The weather was cold and snowy through the state of Montana. Even

117

though we had our winter clothes, we were very uncomfortable because the car heater did not work very well. We wrapped Donna in one of my Navy white wool blankets and Ruby used another one to keep her feet and legs warm. A ferocious wind coming out of the northwest blew the heavy chrome radiator cap off and it sailed off the road. I immediately stopped the car and backed up to where the cap had fallen off. Luckily I was able to find it in spite of having great difficulty walking against the wind. That incident brought to me the reality of just how cold it was. After that I was very appreciative of what heat we did have in the car.

The remainder of our trip home was uneventful. From Billings we dropped south as much as the highway would allow us. We drove through Wyoming and upon leaving it, found the temperature to be much more pleasant through the remaining miles of our homeward journey. When we drove up to our house at 2213 Eastern Avenue, it was great to be back in our own home, even though we knew it would be temporary.

Ruby and I had fallen in love with North Idaho and had decided before we left it that we would move back to the Sandpoint area and start a sporting goods store. We had done some preliminary work before leaving. Carl Tifft happened to be constructing a new building at 211 Cedar Street. He told me of his plans to use only half of the structure for his insurance and real estate business and to rent the other half. I jumped at the opportunity and agreed to a rent of sixty dollars a month for the other part of the building.

So, when we arrived in Davenport, I started preparations for the permanent move West. I resigned from the Fire Department, put our house up for sale and bought a Ford V-8 cattle truck with a stock rack for $500. Everyone thought we were "nuts" for quitting a Civil Service job and moving to Idaho to start a sporting goods store but their comments did not discourage our dream.

We were busy people for the next month making all the necessary arrangements. To start the process of building an inventory, I ran ads in all the papers around for high powered rifles, shotguns, pistols and Mauser actions. There were plenty available in the area because the Rock Island Arsenal, located near Davenport on an island in the Mississippi River, had sold numerous 30-40 Krag and Springfield rifles to local residents. My ads elicited lots of responses and I was able to purchase a large inventory of weapons and actions for my new store.

Besides those I purchased, I also had many on hand. Over the years my collection of antique guns, which included muzzle loaders, rifles and pistols of every sort, had grown to about seventy-five. My personal collection added to the new varieties meant quite a load of guns to haul to Idaho.

After packing everything in boxes, we lined the inside of the truck rack with water proof construction paper and put a canvas tarp over the front and top. We began feeling the pioneer spirit with our modern day covered wagon as soon we headed West. Fortunately, we could count on

Posing in front of my sport shop, my friend Clyde Cox (left) was with me when I caught this 27-pound, 37-inch rainbow trout from Lake Pend Oreille. My store was located in Sandpoint on the western shore of this great natural freshwater lake. We called them Kamloops trout locally and many of the businesses in the Sandpoint area still use this name as part of their business logo.

getting there a little faster than our nineteenth century counterparts.

Three days before we were to depart, I ran an ad in the paper to sell the car I had bought at Farragut for sixty dollars. I'd asked for $250 in the ad. The first person who called bought it for cash. Our lives were hectic those last three days: saying good bye to our many friends and relatives, paying bills and making last minute arrangements for the long drive ahead.

Several friends from the Fire Department helped me load furniture and pack the truck. When the last gun and piece of furniture were loaded, we tied down the tarp with a light rope. The next morning, which happened to be April first, we set out for our new life and new home. After a smooth first day, we stayed the night in a motel in eastern Nebraska.

The second day turned out to be rather interesting. We were traveling west on U.S. Route 20 when we hit a snowstorm that progressed eventually into blizzard conditions. While passing through the communities of Jonestown and Wood Lake, we could see the snow drifting in some areas and piling up. As conditions worsened, we became concerned and dreaded the thought of being stuck on the highway.

Just about that time, a big semi pulled up behind us, so I pulled over to let him pass. Then we moved right in behind him and followed him to the next town, Valentine, Nebraska. Since the truck was an eighteen-wheeler and heavily loaded, I figured it could break the drifts and create a nice pathway for us and it did just that.

At Valentine we spotted a garage right across the street from a small two-story hotel. I drove into the garage and asked if I could park my truck inside during the night. The owner consented. Then we walked to the hotel where we were lucky to get a nice, warm room for the three of us.

The blizzard raged on all night. Huge drifts of snow caused their share of problems for other motorists. According to the men at the garage, at least twenty cars and trucks were stuck along the highway. Many people had to stay the night in their vehicles. With conditions this bad we decided to stay in Valentine for two nights. When the storm ended and the highways were cleared, we set out again.

All went well until we were about fifty miles past Casper, Wyoming, when I heard a sudden pop followed by another noise coming from the back of the truck. I pulled off the road onto the shoulder to investigate and discovered we had blown a tire on the right rear dual wheel. With no spare and considering the load we had, I didn't dare drive with one tire on that side. So I proceeded to get my jack and tools to take the wheel off the truck.

About that time a car pulled in behind me. Its occupant was a salesman who had been stranded in Valentine at our hotel. Recognizing our truck he stopped and agreed to take me back to Casper where I could buy a new tire. He also brought me back to the truck and waited while I installed the wheel. When I tried to pay him for all his trouble, he refused my offer and simply said, "Just help someone else in trouble on the road."

The roads and weather were good the rest of the trip and we traveled three to four hundred miles a day with no more problems. When we arrived in Sandpoint, the building I had rented wasn't quite finished so I had to find a safe place to keep my guns and most of our other personal belongings. Before we had gone back to Iowa, our friends Jack and Eve Knaggs invited us to stay with them until we could find a house in Sandpoint. While we were gone, Jack suffered a heart attack and had passed away.

The Knaggs had leased the old White Lumber Company office the fall before and turned it into a roller skating rink. When we arrived, Eve and her son Paul were running the roller rink, which had a large walk-in safe in the old office part of the building. Eve let me use the area to store my inventory until the building was finished for me to start the store.

Since we didn't have a lot of money to purchase a house, we felt lucky to find a two-story home at 612 Fourth Street completely furnished for three thousand dollars. We bought it and after we had settled into our new home, Carl finished the Tifft Building and I was finally able to go to work on the new store.

There was a barber shop next door operated by a very interesting fellow named Joe LaFond. Joe was an old-timer who loved to hunt and fish. He had the largest set of elk horns I had ever seen, hanging in his wood shed in back of the barber shop.

Next to the barbar shop was a millinery shop, operated by Joe's wife, who made ladies' hats and sold them. She told me that some of her best customers were "ladies of the night" who really liked fancy hats and paid a hundred dollars a piece for them. Yes, there were a few houses in the early days of Sandpoint that had red lights in their windows.

There was another millinery store just a couple of doors down on the west from Mrs. La Fond's. It was operated by the Fee sisters, both very nice ladies who took part in many community affairs. When the Chamber of Commerce put on the Red Hat Dance at the Elk's Club each year during the first week of the fishing season, the Fee sisters knitted small, red, souvenier hats and stuck a small feather in each along with a tiny silhouette of a fish cut out of birch bark. These were sold for a dollar and could be pinned to your coat. If you went to the Red Hat Dance without a red hat you were fined. Having one of these however, filled the bill.

I put a partition across the back end of my new sport shop to make the gun repair room to which I added some storage shelves. I found three eight foot showcases and built a gun display rack across the back of the showroom. The antique rifles and pistols were hung on the wall above the gun rack.

Meanwhile, between the first of April and the twentieth, I contacted all of the wholesale sporting goods businesses in Spokane, including Marshall Wells, Jenson Byrd and Spokane Sporting Goods and bought the merchandise needed to start the store.

With everything in place, Ruby and I had the grand opening of the "Pend Oreille Sport Shop" on April 20, 1946, with more guns for sale than anyone had seen since the beginning of World War II. There never had been a gunsmith shop open to the public in Sandpoint, so lots of local weapons were in need of repair and that meant running the store all day and repairing guns half the night.

One night I was working on a gun and ran into a tang screw that I couldn't budge with a screwdriver. With my hand under the rifle below the area where the screw was located, I put all the pressure I could muster on the screwdriver. Then, for some reason, the gun turned and the screw driver slipped from its position into my hand, its blade piercing into a bone. I almost passed out but was able to get up and walk out the front door. I walked east down to the Von Cannon Bank corner. The fresh crisp air seemed to help me recover. Then I went back to the store, locked up and headed home. It was three o'clock in the morning.

I am sure this injury would not have happened if I hadn't been so tired. Working late nights for several weeks trying to get ready for hunting season had finally taken its toll on my performance. For many years I could get along fine with just three or four hours of sleep each night, but this was physical exhaustion which had brought on carelessness.

Ruby helped me when she could, but we also had a little girl at home who was her first priority. In addition Eve Knaggs assisted me from time to time for about a month. Then I hired a Sandpoint native named Otto Klefstad. He was about my age and he worked for me until hunting season ended. Otto and his wife Della have remained good friends of ours ever since.

During the rest of the winter, I ran the store alone, but it was no big deal because in those days the economy of Sandpoint was built completely around the lumber industry. Men worked in the woods from June first until Christmas. By then everything was snowed in and the roads in the mountains were generally drifted shut. During that time almost everyone was out of work. They drew what was called their "rocking chair money," now known as unemployment compensation. Since the compensation was geared toward providing food on the table and the bare necessities

During the winter, the snow often piled up in front of my shop as shown in this photograph taken after we moved from the Tift Building to our second location on first avenue.

123

for a family, there wasn't much left for buying sporting goods. Wintertime purchases were limited to hand lines, white fish hooks and maggots, all supplied to me by my friend Harold Miller. I also did quite a bit of gun repair that winter, which helped pay the rent and light bill. I only took out enough money each month to buy groceries and pay our bills. Anything above that was used to increase my store inventory.

In June of 1947, our old Davenport neighbors, the Breinichs, came for a visit. Jim had finished his service with the Army. During their visit he started helping me in the store and seemed to enjoy the business. Their original plan was to stay for a short period of time and then return to Iowa. One day Jim asked me if I would sell him half the business. After discussing it at some length, I decided it might be a good idea, for it was hard to find anyone who knew anything about sporting goods. Because

Jim Breinich bought into my sport shop and was a partner for about twelve years until I sold it to him in 1958. We had a real advantage in the number of rifles we carried and the fact that I did the gunsmithing. Jim worked primarily on fishing gear and did the bookkeeping while I was the mainstay on hunting rifles, shotguns and pistols.

I couldn't pay Otto during the winter, he had taken a job with Clyde Cox who owned the Allis Chamber dealership across the street.

After deciding to add Jim as a partner, I offered to take inventory of my stock and fixtures and sell him half the business at exactly half my costs. There was one exception however: my antique guns. We inventoried them at my cost with the understanding that if we ever split up, I could buy his half of the guns back for the same price I paid for them.

Jim and I were partners for twelve years. He did the bookkeeping and all the repair work on fishing reels while I was responsible for all the gunsmithing. We averaged sales of six hundred rifles, pistols and shotguns per year and sold lots of fishing tackle as well.

Our families enjoyed camping and fishing trips around the Idaho Panhandle. I usually did more hunting and fishing than Jim, for he liked to play golf. He did go on several week-long elk hunts with friends to the St. Joe and Clearwater river drainages, however. Although we didn't make much money in our business, we did enjoy the great North Idaho outdoors.

A short time after I started the sport shop, I also began to shoot clay birds: that is, trapshoot, with the Sandpoint Gun Club. They had an area located along the shore of Lake Pend Oreille about a quarter mile north of what is now the Edgewater Restaurant and Motel in Sandpoint. The club had two concrete trap houses and a small club house. We shot east over the lake. Other members of the club who are now considered old-timers in Sandpoint included Jack Cranston, a retired hardware merchant; Art Kalk, a retiree; Bill Parker, Sr., who had served as Sandpoint's chief of police; his son Bill, who was an airline pilot; Stan Maxwell, a partner in the Sandpoint News Bulletin; Glen Bandelin, an attorney and state senator; Fred Schedler, a partner in McFarland Pole Co.; and Louie Schnell, a retiree from Hope. I was elected secretary-treasurer of the group. It was my responsibility to buy the clay birds and ammunition as well as keep track of finances. My responsibilities to that position lasted for fourteen years.

One of the highlights of being involved in the group was our annual trip to Kimberly, British Columbia, for their invitational shoot. The main event was a contest between the Canadian five-man teams and those from the United States. Teams from both sides were made up of

125

citizens of each country. Contestants were allowed to participate on just one team each year. There was a beautiful traveling trophy that stayed with the winning team for a year with the team's names engraved on the plaque.

I not only enjoyed trapshooting but also found it to be good for business. Many of the people I met through the activity became regular customers of our sports shop. I sold lots of trap guns over the years.

Having bought, sold and collected guns as well as having done my share of hunting from the time I was a boy, I was always concerned with firearms safety. My experiences at Farragut really brought this to light. It bothered me a lot whenever I read about gun accidents caused by the careless handling of the weapons. It also bothered me to meet other men in the field while hunting and have them carelessly point their loaded

I've always been proud that our ten-week Firearms & Hunter Safety course was the first Hunter Safety Program of its kind in the United States.

firearm at me or lean on the gun while talking.

Since I was a life member of the National Rifle Association, I received their magazine. In the fall of 1946, I read an article about a group of sportsmen in New Hampshire who had put on a one-day hunter safety program in their area. Their motivation was to try to cut down on the accidental shooting of other hunters through careless handling of guns and ammunition.

This gave me an idea. I contacted our conservation officer Lester Gissel and let him read the article. He thought it was a good idea so we set out to start our own program in the Sandpoint area.

First, we had to find a place to shoot. Charlie Stidwell, the principal at Farmin School, came through and allowed us to use the basement of the old Farmin School building. Next, we needed bullet traps. Clyde Cox, of Cox Implement Company, aided us with this project by building three bullet traps out of quarter-inch steel. The Sandpoint Recreation Board helped us pay for the steel. Clyde donated the welding rod and his labor. With a need for some publicity, we talked with Laurin Pietsch, one of the owners of the Sandpoint News Bulletin, who gladly offered to help.

Les and I then set up a ten-week program for hunter safety. It was open to both boys and girls eleven years old and older. The lecture was followed by a session with each student being allowed to shoot ten shots at targets in front of the bullet traps. The distance was fifty feet, and a coach stood in back of each student. Lots of parents were on hand to provide this help, but we had a rule that parents were not to coach their own children.

Many parents took an active part in our program, but the most active volunteers were Harold and Martha Miller who became involved soon after we started. This dedicated couple continued through the years and guided the program when I was later elected to the legislature and also when I became governor.

At the end of the ten-week course, we gave a written test, observed demonstrations and had an oral test with each student. Those that passed earned a nice patch for their jacket or shirt. It was green with a picture of a buck deer head embroidered in the center. It was inscribed "Sandpoint Safety Ranger."

After about two years in the Farmin School basement, we had to find another location because of a remodeling project. The Eagles Lodge offered their basement. I'm sure that offer came through the influence of Harold and Martha Miller who were long-time Eagle members. About the same time we were making the move to the Eagles, a new bridge was being constructed across Lake Pend Oreille. The crews had torn down the old wooden bridge which had been constructed of six-inch by sixteen-inch full-length treated bridge timbers. These timbers were up to twenty feet long.

I got the idea that we could use the timbers to build an indoor rifle range. Since we would have to find a place to build it I started looking around. Soon I found a lot the City of Sandpoint owned on Pine Street. Then I attended the City Council meeting and presented my plan. At the time Floyd Gray was mayor of Sandpoint. After listening to my presentation, the council and the mayor gave me the go-ahead, stipulating that if we started the project, they would like to see it finished.

The next step was to go back to the people who had been helping us with our program and present the plans to them. They gave their approval and offered all their help to get the project going. I learned that a big pile of bridge timbers had been stored across the lake next to the fish hatchery. The contractor who had torn the bridge down owned the timbers and offered to sell the whole pile to us for five hundred dollars.

That posed a yet another problem, however. Where would we get five hundred dollars? I was serving as chairman of the city recreation board, so I decided to present the dilemma to them. Sure enough, they gave us the five hundred dollars. Everything else that went into the building was donated by somebody. After the foundations were dug and the forms built, we poured the foundation. Several local loggers hauled the bridge timbers as we needed them. Our structure was sixty feet wide and ninety feet long. The walls were sixteen inches thick, built out of bridge timbers. We doubled the timbers on the back wall. All the joints were offset so that no stray bullets could go through.

Someone had loaned us a tractor with a lift for setting the heavy beams in place. When this was done, we nailed them together with twelve-inch spikes, about three to a beam. Once the walls were built eight feet high, we needed a roof. Again a local person jumped in and helped. Dub Lewis, a carpenter, helped me figure out the amount of lumber we needed and took the responsibility of getting volunteers to install the roof. Pack River Lumber Co., owned by Jim Brown, furnished all the lumber for this project, and Bargain Supplies, owned by Dan Deshon, furnished the roofing material.

After the roof was completed, we went to work on a bullet trap for the back end of the building. Someone gave us a huge steel tank which we cut into sheets that were then laid on a cement driveway and flattened out by running a big Caterpillar dozer over them.

To get the cement floor that was needed, we raffled off a nice 30-06 Springfield Sporter with a scope. Again, all this was donated. By selling tickets for a dollar apiece, we made more than seven hundred dollars and were able to pay for the floor which was about thirty by sixty feet.

When the building was completed, we moved our hunter safety classes from the Eagles Lodge to our new rifle range. It was a nice building with a nice story. It had been built with volunteer labor and one-hundred percent donated material.

By 1960 more than fifteen hundred boys and girls had gone through our hunter safety course. That year I was elected to the Idaho State Legislature and I felt good about turning the program over to the many dedicated people who had helped through the years.

I have kept close track since then and, to my knowledge, not one of our students was ever involved in a hunting accident or injury through mishandling a firearm or ammunition. We were extremely proud in 1968 when the National Rifle Association representatives came to Sandpoint and presented Harold Miller, Lester Gissel and me each a nice plaque for starting the first hunter safety program in the United States.

Chapter 11

A Confirmed Mountain Man

From the time I arrived at the Farragut Naval Base in the Idaho Panhandle and saw the beautiful Selkirk, Cabinet and Coeur d'Alene mountain ranges, I became a confirmed mountain man. I loved to hunt in the hills and mountains with all our supplies on our backs for three to ten days at a time. It was my favorite way to spend a vacation.

Backpacking was a great way to enjoy the company of close friends and to learn more and more about the wildlife that inhabited the back country. I made several trips through the Selkirk Range with Stewart Branborg who was doing a study on the mountain goats of Idaho in the early 1950s. As a result of his studies, the Idaho Fish and Game Department printed a book entitled <u>Mountain Goat in Idaho</u> in 1955. On one such trip, Merle Sampson and I spent ten days in and around the Middle Fork of the Salmon River participating on the study. We covered the lower end of the middle fork, many times standing on top of ridges, looking down into the rushing waters of what is better known as the "River of No Return." We had the opportunity to observe goats in their native habitat, watching and recording their actions with movie and 35mm slide cameras.

Times spent such as this, with a full pack on my back hiking through the Selkirk Mountains were very special.

In addition to the Middle Fork, we covered Corn Creek, Horse Creek, Spindle Creek, and the main Salmon River to about six miles below the old town of Shoupe. One interesting highlight of the trip occurred on Horse Creek. This was in April when "Brandy" (Steward Branborg, the biologist) wanted to see if there were any goats at the head of Horse Creek. We lifted our packs to our backs and started up the trail alongside the creek. Having traveled up the trail several miles, we ran into snow which got deeper as we climbed. When we were in over our knees, Brandy suggested that we not go any farther because we hadn't seen any sign of game for the last mile. The snow was crusty besides and that made for tough walking.

When we started back down the trail with me in the lead, I gained about a hundred yards on Brandy and Merle, who were talking about range management. We were down to where the snow was about six inches deep when I was shocked to see tracks of a barefoot man in the trail. I checked back a few feet and found where they came off the north side of the ridge to the trail.

I stopped and waited for Merle and Brandy to catch up. When they did, I pointed to the tracks and asked, "Do you see what I see?"

"That's Cougar Allen," Brandy responded, "an old gentleman who lives in a tar-paper-covered shack on a bar on the south side of the Salmon River, a couple miles below the mouth of Horse Creek. He has a bunch of cougar dogs and hunts cougar in the winter time."

We continued down the trail to a level spot about a quarter mile above the Salmon River. Since it was getting late in the day, we decided to camp there for the night. The following morning while eating breakfast by the campfire, Brandy asked if Merle and I would like to meet Cougar Allen. We both said "yes" at the same time.

We hiked on down to the Salmon River and the main trail where we stashed our sleeping bags and packs in the brush above the trail. Then we headed down the river. Brandy told us the CCCs had built a swinging bridge across the Salmon River to the bar where Cougar had built his residence.

As we reached the bridge and before crossing, Brandy stopped us and said we had better let Cougar know who we were so we wouldn't get shot. He let out a yell, and almost immediately the plank door of the cabin opened. There stood Cougar Allen in a suit of black long johns. Brandy told him who he was and that he had a couple of friends with him.

Cougar yelled back, "Come on over!"

When we arrived, the odor around the shack was pretty strong. He had been catching mice and throwing them outside. The weather was warm with high humidity down along the river and that didn't help the situation much. In addition, several cougar skulls stared at us from the tops of posts or stumps cut off at a high level.

When we got inside, we found that Cougar had been preparing breakfast in his black long johns.

"Sit down," he instructed.

I found a chunk of stove wood which was probably his chopping block and sat down. Brandy sat on a stool, but Merle stood where he was. Cougar said, "Sit on the bed," but when Merle stayed where he was. Cougar said again, "sit on the bed." Finally when Merle didn't head for the bed, Cougar looked at it and saw that it was full of cougar hounds.

"Get the H— out of here!" he yelled. The dogs scattered out the door and windows as if they had been shot out of a gun.

Cougar was a large framed, barrel-chested redhead who stood more than six feet tall. Brandy told us that old-timers who knew him in his prime recalled that he would put a hundred-pound pack on his back and head up a trail, never stopping until he reached the top.

One of our first observations when we walked into the cabin was that he had his chest bandaged up. The bandages could be seen between the buttons on the tops of his long johns. Brandy asked him about the wound.

Cougar responded with the following story: The week before, he had taken his dogs and hiked up Horse Creek to see if he could find a cougar. Soon they jumped one and the pack of dogs were on its trail. He had one young hound in the bunch that decided to take a short cut. It ran into the big male mountain lion by itself. Consequently, the cat took after the dog, which, in turn, hit the Forest Service trail and headed toward its master for protection.

The problem was that Cougar was on a narrow ledge of a trail with a rock wall on one side and approximately a twenty-foot drop on the other. Here came the dog straight down the trail with the mountain lion in pursuit right behind it. Cougar was carrying a .32 caliber, single-shot rifle. The dog ran between Cougar Allen's legs and the mountain lion leaped into the air straight at the man.

Raising the rifle, he shot "from the hip" and hit the cat in the chest, killing it in mid-air. The momentum of the animal carried it right on top of Cougar Allen, knocking him into the rocks on the trail. The impact broke a couple of his ribs. Cougar said he was lucky to stay on the trail, but the cougar hit him and rolled over the ledge, landing on the rocks in the creek some twenty feet below.

Following this exciting tale, the three of us listened to stories of the gold rush days in and around the Shoupe area of the Salmon River. From these yarns, we learned that more than eight thousand Chinese had prospected gold in that area during the late 1800s. He also wanted to sell us gold placer claims that he said had "ten million dollars worth of gold" in them. His price was "one hundred thousand dollars!" Cougar Allen was definitely a great story teller — parts of which were probably true and some of which were figments of his imagination. Whatever the case, he certainly kept us entertained.

After three hours of enjoying his tales, we headed back up the trail to retrieve our packs and set out for our cars at the end of the road, eventually destined for Sandpoint and home. I asked Stewart about Cougar Allen's walking bare foot in the snow. He didn't have shoes or

This photograph of a North Idaho cougar taken with a customer of mine in front of my sport shop gives you an idea of the size of the animal Cougar Allen delt with just a week before our visit.

133

socks on in the cabin; but because we were inside on a wooden floor, I didn't think much of it, though the tracks I'd seen in the snow earlier had me wondering. Stewart said as far as he knew, "Cougar Allen doesn't wear shoes anytime of the year," and left it at that.

About the same time I moved to Sandpoint and started the Pend Oreille Sport Shop, the Idaho Fish and Game Department assigned Lester Gissel as conservation officer in Bonner County. Les was an outdoorsman from the soles of his shoes to the top of his head. We became very good friends and spent many hours, traveling many miles throughout the mountains of North Idaho. In fact, there is hardly a ridge or mountain peak in the Idaho Panhandle that we haven't stood on. We have traveled through the mountains on snow shoes in minus ten to minus twenty degrees below zero weather. We have also fished most of the high mountain lakes in North Idaho as well as the majority of the streams.

Both of us were very interested in wildlife, so I spent a lot of time with Les on weekends and holidays checking the winter ranges of deer and elk. In winter, we covered the territory on snowshoes. One of the problems during this time of year is coyotes or cougars killing deer and elk when the snow is deep and the game animals are yarded up, usually on the south exposure of a mountain or high hill. Another problem throughout our state was caused by "spotlighters," poachers who use spotlights on their cars or pickups to search the fields for deer at night close to timbered areas. Many also used powerful flashlights or lanterns. Once they spotted a deer, they would shoot it from the road. Often these game lawbreakers would compound their crime by shooting (hopefully by mistake) and killing cows or horses.

I rode with Les Gissel and Paul Flynn, the conservation officer from Boundary county, on many a night in efforts to catch spotlighters. Night after night, we would drive through the farm areas from the first darkness until three or four the next morning.

Here is a true story about spotlighting told to me by a farmer friend of mine about himself: He had bought a farm north of Sandpoint and moved from another farm which he had been renting. When he started to move to the new place, one of his neighbors came over and helped him unload and carry furniture and other items. Upon finishing, they sat in the kitchen visiting over a cup of coffee and piece of cake.

My friend's new neighbor asked if he had ever done any spotlighting of deer. My friend responded, "No."

Then the neighbor asked if he would like to go. Not wanting to offend him, my friend said he would.

The neighbor left to go home and do his chores; but upon leaving, announced, "I'll pick you up about seven thirty tonight."

That evening, the man came into the driveway with his pickup, complete with spotlight. When my friend was comfortably seated in the truck, the neighbor said, "You have an old apple orchard on the back of your place, and deer come in to eat the fallen apples. Is it okay if we start there?"

My friend said that would be all right, so down a side road they went to where they pulled-up alongside the fence. The neighbor turned on the spotlight and at the other end of the orchard were two sets of eyes looking back. The fellow grabbed his high-powered rifle and jumped out of the pickup. My friend got out on the other side.

The neighbor said, "You get the little one and I'll get the big one."

My friend was reluctant to shoot, so he stalled for time. Meanwhile, the neighbor took a shot and down went the animal.

He yelled to my friend, "Get the other one!"

But my friend froze.

"I knew everyone in Boundary county heard that shot," he told me later. Shaking with fear, he urged his neighbor not to shoot the other animal.

When they climbed the fence and walked over to dress out the "deer" — low and behold — it turned out to be one of my friend's horses. The other set of eyes belonged to his son's pony. It seems that there was a fenced-in lane that led from the barnyard to the old orchard area.

This plot of land was being used as a pasture. My friend had put the horses and cattle in the barnyard earlier, under the impression that the gates were closed. Since it was a new place, he had forgotten about the lane. Needless to say, my friend became one of the most rabid opponents of spotlighting in the county after that incident.

Besides this story, I experienced some real eye-openers while stalking spotlighters with Les Gissel. Another adventure with him took us on a backpacking trip through the northwest corner of Boundary county near the Canadian line.

The fish and game biologist had asked Les to get him some scale samples of the fish in Grass Creek and Cow Creek. He also wanted us to check on the goats and other game in that area. I volunteered to accompany him for the week. We left on a Sunday morning, going through Bonners Ferry to Port Hill. We crossed the Kootenai River via the ferry at Port Hill, then followed Myrtle Creek to Boundary Creek and finally arrived at Grass Creek.

There had been a molybdenum mine at the head of Grass Creek many years before and the miner had put in a road up the drainage. It is about fifteen miles from the mouth of Grass Creek to the old mine. Les drove the pickup up the old road about ten miles until we came to a creek that

cut our road and ran into Grass Creek. Its bank was about four feet deep and ten feet from side to side. Someone had constructed a bridge out of three poles for each track. Wired together at close intervals, the two-track bridge appeared to be very strong, so we proceeded to drive across. All went well until the two front wheels were on the ground on the other side. This put all the power on one of the rear wheels, and it kicked the poles out from the left side. The

Hunting in the mountains of North Idaho was one of my favorite outdoor activities. I took this billy goat in the Lion Creek drainage in the Selkirk Mountains above Priest Lake about thirty miles north of my home by the way a crow flies.

truck stopped, hanging in the air and perched on three wheels. What a revolting development, considering that we were about thirty-five miles from the closest civilization!

Fortunately, there was a nice spot to set up our tent and camp about fifty feet behind the truck. We decided it was best to first set up camp, which we proceeded to do, all the time being very careful as we removed equipment from the pickup. While we were trying to figure out a way to get the truck back on "terra firma" without having it turn over on its side in the creek, I don't think we said a word to one another until the campsite was completed.

Once that was done, we turned our attention to the problem at hand. Since we didn't have a jack, we decided to cut a long, strong pole to use as a lever. Then we found a big rock and moved it to the edge of the bank at the back of the truck. Placing the end of the pole under the back end of the truck, we used the rock as a fulcrum. The pole served as a lever to raise the rear of the vehicle high enough to return the poles to their rightful place under the left rear wheel. Then Les got in the truck, started the motor, and very carefully, very slowly backed it off the poles. I watched the poles, while Les moved the truck inch by inch. We both heaved a sigh of relief when the truck was finally back on all four wheels on solid ground.

The next day we fished Grass Creek both above and below camp. We caught and released a lot of fish, keeping only those that had been too greedy by swallowing our flies. These were mountain brook trout and our largest "lunker" was about ten inches. We kept enough to fry over the campfire that evening.

On the third day, we hiked up to the molybdenum mine, which was in pretty bad shape, caved in from heavy snows and lack of maintenance. There were four log cabins sitting in a row a short distance from the mine. I'm sure they were the bunkhouses for the men who had once worked there. The doors and windows were open, but the roofs were in good shape and the cabins were dry inside.

One of the buildings had forty cases of 40% dynamite stacked against one wall. The explosives had been there so long that gelatin was running out of the boxes and forming crystals on the outside. Dynamite is very dangerous to handle in that condition. To make matters worse, several boxes of dynamite caps and rolls of fuse sat near it.

Across Grass Creek about a hundred yards away was a large metal building, and in the middle of its dirt floor were seventeen more cases of dynamite. We also discovered deer tracks inside the building and could see that the deer had been eating on the explosives. The gelatin was leaking from these cases and it was probably the salt within that attracted the deer.

That night we camped at the head of Grass Greek, and the next morning we started toward a mountain known as Phoebe's Tip. We saw seven mountain goats feeding along its west rock face and watched them through the binoculars for more than an hour. From there, we hit the ridge that took us to the top of Phoebe's Tip. At that point, we enjoyed watching a couple of black bear wallow in the pond about half a mile below us. We could also see Mollie's Lookout at the end of the ridge about a mile southeast of us and decided to hike over there and spend the night in the lookout.

When we arrived at our destination, we discovered that the lookout had been abandoned. We saw goat hair all along the railing and on several clumps of brush around the lookout which sat directly on the rocks. Because it was built on the ground and not up on the usual tower that most lookouts had, it was open for the goats to use at their pleasure.

Since there was no water at the lookout, Les volunteered to find some while I gathered firewood. I had the better deal because there was lots of wood lying about on the ground around the lookout. Les had to drop down nearly a quarter mile to find a spring. Once we had water, we made coffee and cooked dinner amid the beautiful scenery. Our view included Upper Priest Lake and the north end of Priest Lake.

The next morning we headed northeast and dropped into the head of Cow Creek, where we found several old prospect holes and some old mine cabins. One was located right alongside Cow Creek, close to its source. It was well preserved, and still had a good roof. The door was open, but much of the inside of the cabin indicated that the owner or at least the last person there had left behind numerous items many years before. Of course the pack rats had messed the place up and their presence was evident everywhere.

When we made breakfast that morning at Molly's Lookout, we used the last of our coffee. I had misjudged the amount we would need for a week. Looking around the cabin, we spied an old single coil bed-spring wired to the ceiling. We could see that there were several items on it, so I found a chopping block to stand where I could reach them. One was a sack of white beans; another was a sack of flour; and, believe it or not, the other was a one-pound can of Folger's coffee, complete with the key to open the can! It was covered with dust about half an inch thick, but we felt pretty lucky because the can showed no sign of rust. After dusting it off thoroughly and inserting the key, we broke the seal. Hearing the air go in, we were sure that it was okay.

To get away from the pack rats, we decided to hike downstream about a hundred yards and camp. The flip of a coin determined who would start a fire and supper and who would catch a mess of fish for the meal. Winning the toss to go fishing, I took off. Catching six nice 8- to 10-inch brook trout took just fifteen minutes.

When I returned to camp with the half dozen trout, Les had the fire going and the coffee boiling. We got our cups out and after pouring a bit of cold water on top to settle the grounds, we each filled a cup with coffee. Wow! To our surprise, it was exceptionally strong and very bitter. In fact, it was so bad we couldn't drink it. That was a great disappointment because we both enjoyed our cups of coffee sitting around campfires after dinner and a long day in the mountains.

We never understood why the coffee was so bad until later when a grocer friend explained that the can of coffee had probably been on that bed spring high in the mountains for at least twenty years. Lying close under the roof, as it did, the extreme cold in the winter and the heat in the summer probably caused all the oil in the coffee beans to work toward the bottom of the can, where it likely became concentrated. Since the can had been stored upside down, the concentrate was on top when we opened it. He explained that if we had stirred it up, the coffee probably would have been okay and that if we had taken it by chance from the other end, the coffee would probably have been very weak.

The next morning we caught a few more fish for breakfast and took scale samples while dressing them. We also spent some time around the head of Cow Creek checking out the prospect holes and several other cabins. This area is a basin where lots of springs converge to make up the main creek. It was covered with ferns taller than we were.

Les and I were wandering around in the ferns when we almost stepped in a pile of fresh bear dung. Then we saw the animal's tracks with long extended claws. It was a grizzly bear, definitely. All we had for defending ourselves were our two fishing poles. Several paths leading through the ferns indicated that grizzly had been living in the basin at the head of Cow Creek for some time.

As we made our way out through the ferns, I jumped across a small stream about eighteen inches wide and ran into the side of a martin trapper's cabin which had been made out of small poles. The structure was about six feet wide and eight to ten feet long. It stood not more than five feet high. Inside, we found a pole bed on one side and an earth stove in the corner behind the door. The ferns were so thick and tall that I hadn't seen the cabin until I met it face to face. It was somewhat of a shock to come to such a sudden stop.

From the cabin, we hiked up over the ridge, down past the molybdenum mine and the cabins, and back to our original camp and the pickup. We spent the next couple of days hiking over the ridge toward Blue Joe Creek and the old Continental Mine. We felt fortunate to have beautiful weather for the entire week. We saw lots of birds, deer and goats besides enjoying fresh fish for almost every meal. At the end of the week, we headed home with our mission accomplished.

Les Gissel and I made many backpacking trips through the mountains together. These ranged from one-day trips up to sometimes a week with all our food and sleeping bags on our back. Some of these experiences were easy and pleasant, while others were challenging. I liked hiking in the mountains with Les for several reasons. We hiked about the same speed. No matter how bad the weather became, he never complained. We were also pretty adept at spotting animals, and we each had a deep commitment to wildlife and range management. Finally, Les studied his area and knew it better than most people know their backyard. I considered it educational and a great opportunity for an old Illinois farm boy to go to the mountains with this dedicated man.

We took another memorable trip through the north end of the Selkirk Mountains northwest of Sandpoint. This nine-day adventure started at the Canadian line and ended at the end of the road on Pack River. The three of us—Les, Carl Greif and I—carried everything on our backs with pack boards.

Carl Grief worked for the Hitchner and Hitchner Cedar Pole Company in Sandpoint. He was slight of build but in excellent condition. The night before our trip we divided our supplies among the three of us. Setting a kitchen scale on the floor of our living room, we separated the items by weight. Carl insisted on his share of the load and never lagged behind or complained once on the nine-day trip.

A bad rain and windstorm hit us the first night out. All three of us got soaking wet trying to find shelter without getting under a tree. Lighting flashed around us, making the whole situation rather tense as darkness was approaching. We finally found a shelter under a rock cliff for protection. There were no complaints from anyone. We had figured the food right down to the last. When we hit the end of the trail, we had just enough for one more meal. On this trek we covered more than sixty-five miles which took us to creek bottoms twice and up and down several mountains. Throughout our journey, we again saw our share of birds

One of our wives took this photograph of the three of us with full packs on our backs just prior to heading out from the Dirt Oven area on Smith Creek for our nine-day trip across the Selkirks. Les Gissel is in the middle and Carl Grief is on the right.

and wildlife, including goats.

I had an interesting experience with a goat on the east side of Abandon Mountain near the top. Les, Carl and I were walking down the main ridge when we spotted four mountain goats feeding in a meadow about a hundred and fifty yards down the mountain. Since I had an 8mm movie camera, we decided to try to get close enough to take some pictures. Our plan called for Les and Carl to go down the ridge to a saddle where they would leave their packs. Then, they would contour below where the goats were feeding. Between me and the goats were a series of block faults through which I planned to work my way down toward the goats. When I reached the bottom, Carl and Les were to spook the goats, which generally run uphill. The plan was for me to be behind one of those block fault ridges where I was sure to get some good pictures.

All went well, and I was almost down to where I planned to stop and wait for Les and Carl to drive the goats my way. Slowly and quietly, I crept up to the top of a little ridge, planning to drop over it and wait. Just as I peered over the ridge, I looked straight into the eyes of an old billy about three feet away. I don't know which one of us was the most surprised! He took off "post haste" and scared the other goats which disappeared around the corner of Abandon Mountain with him.

I was so surprised that I was all thumbs trying to get my camera out of the case. I did get a shot of his south end however, going north around the corner. My hopes of being a premier wildlife photographer went with him.

Another incident occurred the next day when we dropped off the mountain, crossed Lion Creek, which runs into Priest Lake, and climbed the mountain on the other side to Kent Lake. We fought snow brush all the way up the mountain from Lion Creek to the lake. When we got there, the lake was so shallow we could see the bottom everywhere. We had planned to camp by the lake that night, but the mosquitoes were so thick, it was hard to tell what color our jackets or shirts were. We doped our hands and faces with repellent, but that didn't help much. The critters would fly into our faces and eyes anyway.

With the mosquito problem persisting, we decided to climb up on the ridge about a thousand feet above the lake to camp. We wound our way up the ridge, being very quiet as we walked through some house-sized boulders looking for a level place to camp for the night. Just as we came around one boulder at the top of the ridge, we saw a large flat rock with a goat curled up on it, sleeping. He stood up and looked at us for a couple of seconds and for some reason or another decided to depart.

We found an ideal spot to camp for the night, complete with a ten-by-twelve-foot flat granite rock with a wash basin carved in it already full of water. There were several gallons of warm, clean rainwater that we could use to wash our hands and faces — oh so refreshing after the tough climb we had just completed!

I took this photo of Carl (left) and Les cleaning fish at West Fork Lake near the Canadian border on that trip. Sadly it was the last trip either Les or I got to take with Carl Grief.

I always enjoyed going to the mountains with Les and Carl because they were such great company and so adept at facing the obstacles when there were no trails and the going was tough. When the three of us were together, no one ever complained or became crabby.

We planned to take another trip together the following year, but just two weeks before our planned departure, Carl became very ill with bulbar polio and died within just a few days. We regretted the loss of this special friend with whom we had experienced many pleasant memories. Les and I have talked about Carl many times since that last trip. He was really a great guy to be with, especially when the going got tough.

One day Les contacted me and asked if I could get away for three or four days to count the goats around the Scotchman Peak area east of Clark Fork, Idaho. After making arrangements to be away from the store for several days, I joined Les and we loaded our packs with food, threw them in his truck and headed for Clark Fork. We drove up the Big Lightning Creek Road to the Mosquito Creek Road and left his pickup at the bottom of the trail leading up the ridges to the Old Scotchman Lookout.

We arrived at the lookout around five o'clock in the afternoon and decided to camp there for the night because it was the highest point, allowing us to see in all directions. We set up camp on a large, level, flat rock just below the old lookout because the structure itself had signs of pack rats throughout. We found a snowdrift on the north side of the ridge and melted the snow to make coffee and wash dishes. After dinner, we used our binoculars to scan the rocky hillsides all around us for goats, but to no avail. We continued our fruitless observation until it became too dark to see.

The next morning after breakfast we packed our gear and headed toward Scotchman No. 2 and Black Mountain. About ten o'clock that morning, we rounded a cliff and jumped a big billy goat. He bounded for higher ground and found himself stranded on a ledge which extended straight up behind him and ended against a wall of rocks a short distance away.

Les and I stood below him, blocking his only escape route. Having trapped him in this way, we enjoyed taking pictures of him for about half-an-hour as he pranced back and forth on the narrow ledge trying to find

Les Gissel peeks around the rock ledge at the young goat he saved from the talons of a bald eagle. We were counting mountain goats in the Scotchman's Peak area east of Clark Fork in North Idaho.

a way out. Once we had snapped all the pictures we wanted, we left him, moved over to Black Mountain, and hiked down to Spar Lake, just over the Idaho line into Montana. Late that afternoon, we hiked back up the mountain and found a nice place to camp on top of a ridge at the head of Blue Creek.

Running through the top of this ridge are two fresh water springs that form the headwaters of Blue Creek. One spring flows south and forms a branch of the creek, while the other flows north around the east side of the mountain to join the other fork some distance down the canyon. The springs are only about fifty feet apart at the top of the ridge, however. We brewed the coffee, cooked dinner over our campfire, and made our beds out of bear grass to cushion our sleeping bags from the hard ground.

The next morning turned out to be another beautiful day. We crawled out of our sleeping bags to stoke up the fire and enjoyed spectacular scenery. After years of traveling together, Les and I have agreed on a working arrangement. He does the cooking and I wash the dishes. On this particular morning, he made breakfast and packed his gear afterward. When I finished washing dishes, I started putting my things together and was just starting to tie them to the pack board. Les was standing off to one side watching a bald eagle silently sail in over the ridge. Suddenly, the eagle folded its wings and started to dive toward the rocks on the ground. Les carried a .22 automatic pistol in a holster on his belt. Pulling it out, he started shooting in the air, and the eagle took off. The bird had been diving on a young goat, which it would have killed if Les had not scared it off.

Les started running toward the little goat and yelled back at me, "Get your cameras and come on!"

I did just that while Les ran the little fellow out on a small rock cliff. Having determined where he was heading, I ran down the side of the mountain and got to the bottom of the cliff. The goat had gone over the edge and was standing on a three-foot-wide ledge about fifteen feet from the top.

Slowly and quietly, we worked our way toward him with Les descending from the top and me climbing from below. The animal would look at Les and then at me and stomp his front feet. We worked to within six feet of him, taking 8mm movies and 35mm slides all the time. Finally the little guy got tired of our monkey business and walked over to the edge of the ledge where he cocked his head and looked over. Suddenly, he went over, hitting little projections with his feet all the way to the bottom of a thirty-five-foot straight-up-and-down cliff without falling. When he hit bottom and fairly flat ground, he took off on a trot with his little tail in the air waving "good-bye" to us.

After this great experience, we climbed back to our camping spot on top of the ridge. I finished packing my gear and got our last cold drink of water from one of the springs at the head of Blue Creek. We hung our pack boards on our backs and headed northwest toward a pass leading to the headwaters of the East Fork of Big Lightning Creek. At one point while descending a steep slope at the head of the East Fork, we passed a large bull pine which had been marked as a section corner during the original survey of that portion of Bonner County probably in the late 1880s or early 1890s as Idaho became a state in 1891.

We also passed an old mine and saw several pieces of mining equipment that had rusted away with the years. About five o'clock in the afternoon, we welcomed the sight of the Big Lightning Creek Road. The view of the fish and game truck further down the road signaled the end to another three grand and exciting days in a beautiful area.

Chapter 12

Close to Nature in the Mountains

While I owned the Pend Oreille Sports Shop, my main source of revenue came from buying and selling guns, ammunition and accessories. From the start, my being a gunsmith put us ahead of the competition in our area because we could buy broken or defective guns and I could repair them for resale. I re-barreled and converted many of the long-barreled Winchester and Marlin 30-30's to short-barreled carbines. I was authorized by Winchester, Remington, Colt, Smith & Wesson, Stevens and all the other gun manufacturers to buy and install their parts. We kept a good inventory of parts after they became available at the conclusion of World War II.

For several years after the war, I had to repair, build up the wear by welding and heat-treating parts or even make new parts from scratch. When new parts were available, it was great because they saved time for me and money for our customers.

We sold a lot of telescopic sights because I could install them. We generally mounted the scope for free whenever customers purchased scopes and mounts from us. Another advantage for us was that I was authorized to buy and install scope parts. I could re-seal leaking scopes after taking the moisture out of them with heat. I used silicon grease to reseal them after they dried out and before I put them back together.

Firearms, both antique and modern, have been a part of my life since I purchased my first .22 Crack-Shot single shot rifle when I was about ten years old. I had about twenty-five rifles, shotguns and pistols when Ruby and I were married. In this past year I sold my collection of antique guns. I kept my personal hunting rifles and shotguns for my continued enjoyment. I enjoy trap shooting, target shooting and hunting just as others enjoy golf and tennis.

In my early years, running a trap line provided the money to buy my clothes and provide me with a dollar or two to go to a dance once or twice a month. Rabbits, squirrels and quail helped with the food bill and helped

147

Once my longtime friend, Ross Hall, and I hiked from the Baldy Lookout in back of what is now Schweitzer Mountain Ski Resort over Long Mountain down to a spot near the Sandpoint Airport. Ross, who took this photograph of me taking a break on that hike, turned out to be one of the great photographers of our time. Many of his photographs illustrated historical events and character and still sell in galaries around the U.S., partly thanks to his son, Dan who has carried on the legacy with fine art prints from Ross's many negatives. This was one of my favorites of me because it illustrates my timeless love for the mountains of North Idaho.

stretch our egg and cream checks from which my folks bought staples and groceries during the week.

None of the game was ever wasted. It was cleaned in the field or as soon as we arrived home.

When we moved to Idaho and started the sport shop we didn't have much money so the deer and elk I bagged really helped us through each year.

The experience and skill that I developed from hunting each year helped me evaluate many new guns and ammunition as they came on the market. I would buy the first new gun in a new caliber and use it on game to see how it handled and performed in the field. I tried different weights of bullets on various kinds of game.

I always tried to be a good enough shot so I could drop game without a second shot. I did have some bad experiences with some guns and ammunition. These episodes helped me advise my customers as to what worked best.

One of my experiences was with a 300 H.H. Magnum rifle. One morning I was walking up a draw east of Naples, Idaho. There was a skiff of snow on the ground that morning. It was just getting light enough to see clearly when I spotted a small forked horn buck and doe feeding above me about a hundred yards away on the opposite side of the draw. I stopped and watched them for about five minutes. Their tails were headed toward me so I just watched. Finally the buck turned sideways. I held the sights in back of its front legs where its heart should be.

I pulled the trigger firing the gun and the deer took off on a dead run. The buck ran straight ahead and the doe took off in the other direction.

I stood there with my mouth open and watched them run. I knew my hold was good. That buck should have dropped right there in his tracks.

I walked over to where it was standing when I shot. There was a small piece of its heart laying in the snow so I knew I had hit it where I was aiming. I followed the tracks and learned that the buck had run about a hundred yards before dropping, where it then slid in the snow about ten feet.

I was using 180-grain bullets that just bored their way through and didn't provide the shocking power for an instant kill. Needless to say I never used that gun or ammunition on deer again. My favorite gun for deer, coyotes and other small game is a Model 70 Winchester Featherweight firing .243 100-grain soft point bullets.

I might mention that I hunted with black powder "cap and ball muzzle-loading" rifles for many years, too. These were the old Kentucky squirrel rifles.

The best part of hunting is just working your way through the woods as quietly as you can, keeping to game trails, watching the pine squirrels, snowshoe rabbits and grouse from time to time. Over the years, I have observed all kinds of animals and birds while contouring the mountains in beautiful virgin timber.

One experience I'll never forget involved a downed tree about a foot in diameter. It was lying flat on the ground, and standing on it gave me a little advantage in looking over the country around me. Suddenly, I noticed some movement at the far end of the log. It was a pine marten with the little orange patch on his chest. Jumping up on the log, it ran right toward me. About five feet from me, it stopped for a few seconds and looked me over thoroughly. Then it jumped off the log, went around me, jumped back on behind me and finally went on its way. Throughout the whole experience, I stood like a statue, only moving my eyes. The animal never looked back as it disappeared into the brush behind a big tree. It had to be about twenty-four inches long with its shiny, beautiful brownish-black pelt, beady black eyes and cat-like ears. What a thrill when it actually jumped back on the log just two feet from me.

That reminds me of another time when my friend Les Gissel asked me to go with him and his son Con to check on some mountain goats in an area close to the Canadian line in Idaho's Panhandle. He was the conservation officer for Bonner County at the time. I agreed to accompany Les and Con to the Parker Creek Area, northwest of Bonners Ferry. We followed the Parker Peak trail for about a mile until Les suggested going up the creek a ways. From there, we could follow a couple of ridges from the creek up to where the Parker Peak Trail follows the main ridge.

Les and Con left me at the foot of the first ridge, suggesting that I give them about thirty minutes to get over to the foot of the second ridge. It was about a quarter mile across the rocks to the foot of their ridge, which ended just above Parker Creek. We would both climb our individual ridge toward the main ridge leading to Parker Peak and the old lookout. It was probably about a mile from the bottom of the ridge to the trail that ran up the main ridge to the mountaintop.

When the half hour was up, I started climbing slowly, watching both sides for game. My climb to the top was uneventful, for I observed only a couple of blue grouse and several chipmunks.

Upon reaching the ridge trail, I decided to walk up and wait for Les and Con at the top of the ridge they were climbing. When I arrived at the top, there was no sign of them.

I found a nice flat rock about six feet from where their ridge joined the trail. I sat down to enjoy a beautiful view of the Kootenai River Bottoms and Creston, British Columbia, just above the Canadian border. I sat quietly on the rock for about ten minutes until I heard rocks rolling behind me. I figured it to be Les and Con coming, so I just sat there looking over the valley and the distant mountains with my binoculars.

The silence that followed struck me however. I turned my head around fully expecting to see my friends. Instead, each of the intruders had four legs! Less than six feet from me were two adult mountain goats, checking me out. I carried an 8mm movie camera in a case under my arm and since they hadn't bolted right away, I tried to slip the camera out of the case, very slowly. When it was about halfway out, they decided to make a quick exit and were gone. They were beautiful animals with clean white hair — perfect for a picture.

Within about ten minutes, Les and Con joined me. Undoubtedly they had scared the two goats my direction but had not spotted them. After telling them what they had missed and enjoying some more of the view, we headed down the trail to the car.

It was spring. On the way down, the trail went by a large tree on the side of the mountain. The tree held a bald eagle's nest. When we came around the mountain above the tree, its occupant flew from the nest. Our position allowed us to look down on the eggs in the nest. We stopped just long enough to take a couple of pictures before continuing down the mountain. We did not want to disturb the eagle and keep her off her eggs too long.

Our trips to the mountains were not limited to spring, summer and fall. During the winter of 1954 or '55, Les kept getting reports of coyotes killing deer at Priest Lake. The lake freezes over in the winter and during this year the temperature had dropped to about ten below zero where it remained for several weeks. We also had several feet of snow on the level.

One morning Les came into the sports shop and asked, "How would you like to go on a snowshoe trip to the thoroughfare of Priest Lake tomorrow?" He said we could take off from Stevens Resort in the narrows and that he had the keys to a cabin at the north end of the lake close to the thoroughfare, a two-mile stretch of river between the main Priest Lake and Upper Priest Lake. Actually, the thoroughfare is a part of Priest River which starts in Canada and flows about eighteen miles from the Canadian line before entering Upper Priest Lake which it flows through and becomes the thoroughfare into Priest Lake. Priest River then exits at the south end of Priest Lake and continues about twenty miles to its mouth where it enters the Pend Oreille River a short distance east of the town of Priest River, Idaho.

Les told me that our drive to Stevens and the snowshoe trip would take most of the day. We would spend the following day checking the upper end of the lake and return the third day, he said. I made arrangements with my partner to take the shop while I went with Les.

At the time Les was explaining his plans, a mutual friend of ours, Merle Sampson, happened to be there. He heard Les and said the trip sounded interesting. Les invited him along. Merle was the county agricultural agent.

That evening we put our food together with our snowshoes, sleeping bags and other equipment. Les carried his 303 Savage and I took a 30-06 rifle with a box of 110-grain bullets in case we encountered coyotes on the trip.

The following morning we took off early. Our packboards and snowshoes were in the back of the Fish and Game pickup. On the way, we stopped at a restaurant and finished off a big breakfast, knowing full well we couldn't eat again until we reached the cabin at the far end of the lake.

Stevens Resort was closed when we arrived, but Les had made arrangements to leave his pickup on their property while we were gone. The temperature was just ten below zero when we were stepping into our snowshoes. There was about a foot of loose snow on the ice, but the cold temperature made it like feathers. It didn't cause us any problems.

We covered about eight to ten miles before reaching the cabin. The snow was cold and every once in a while, the ice would crack as we trudged along. At that time of year, darkness set in at around four in the afternoon. We arrived at the cabin around three-thirty and found it almost buried from blowing and drifting snow. In fact, we had to dig our way to the door by hand. Inside, the cabin seemed colder than the outdoors.

Next we had to start a fire and get the place warmed up. After lighting some newspaper in the fireplace, we soon discovered that the chimney was covered with snow. Checking the stove pipe in the kitchen range, we found the same problem. Les volunteered to climb up on the roof and clean the snow out of both chimneys. That's an interesting job when it's ten below zero and daylight is quickly diminishing. While Les was on the roof, Merle and I started preparing paper and wood for the two fires.

Les found an old wooden ladder in the woodshed and climbed to the roof which was covered with several feet of snow. As he was cleaning, some snow came down the fireplace chimney. We quickly scooped it up and threw it out the front door, but the chimney from the kitchen stove presented a different challenge. As Les cleared it at the top, some snow fell down and plugged up the stove pipe leading to the chimney. As a result, we had to take the stove pipes down and clean out the bottom of the chimney by reaching in and scooping the snow into a basket with our hands. This all took about an hour, but finally we got the fires going.

The fireplace was made from water-worn, round rocks. When we started the fire, it began putting out some heat. The rocks were coated with frost, and the heat caused them to look like they were covered with white feathers. The effect lasted about an hour and was a fascinating, beautiful sight to watch.

Warming the cabin took most of the evening. We made a big pot of coffee and fixed dinner. Kerosene lamps aided us in cooking and moving around. After dinner we put our sleeping bags on the floor in front of the fireplace. Any time someone awakened, he threw another chunk of wood on the fire. The next morning broke bright and clear. It was a beautiful crisp day, still ten below zero.

Following breakfast, we dressed in our heavy warm clothes and slipped into our snowshoes. We headed out to cover as much of the northern shoreline as possible, looking for deer kills or signs of coyotes, cougar or bobcats. The sky was blue. We felt no wind and the snow was perfect for snowshoeing. We covered a lot of shoreline before heading back to the cabin.

We didn't find one deer kill. We also failed to see any coyote or cougar tracks. We even took a jaunt through some of the flats on shore above the lake and traveled up the Lion Creek trail for a short distance looking for predators.

Back at the cabin, we were much more comfortable than we had been the previous night. It didn't take long to get some good fires going in both the fireplace and the stove. Les and Merle prepared a good dinner, and I washed dishes that evening. After sitting down to relax, we spun some stories around the fireplace talking about our outdoor experiences. Then, we rolled out the sleeping bags and called it a night.

The next morning after breakfast, we packed our gear and put out the fires. Les climbed up on the roof and put a cap on both chimneys to keep the snow out. On the way back to Stevens Resort we followed the east shore of the lake, looking for coyote and deer signs. When the three days were over, we had covered a lot of territory but found no deer kills.

The trip back to Sandpoint was uneventful except that the temperature still hovered in the minus ten range. Several weeks after that, the temperature dropped to around thirty-degrees below zero.

Later, Les had received several phone calls, from the Coolin and Cavanaugh Bay area at the south end of Priest Lake, telling him that coyotes were still killing deer on the lake in that area. He called and asked if I'd like to go with him to check it out. I agreed and again put my gear together. This time we wouldn't stay all night.

Les also mentioned our plans to Stan Maxwell, one of the owners of the <u>Sandpoint News Bulletin</u>, who wanted to join us. The three of us left Sandpoint early in the morning and drove to the Cavanaugh Bay area of Priest Lake. We took off on our snowshoes through about two feet of snow, covering areas along the east side of the bay. Eventually, we made a big loop through the timbered areas.

About three-thirty that afternoon, we came back on the East Side

Road, which led us to Les' pickup. We hadn't found any deer kills, even though we saw sign of deer in some virgin timber stands. Under the heavy canopy of the magnificent timber, we found very little snow. Therefore, the deer could outrun the coyotes and were not in too much danger.

The problem with coyotes killing deer intensifies when deer travel an area where the snow is deep and crusty. Coyotes then have an advantage because they can run across the top of the snow. The difference in weight obviously puts a deer at a disadvantage under such conditions.

On the way back to our vehicle, we met an old gentleman coming out to the road to his mailbox. He was wearing a fur hat with ear muffs and a long, heavy black overcoat that hung to his ankles. His heavy boots and gloves completed the picture of a man who wanted to stay warm.

The three of us on snowshoes met him as he reached the mailbox. We stopped a minute to pass the time of day with him. We were dressed warmly, but our coats were open from our working so hard snowshoeing.

Looking us over, the old gentleman asked, "Do you know how cold it is ?"

"No," one of us responded.

"When I left the house a few minutes ago, it was thirty-five degrees below!"

It surely didn't seem that cold to us. There was no wind and we had been so active, we hadn't noticed that it was that cold. We hadn't found a deer kill that day despite the fact the three of us had covered a lot of ground, but that didn't mean there were no coyote-deer kills.

Once I was invited to go snowshoeing from East Hope to Round Top Mountain with another group of men. The trip was organized by Dr. Neal Wendle and Art Pederson. Ross Hall, Matt Schmidt, and I rounded out the group. Dr. Wendle was a physician in Sandpoint who loved hiking in the mountains and fly fishing. Art Pederson, who lived in East Hope, was Bonner County's Shell Oil Dealer. Ross Hall owned a photography studio bearing his name and had earned a fine reputation as a photographer. Matt Schmidt was also a talented photographer who spent a lot of time, winter and summer, in the mountains of North Idaho. Matt was a gunsmith and avid hunter who loved to shoot targets and test rifles for accuracy.

We left Art Pederson's home in East Hope and started up the mountain behind their place. The snow was about four feet deep at the bottom of the mountain, and it increased as we gained altitude. We carried our food and sleeping bags on a packboard. The weather was cold but not below zero. It was probably about twenty degrees above zero when we started. The snow was great for snowshoeing and we were all in pretty good condition.

That evening we had nearly reached the top of the mountain and found a sheltered area under some virgin timber to make a fire and cook dinner. To cook the steaks, we dangled them from a forked stick over the fire. Our meal was all finger food, so to speak, so we had no dishes or pans to wash. There was a drift of packed snow in a sheltered spot among the trees. It had an abrupt edge about three feet high, so we burrowed into it and built a small cave just large enough for our sleeping bags. Each person built his own cave in the snow. We also carried a small waterproof tarp to prevent any moisture from getting on our bags during the night. This provided a warm, comfortable bed for the night. We stacked our boots and heavy clothing under the

Ross Hall, Art Pederson, Dr. Neal Wendle and I were photographed from a tripod as we snowshoed up Round Top Mountain in the Cabinet Range behind Hope, Idaho. It was my first experience staying overnight in a self-dug snow cave. The picture gives you some idea of how really beautiful it is in the mountains in the middle of winter. It was a fantastic experience for an old farm boy from the flat lands of Illinois. All of the men on that trip became my life long friends.

tarp alongside our sleeping bags to keep them dry and warm. When it was time for bed, we crawled into our sleeping bags with most of our clothes on, including our wool socks.

The Cox Implement Company owned by Clyde Cox was directly across the street from my sportshop. During my second year in the store, Clyde came over and asked me if I would like to go elk hunting with his group that fall. He explained that they packed into Spruce Creek in Idaho from Lost Horse Campground in Montana. Lost Horse was on a ridge close to the Idaho line west of Darby, Montana.

Clyde Cox and Floyd Schwin had hunted together for many years. I had sold half interest in the sports shop to Jim Breinich so I could get away occasionally. Jim encouraged me to go ahead and join them.

It turned out that the wives went along also, making a group of six packing into the camp at Spruce Creek.

Clyde and Floyd had hired a packer from Stevensville, Montana, to pack us in and out of camp. He turned out to be a real character. Glen Hackney was a great guy but a typical cowpoke: tall, skinny and gangly. He always had a crude, roll-your-own cigarette hanging out the corner of his mouth to complete the stereotypical picture. He seemed to live in the saddle, packing hunters in and out of the mountains during the season. I don't think he ever changed clothes or shaved from the beginning of elk season until it ended. His base camp was located at Lost Horse.

Our party included Clyde and Anna Cox, Floyd and Mary Schwin, and Ruby and me. We loaded tents, sleeping bags, food and our hunting gear into a caravan of pickup trucks and headed for Lost Horse. The trip took most of the day. That night we slept on cots and tarps on the ground at Glen's base camp.

The next morning Glen and his crew loaded our gear on pack horses, saddled up others for each of us to ride, and got us going for our camping spot on Spruce Creek. With our destination miles away, we traveled down into one creek draw, up the mountain through a pass and finally down to Spruce Creek. It was one day before the season opened.

Upon arriving at our hunting camp, we all pitched in, setting up tents, stove, and all the comforts we could arrange for our stay in the back country. When camp was set up, we still had a couple of hours of daylight left. Therefore, we decided to scout-out hunting areas for the next day. After spotting a lot of fresh elk sign, we headed back to prepare dinner. Our camp was very comfortable, even though it snowed about six inches that night.

We woke up about four the next morning. After enjoying a breakfast of hotcakes, bacon and fried potatoes, we packed individual lunches and put them in our packsacks along with our hand-axes, hunting knives and matches. We three men left camp just before daybreak. The wives kept the fires going and did some housekeeping.

Since we planned to stay a week, we were in no hurry to bag our elk. Besides, the odds were excellent, considering that we were the only hunters in the drainage, which seemed to teem with elk. Our packer left us a couple of pack horses with plenty of feed so we could pack our elk into camp and hang them on the meat pole we had wired between two trees.

Clyde and Floyd each killed their elk on the second day. The next day they went back with the pack horses, finished dressing the elk and packed them back to camp. They insisted that I continue hunting while they did their packing.

About three o'clock that afternoon, I was heading off the mountain toward camp when I reached an opening in the trees. About a hundred

Clyde Cox's wife, Anna, and Ruby are shown here doing the camp dishes. Floyd and Mary Schwin also accompanied us on this elk hunt up Spruce Creek in Idaho west of Darby, Montana.

yards below me was a small meadow with a cow elk feeding. I aimed at the vital spot back of its front legs and pulled the trigger. The cow dropped as if she had been hit in the head with a sledge hammer. I put another shell in the chamber and stood still, watching for several minutes. The animal did not move, however, so I worked my way down the mountain toward her.

When I reached the elk, she hadn't moved an inch. Taking off my pack, I proceeded to dress my prize. This was the largest animal I had ever attempted to dress-out in the field. The cow was big and fat, weighing from 600-700 pounds on the hoof. When I tried to untangle the carcass from the brush, it fell in further yet and I couldn't budge it. Finally, pulling one leg at a time, I managed to get the body straightened out so I could begin the dressing-out process. By this time, I was covered with blood from the tips of my fingers to my chin. Looking back, I'd give anything for a video of that experience. By the time I finished the whole process, it was dark and I was still almost three quarters of a mile from camp.

Dinner was ready upon my arrival but I had to practically take a bath in the creek to get cleaned up before anyone would let me inside the tent.

The next day Clyde and Floyd helped me finish skinning my elk where upon we quartered it, and packed it back to camp.

We sent out word through another packer that we would be ready to come out on Friday or Saturday.

Glen Hackney came in with his pack string Friday afternoon and stayed with us that night. We spent an hour after dinner listening to Glen tell us about the Spruce Creek and Cub Creek areas where we were hunting. Having had a busy day, everyone was ready for bed after his stories. Early the next morning, we packed up and headed for the base camp at Lost Horse.

When we arrived at camp, we unloaded the horses, packed our meat, gear and horns into the trucks, and began the trip back to Sandpoint. We were three happy, contented couples who had spent a week in the back country of Idaho.

The next year Clyde and Floyd invited me again. I was happy to accept their invitation. Mary Schwin and Ruby couldn't go so Harold Harford joined us. Anna Cox was the only lady in our group. That year we went two days before the season opened to do some fishing. All our plans had gone well until we arrived to set up camp at Spruce Creek.

Lo and behold! The afternoon before the season opened, ten men from Buhl, Idaho, showed up at our camp with their pack and saddle horses. They made no secret of their disgust toward us for occupying that camping spot, though it was the same one Floyd and Clyde had used for years.

After fussing around for about half an hour, they started unloading their horses and set up camp right next to us, a move which completely goes against the grain in hunting etiquette. They could have gone up or down the trail either way but they showed no respect for us.

As soon as their camp was half set-up, four of them put sleeping bags on their backs and, with rifles in hand, headed up the mountain. We learned later that they had assigned four of their group to spend the night in each of the two mountain passes. Just about daylight, the other six hunters spread out and headed up the mountain toward the two passes, talking, yelling and making all kinds of noise. Their motive was to drive the elk to their buddies stationed at the passes.

Their unsportsman-like behavior took the heart out of our small group. Nevertheless, we headed down the canyon a ways and proceeded up the mountain on the south side of the creek. That afternoon I turned back east on the side of the mountain toward the direction of the Buhl group.

About two o'clock, as I walked along an open hillside I noticed another hunter coming directly toward me through the timber. He was about 200 yards away. I had walked about fifty feet more when he suddenly spotted me, threw up his rifle and pointed it at me. I yelled and waved my arms immediately.

He finally put the gun down and changed his direction. Within a minute or two, he was out of sight. The very next day, Harold Harford was hunting in the same area when he decided to cut through a narrow alder thicket in a draw running up and down the mountain. Suddenly, a shot rang out. Harold felt something hit his chest and his face. He put his hand to his face. It came back bloody. Instantly, he yelled, "I've been shot! Come and help me, or I'll come and get you!"

In a few minutes, the hunter appeared through the brush. His glasses told the story. They appeared to be half an inch thick. Harold carried a first-aid kit in his pack, and the guy helped him cover the wounds with Mercurochrome and band-aids. Fortunately, none of the wounds were deep because the bullet had hit a big rock right in front of Harold. It broke up and splattered him. He was one lucky guy to have stepped behind the big rock just as the hunter shot. Harold was wearing a bright red hat and bright red plaid jacket. The other hunter had simply seen the brush move and shot at it.

Harold made it back to camp with no problems. We went over to the Buhl camp and told the men there what had happened. The next morning they packed up and headed home. Thank God!

Later, Harold described the man who shot him. He was dressed exactly like the one who had pointed the rifle at me the previous day.

After they pulled out, the woods were again calm and quiet. That same day, we took a hike up through where they had made their drive the opening day of elk season. We found a dead spike bull in one spot that one of them had shot. It appeared they never even checked to see if he had been hit. And to make matters worse, we discovered a dead cow near one of the mountain passes. They had neglected her too. Yet both animals were out in the open where they could have easily been spotted, if the hunters had just bothered to look for them. What a tremendous waste of meat and elk! What a bunch of sportsmen!?

The four of us killed an elk apiece two days later not far from camp in the same vicinity where the fellow had shot Harold.

This is another photograph taken by my friend Ross Hall. I was fishing the pool beneath Char Falls on Big Lightning Creek northeast of Clark Fork. Like many of his other photographs, this one shows the appreciation one develops for the mountain country of North Idaho.

161

Chapter 13

Above and Below Ground

Although several interesting and important events occurred in my life between 1948 and 1958, the most meaningful was the birth of our son Steve. The old Stackhouse Hospital on the east side of North Second Avenue in Sandpoint provided the setting for his welcome to the world on June 3, 1948. The facility was situated on the bank of Sand Creek just east of where Bonner General Hospital now stands. Dr. Wilbur Hayden, our personal friend and family doctor, delivered Steve. Needless to say, Steve's arrival was a very happy day for Ruby and me.

Our son became my fishing, hunting, prospecting and backpacking partner at an early age. We covered most of the creeks in Bonner County as well as much of the back country on prospecting trips. We also spent many a night in the mountains on backpacking trips.

Steve was around six years old when we hiked into Harrison Lake, about six and a half miles from the end of the Pack River Road northwest of Sandpoint. During the time that we marched up one hill and down another, a loyal "party-colored, four-legged" friend followed our every footstep. Twink, as we called her, was the same Cocker Spaniel who hiked with Donna and me up to Chimney Rock. That little dog loved the mountains as much as Steve and I did.

We built bough beds and slept out in the open after catching and cooking trout over the campfire. The next day we packed up and climbed to the top of the ridge between Pack River and the Priest Lake drainage. After following the ridge south to Little Harrison Lake, Steve caught enough fish for that night's dinner. Again, we set up camp in the open and slept out under the stars. The next day we fished a bit before packing up and heading south over another rocky ridge to Beehive Lake. After fishing for about an hour with no luck, we decided there were no fish in the lake. Possibly they had been winter-killed. At one point, we found an overgrown trail leading off the mountain down to Pack River, close to where we had left our little yellow Jeep three days before.

Steve was a good hiker in the mountains. I have many pleasant memories of our trips, especially one of sitting on a rock by a campfire way back in the mountains. Everything was quiet except for an occasional coyote yelp breaking the silence.

When Steve was about three years old, he became quite ill. Dr. Hayden and Dr. Helen Peterson worked with him for several weeks without any success. He developed a fever of at least 102 degrees every other day. Dr. Hayden finally made an appointment with a specialist in Spokane. We took him in early one morning and they checked him over thoroughly, taking blood tests, etc. Then, the doctor told us to go have breakfast and come back to his office later. When we returned, he invited us into his private office and informed us that the tests had been evaluated. The results were a shock.

He told us that Steve had either leukemia or mononucleosis, but that they wouldn't be able to pinpoint the exact diagnosis for another five or six weeks. After much worry, we were finally relieved to discover that his illness was mononucleosis. Tragically, it had already done permanent damage to him. The high fevers had injured Steve's pancreas with the consequence that by the time he was six years old he had developed diabetes.

There were some tough times, but Steve made it through grade school and high school just fine. He then spent a year at the University of Idaho. When I was elected governor, he moved to Boise with us and pursued a degree in nursing at what was then Boise State College (It is now Boise University). After graduating as a registered nurse, he worked in St. Luke's Hospital for about fifteen years. The last seven of those years were spent nursing patients in the recovery room after surgery.

In 1971, he married Karen Lee from Weiser. They now have two fine sons, Michael and Rick. I think Steve was very fortunate to marry a nice, talented person like Karen. She has a degree in both business and education. She works as insurance adjuster for the Idaho Plumbers' Union.

The stress of Steve's nursing job along with diabetes has taken its toll on him. In 1987 he underwent an "angioplasty" on three blood vessels at Stanford Medical Center. A year later during another bypass operation in Boise, one of his blood vessels ruptured. That time the doctors had to perform emergency coronary artery bypass surgery. And again a year after that, they had to do another angioplasty for another artery blockage. This time they were successful.

At the time, Steve's doctors suggested that he get out of nursing and into a less stressful career. Since then, he's gone through rehab training and currently works in the electronics division at Hewlett-Packard in Boise.

Steve, Karen, Mike and Rick are a close-knit family. Both boys are good students and recently started gaining experience in the free-enterprise system by having paper routes.

During the years that Steve was growing up, my life changed in another way too. I took flying lessons and earned my private pilot's license. My training became possible because of the G.I. Education Bill. I took my training at the Sandpoint Airport under the tutelage of Don Kramer, who managed the Sandpoint Airport at the time. Don started me out in a J3 Cub airplane. Several other instructors, including Jay Dee Clark, J.R. Morrison and J.O. Doyle worked with us from time to time. My first flying lesson was March 3, 1947. Since I enjoyed flying in the early morning when the air was cool and heavy, I was usually at the airport by six a.m. for my hour of flight.

During my early training I suffered from air-sickness every time we did something new. Just prior to the first time we performed stalls, for example, I had eaten a piece of huckleberry pie. Immediately after the first stall, I stuck my head out the side of the airplane and covered it with huckleberries. When we did spins, I also became ill. It has always been interesting to me however, that I never suffered air sickness again from any particular maneuver once I got through it the first time.

Don Kramer was an old bush pilot and had spent many years flying in and out of mountain airstrips, so he was a great instructor for the kind of flying I wanted to do. He explained to me about air currents in the mountains and how to fly in them safely.

I had several interesting experiences during training, including two dead-stick landings. These occur when the motor quits and the pilot must land without power. The first one, thank the Lord, happened when Don was with me. We came into the airport pattern to land, and our altitude was 800 feet. I pulled the carburetor heat lever on a few minutes before cutting the throttle to glide down to the runway. Upon cutting the throttle, I heard the motor backfire and stop. It was a very funny feeling to see the propeller standing still.

Don assured me that I was okay and to simply go ahead and land as if the motor were running. He warned me not to lose elevation too fast or I would land before getting to the end of the runway. With his assurance, I was able to make a good landing. Fortunately all went well.

When we landed and got out of the plane, Don checked the carburetor heat lever and found that it had broken off. Apparently when I pulled the lever to put heat on the carburetor, it had broken and iced up, thus killing the motor. About three months later the same thing happened when I was flying alone. It was a different airplane but I had no problem landing it without power because I knew what to do.

One of the J3 cubs that we flew was a great climber. Someone told me that 10,000 feet was the limit the plane could ascend. One July morning I decided to see how high I could take the plane. I trimmed it to climb and headed north over the Selkirk range toward the Canadian border. About halfway between Bonners Ferry and the Canadian line, I reached the 10,000-foot level. It was still climbing so I let it go. Before long, I was at 11,000 and still going upward—then 12,000. By this time, I had reached the Canadian border and could see the 110-foot-wide strip that had been cleared to mark the boundary between the United States and Canada.

I was enjoying the scenery so much, I forgot about the altimeter for a while until I realized my feet were getting cold. By then I was over Creston, British Columbia, and could see Kootenai Lake and the beautiful mountains that surround it. When I glanced at the altimeter, it read 13,000 feet! I turned the plane around and set it into a glide toward Sandpoint at a speed just below the red line — a speed indicator that reports the maximum speed allowable for that particular plane. Each airplane will stand only so much stress, so the pilot shouldn't exceed the speed beyond the red line. Upon arriving at Sandpoint, I was still 5,000 feet above the ground, so I put it in a spin to lose altitude and get back to earth. It seemed almost a shame because it had been a beautiful morning of flying.

In May of 1948, I had to take my cross-country flight. I decided to fly back to Illinois to see my folks. Don Kramer assigned J.O. Doyle, one of his instructors, to go with me. We set a course east over Missoula, Montana, then southeast. When we ran into a snowstorm, we tried to skirt it by going south. My instructor was supposed to be showing me how to navigate across the country, but he became disoriented and didn't know where we were. Suddenly, I spotted Devil's Tower at Spotted Horse, Wyoming. At that point, he decided that we should head further south into Wyoming, but the snow continued to get heavier and more dense as we flew. We spotted the lights of a town and headed toward them, hoping to find an airport where we could set down for the night until the storm passed.

Circling the edge of town at a fairly low elevation, we continued searching for an airport. Finally, we spotted a couple of hangars and a wind sock on one of the buildings. By this time, the snowflakes were the size of quarters and extremely thick. When we flew past the wind sock looking for the runway, we noticed it had the word "HELL" on it. At this point, we were really wondering where we were!

After landing, we learned that we were in Gillette, Wyoming, and the wind sock had been put out by the Shell Oil Co. Apparently, the "S" had been whipped off by the wind. That knowledge was a relief to us. We found a motel close to the airport, had dinner and went to bed — two exhausted guys!

The next morning we fueled up the Taylorcraft and headed east. The storm had ended and flying was great except for a stiff headwind. Our destination was an air base in Rapid City, South Dakota. Somehow Doyle had allowed us to drift south. At that point we were fighting head winds, and it was starting to get dark.

We were flying low over the grain fields of South Dakota and talking about landing in one of the fields for the night when we saw a glare of lights over a hill. We headed for it. Low and behold, there was a small airport about a block from the center of the little town of Custer, South Dakota. We could see a wind sock on a barn, but the runway didn't look like it had been used for some time.

We then flew low over the runway. Not seeing any ditches in it, we decided to land. After touching down, we taxied up to the barn. As I remember, there were five small airplanes hanging in the barn by their

166

tails.

From the air we had spotted a restaurant and hotel about a block from the airport so that's where we headed to spend the night. The next morning after breakfast we walked back to the plane, checked it out and decided to take off. Doyle, and I talked about flying straight out from the end of the runway. If we took off and turned right, we would head directly into a small hill full of oak trees about fifty to sixty feet tall. We decided the safest plan was to go straight, where there were no obstructions.

"Maybe you should let me take it off from this airport," he said. As my instructor he was responsible for whatever happened.

"If you think you should, okay," I responded.

Well, he started the motor, let it warm up and then checked the switches and mags. He taxied down the runway and lifted off in good shape. Instead of going straight out though, he turned the plane to the right and headed directly toward the hill! We were barely maintaining flying speed. The wheels of the airplane were touching leaves and small limbs of the tree. We just made it over the hill, and he was able to drop the nose, picking up enough flying speed to keep us in the air. There is no doubt in my mind that someone had His hand on both our shoulders that time!

The rest of the trip was uneventful. Once we reached Illinois, we landed on an airstrip belonging to one of my former friends who was also a distant relative. After spending the day with my family, we headed home.

I might add that several years later my instructor on that cross-country flight, J. O. Doyle, died trying to take off from Coeur d'Alene Airport in heavy fog. Apparently his plane stalled and went to the ground on its nose, killing him along with his mother and father.

My pilot's license allowed me many opportunities to fly all kinds of airplanes, including an F4C Phantom Jet at Mountain Air Force Base in Mountain Home, Idaho. The instructor who took me up was Doug Pennington. He took the plane to about 20,000 feet where he turned on the after-burner and boosted us to a speed of 1040 miles per hour. We went through the sound barrier at around 900 mph. At this point, Doug told me to watch the instruments. When we hit the actual barrier, the

Suited up for flying high, I rode this RF-4C Phantom jet out of Mountain Home Air Force Base at 1040 mph and flew it myself for forty-five minutes at 550 mph.

instruments all went crazy. Then they settled back to normal.

Doug then slowed the plane down to about 550 mph and asked me if I would like to fly it. I jumped at the invitation! I flew the plane for about forty-five minutes and took pictures of the State Capitol with the cameras in the plane.

On another occasion I flew a Leer jet from Cape Kennedy to Miami, Florida. I have also taken the controls of Jet Ranger, Bell helicopters as well as a double-rotor Skycorsky helicopter. I flew the latter during an hour-long fishery patrol with the U.S. Coast Guard. Flying has always been one of the highlights of my life.

In 1958 I sold my interest in the Pend Oreille Sport Shop to my partner, Jim Brenich. We had been selling some mining equipment such as mineral lights, rock drills, and gold pans during the last two years. I decided to keep this part of the business, calling it the Don Samuelson Equipment Co.

My featured item was the Cobra rock drill which was made in

Sweden. I also served as the fire fighter fire equipment distributor for Idaho, Montana, and ten counties in Washington. I sold Hi Lift jacks, drill steel, and offered my customers new items from time to time. I was also the first salesman outside the Atlas Copco Company who was set up as a dealer.

Atlas Copco had their own sales force that called on the mines, large contractors and construction companies. They sold the gasoline-operated rock drill but were calling on the wrong people to sell them. The drill couldn't be used underground because of the carbon monoxide gas it created. Besides, it was too small for the large contractors.

At the sportshop, our featured piece of mining equipment was a gasoline rock drill made in the United States by Syntron. This machine weighed one hundred and fifteen pounds. I sold a few of these machines and bought the drill steel to use with them from Atlas Copco in Spokane, Washington about seventy-five miles southwest of Sandpoint.

One day when I stopped to pick up some steel, the manager, Carlos Miliner showed me the new Cobra rock drill that had just been sent to them from their factory in Sweden. It weighed only fifty-three pounds and out-performed the Syntron machine two-to-one. I told Miliner that if they would let me have the Cobra rock drill, I would show them how to sell it.

After I had talked to Miliner, the company's district manager brought me a demonstrator. That was right after Christmas in 1959. Carlos told me, "I'll leave it with you for three months — we'll see what you can do."

To make a long story short, I sold more Cobras in Idaho, Montana, and the ten Washington counties than the company sold in the entire United States, Canada, Alaska, and Mexico put together. My success stemmed from contacting both large and small logging contractors and demonstrating the machine. It was about one-fifth the price of a compressor, jack hammer and the drill steel. For small jobs out in the open air, the gasoline rock drill worked great. It was also beneficial to country road crews for their small jobs and to power companies for drilling and blasting rocks while making holes for power line poles. In other words, I contacted people who could use this type of equipment to their advantage and showed them how to do it.

I really enjoyed that business. Ruby and I worked together at it. I sold the equipment and did repair work while Ruby ran the office and sent out parts. Traveling Monday through Thursday, I called on loggers in three states and went back in the mountains on logging jobs to demonstrate the rock drill. I also contacted small mine prospectors, county road foremen and small construction companies to give demonstrations. It was not unusual for me to meet logging contractors at four in the morning and follow them in to their logging operations anywhere from twenty-five to seventy-five miles back in the mountains.

The Forest Service required a fire extinguisher on every piece of equipment in the woods. As a distributor, I could sell fire equipment at wholesale prices. These extra sales not only helped me with my road expenses but also aided the loggers and contractors.

Because of my love for the outdoors this job was right up my alley. I saw lots of game while traveling the back roads and mountains.

During those years (1959-1966) the prices of motels, meals and gasoline contrasted drastically with what we know today. Motel rooms averaged from four to six dollars per night. Most meals were under a dollar. A good steak dinner ran about a dollar and a half and gasoline sold for about fifty cents a gallon.

During that time, I was very interested in mining. Throughout my travels I kept my ear to the ground in regard to mining property and new mines. A good friend, Ralph Thurston, was a mining engineer and geologist who represented six companies. I scouted for him. If I found anything interesting, I would call Ralph and he would fly to Sandpoint to pick me up. From there we would go look at the property. We crawled into some very interesting old mines with rocks as big as a Volkswagon Bug hanging from the ceiling. They were not comfortable places to be for very long.

Ralph once mentioned that he had a customer who wanted him to find a natural cave to develop into a tourist trap. On one of my trips to Riggins, Idaho, I heard about a new cave a fellow named Jim Specklemeyer and his brother had found in the Seven Devils Mountains south of Riggins. I contacted Jim and got all the information I could, to pass on to Ralph Thurston. Jim said he would take us through the cave any time Ralph could make it to Riggins.

I called Ralph at his home in Lander, Wyoming, and told him about the cave. He set a date to come and I subsequently made the appointment with Jim. When we arrived in Riggins, Jim had some complications develop which made it impossible for him to go with us. Fortunately, he had made arrangements for a friend of his, Ben Cook, to accompany us. The cave was on Papoos Creek so it was called Papoos Cave.

When we got there Ben, Ralph and I headed up the Seven Devils Road to a spot above the entrance to the cave where we could park the car. Armed with lights, packsacks and rock picks we hiked down a small dry creek bed to a rock ledge. At the base of the ledge was a hole leading into the mountain. A heavy hay rope was tied to a large rock outside the hole, which dropped straight down for about fifteen feet. At the bottom of the hole was a large flat rock about ten feet square. The cave floor was covered with all sizes of larger rocks which sloped at a forty-five degree angle downward for another hundred and fifty feet.

Since Ben had been in the cave before, he said he would go down the rope first. He made it down okay, so I was next. Ralph helped me square away my pack and then I started down the rope. It was pitch black while I slid downward. Suddenly, the rope broke and down I went. As luck would have it, I had dropped only three or four feet before landing on my feet. If I had lost my balance and gone backward, I would surely have landed on my back and head in a pile of sharp rocks about the size of a bushel basket. Thank God, I didn't!

Ralph was still outside the cave, which helped. We checked to see what had happened to the rope. The rope was a new one-inch thick hemp rope that had been hanging against the cave wall all winter. The spot where it broke though was blackish-brown. Iron pyrite crystals in the rock where it lay had mixed with water to form sulfuric acid. In this way it slowly burned the rope and weakened it.

We didn't have enough good rope to tie together for climbing back out, but Ben remembered another sixty feet that was down below us in the next part of the cave. Ben and I took our flashlights and worked our way down to the other rope. As we untied it from a big rock and started pulling it up, it broke from its own weight. Fortunately, we wound up with a piece about fifteen feet long that was strong enough. Then we climbed back up to the big rock.

Meanwhile, Ralph found a cord long enough to reach us. Tying the rope pieces on his cord, he pulled them out and fastened them all together to make a kind of rough rope ladder for Ben and me to use to climb out. Needless to say, aside from being another close shave, that was the end of our spelunking. If either of us had gone backward off the large rock when the rope broke, we wouldn't have had a chance. Shortly after that, the Forest Service took over the cave and closed it to the public. Since then however, I have talked with several "spelunkers" who obtained a permit to explore and map the cave.

Ralph was a close friend and a really nice guy, but he pushed himself really hard. He flew a Beach Bonanza airplane. I soon learned to watch him closely when I was flying with him. Whenever his eyes became narrow slits, I would say, "Ralph, turn the plane over to me and let me fly it."

He would turn it over to me and then sleep for fifteen or twenty minutes. Afterward, he was fine for the rest of the trip.

I lost a good friend in 1970 when Ralph went to sleep at the wrong time and crashed into the top of a mountain in Nevada. He was flying to check out some mining property.

Working our own mine prospect, I'm seen here with Les Gissel's son Norman and my faithful companion Twink. The prospect was uranium. The mine was located east of Elmira in North Idaho.

My enjoyment of the mining business probably stemmed from a hobby that began in 1924 when I was old enough to join the Boy Scouts in Woodhull, Illinois. I was eleven years old at the time. That summer our scoutmaster organized a week long camping trip to Wisconsin. Our trip took us to the shores of Lake Superior, where we camped close to the beach. Once while walking along the sand, one of our scouts found a small banded agate. The discovery inspired us all to search for agates. From that time on, I was interested in pretty rocks. I still have the small banded agate that I picked up on that beach sixty-six years ago.

While living in Illinois and Iowa, not too many rocks interested me; but when I moved to the *Gem State,* (Idaho) I became very interested in rock hounding. The star garnets at Fernwood, about a hundred miles south of Sandpoint have received a lot of my attention. I must have at least one hundred pounds of garnet today. I used to go down and dig for them several times every year bringing back about twenty pounds each time.

The first piece of rock equipment I owned was a tumbler, which I used to polish garnet, agate and jasper for use in bracelets and necklaces. Next I purchased a rock saw and a grinding and polishing unit from Frantom Lapidary Supply. With that equipment, I made cabachons and shape stones to fit in silver and gold rings, pendants and earrings.

When I started traveling with the equipment business, I was able to

My interest in rockhounding developed into a serious hobby of jewelry making. I made these necklaces as well as many other types of jewelry out of gold, silver and gems, and still carry on the practice in my retirement years.

173

increase my inventory of rocks and gems by becoming acquainted with new sources throughout Idaho, Montana and Eastern Washington. Later during my term as governor, I made and gave away many garnet bracelets to Miss Idaho representatives, rodeo royalty and other ladies or young women selected for an honor or selected to represent their area.

When the World Boy Scout Jamboree was held at Farragut, Boy Scout groups in the Boise area helped me tumble small pieces of jasper from a mine close to Eagle, Idaho. We had a small card printed with my picture on it welcoming scouts and their leaders to Idaho. A small piece of polished jasper was glued to each card. I also kept a glass bowl of polished stones from Idaho on my desk and gave one to anyone interested in a souvenir from Idaho.

After leaving the governor's office and going to work for the U.S. Department of Transportation in Seattle, I became interested in faceting precious gems. Wayne Anderson, a good friend of mine in Spokane, and I had been considering it for some time. He called me one day and told me that he had bought a prismatic faceting machine. After visiting him on my travels to Spokane, I bought one. With such a machine, one can cut all kinds of stones and polish them, similar to the way diamonds are cut.

I could store the machine in a closet, then take it out and set it on a table if I wanted to cut and polish a gem. I bought the machine in 1971, so I've been able to facet stones for about twenty-one years. It seems that I just kept getting deeper and deeper into the rock and gem hobby every year. First, it was silversmithing, then goldsmithing. Now I do the whole procedure from raw stone to finished jewelry.

I like to design jewelry items out of wax. I use the lost wax process in casting the item in gold or silver. It is a process where the wax item is placed in a metal flask and investment (a substance similar to plaster of paris) is poured over it. When it hardens the flask is placed in a furnace for an hour and a half to burn out the wax, leaving the impression of the item inside the flask. The flask is placed in a centrifugal casting machine while it is still hot. Gold or silver is then placed in a crucible that is attached to the flask. The metal is melted and when the casting machine is released, the metal is thrown into the flask, filling the void where the stem was. When the flask cools it is dunked into a bucket of water that washes away the investment. The item goes to the bottom of the bucket. At this point the sprue (or tail) is cut off and the item is ready to clean and polish.

Now I can make a piece of jewelry from scratch. I love working with my hands and designing a one of a kind piece of jewelry. Needless to say, Ruby has a good selection of jewelry.

Chapter 14

Entering into Politics

My involvement in politics stemmed from participating in a variety of state and local organizations and governing boards. For example, I had been with in the Idaho Wildlife Federation, where I served on the Northern District board of directors. I was also their president for two years and two years on their state board of directors, as vice chairman. Some of my other activities included the Bonner County Sportsmen's Association, the Sandpoint Recreation Board (where I served as Chairman) and the Sandpoint Chamber of Commerce. I was also a member of the chamber's board of directors and served as their president for one year.

My association with these public service organizations thrust me into the political circles at all levels. I was becoming more and more concerned about the direction our state and federal governments were going. I didn't think I had the right to criticize without trying to do something about what was happening.

In 1958, I picked up a petition to run for the House of Representatives from Bonner County on the Republican ticket. First, I contacted the Bonner County Republican Central Committee, which was comprised of three elderly gentlemen who met only when needed to recommend an appointment to fill a vacancy. Contacting the chairman, I arranged for a time and date to meet with them. When we got together at the Community Hall in Sandpoint, they listened to my plan. When I finished, they wished me good luck and that was the last I heard from them.

Next, I contacted my friend Laurin Pietsch, one of the owners and the editor of the Sandpoint News Bulletin. He assisted me in assembling campaign folders and printed cards for me to pass out to voters.

My opponent was Robert "Bob" Doolittle from Priest River. He had served in the House of Representatives for fourteen years. He was also in line to be Speaker of the House upon his re-election.

After putting together a program designed to work with and truly represent the Bonner County constituency, I contacted all the organizations within the county, asking for a few minutes of their time. I promised not to talk politics, to limit my talk to five minutes and to answer any questions.

My program was simple. It involved targeting all the groups representing the economic and social make up of Bonner county — loggers, cattlemen-ranchers, lumber mill workers, milk producers, sportsmen, women and miners interests.

Most of the organizations invited me to speak. My talk always began with the statement that I believed in and supported the two-party system. I also said that we needed good, solid, honest people in each party to participate in our government. Next, I named the seven groups and told them that if I were elected I would set up a public meeting with each — not to talk to them, but to listen. I wanted each group to advise me about legislation that needed to be presented or legislation that needed correcting. I assured them that this information would go with me, and I would do my best to get it presented during the session. Finally, I told them I would come back to Bonner county on a Saturday in the middle of the legislative session to inform them about what bills had been introduced and how they would affect each group. During these meetings, I was careful to never mention my opponent. I just presented my program. I have always believed that you can not build yourself up by tearing someone else down. Each person attending these meetings received a folder with my picture and a detailed explanation of my program. My strategy also included the door-to-door approach, leaving information on cars at the county fair and other events that drew crowds.

Ruby didn't want anything to do with politics, so our daughter Donna assisted as campaign manager. She was in high school at the time and enjoyed helping me. Lauren Pietsch continued advising me and was very encouraging through all my races, including my election as Governor.

In the primary election I ran unopposed, so I was the Republican candidate for the House of Representatives. The Democratic candidate received two votes to my one, however. In the November general election, I lost by forty-three votes.

An interesting sidelight during the few weeks that followed the election was that a number of my Republican friends confessed they didn't think I had a chance so they voted for my opponent. One member of a large Republican family said, "If I'd known that you would come that close, I'd have voted for you."

In 1960, many of those same people encouraged me to change and run for the Idaho State Senate. "This time we will help you," they said.

That year my opponent was an attorney named Glen Bandelin. Glen was quite a leader in Democratic politics in Idaho as well as at the national level. In fact, there had even been some talk about his being

considered as a Vice Presidential candidate at the national level.

I picked up my petition and had no problem getting it signed. The petition was filed and the race was on!

I followed the same program as I had during the prior election. Again, I talked to most of the organizations in Bonner county. I never mentioned my opponent. I ran unopposed in the primary. Just as before, when the votes were counted, my opponent had two votes to my one. Our state primary elections require that voters select one party ticket or the other.

This is one of my first campaign pictures I used when I ran for State Senator in 1960.

After the primary, I worked hard, going door-to-door throughout the county. This time the entire family pitched in to help me. When the general election votes were counted, I had won by just over 700 votes. Knowing that I was the first Republican legislator elected from Bonner County in many years added sweetness to the victory.

In keeping with my campaign promise, I held meetings with the seven groups of people that represented Bonner county. The county commissioners allowed me to use courthouse meeting rooms. Both the Sandpoint and Priest River papers advertised the meetings and attendance was excellent. I was able to gather lots of valuable information, which helped me truly represent the people of my county during the session set to begin in Boise in January 1961.

This was a completely new experience for Ruby and me. We had to close up the house for a couple of months, rent a place to live in Boise and make plans for our son (who was in grade school at the time) to transfer to a new school there. We were able to rent a house quite near a school for Steve. Our daughter was attending nursing school at Deaconess Hospital in Spokane. All the planning made for some busy weeks.

I took on the role of freshman senator when the Legislature convened in early January, joining a group of older, seasoned legislators. Some had served for more than twenty years.

Since I wanted to get on at least one of the important committees like the finance committee, I talked to several of the "wheels" in the Senate like "Casey" Barlow, Tom Heath, and Fred Cooper. Casey informed me that in no way would they put me on the finance committee as a freshman.

This upset me. I told them in no uncertain terms that if I was ever to be re-elected to the Legislature from my Democratic county, I needed to be appointed to one of the strongest, most important committees — specifically the Senate Finance Committee.

About two days later, Casey called me to his desk and said, "We are assigning you to the finance committee. But, by God, you'd better do what we tell you." I served on the Senate Finance Committee for my entire six years in the Senate, and no one — not even Casey — tried to tell me what to do or how to vote on anything.

I also served as chairman for the Senate Public Resources and Public Recreation Committee during my Senate career. In fact, I gained experience on all the committees except for State Affairs. Every year I took different committees along with the two regulars. Each Senator generally participated on four committees during each session.

The Senate Finance Committee held the most interest for me because it dealt with every agency of state government — all of the money each agency spent and how they spent it. We worked with the agency heads and knew who the good business managers were as well as the poor ones. The information I gained while working on this committee paid off later when I ran for Governor. I knew who tried to manage money and who tended to waste it. I also found out who was having the three-martini lunches and charging them to their departments and, of course, the state taxpayers.

One of the hot items on the Legislative agenda during my first year was the "Green Stamp" bill, which had been introduced to make the stamps illegal.

Sperry-Hutchenson was the dominant stamp company and their stamps were green in color. Many businesses gave stamps to customers at the rate of one for each dollar purchase. The customer was given a book to paste the stamps in. When the book was full of stamps it had a value toward items in a catalog furnished by the stamp company. For instance, when you had five books you could turn them in for a toaster or a set of pots and pans, or dishes. There were many things in the catalog and they varied in the number of books required to get a particular item. As I remember it, some items were exchanged for one book. Others took up to twenty or thirty books to obtain.

The problem with the stamps was that merchants had to pay for the stamps which meant they had to raise their prices on whatever they sold. This increased grocery bills, clothing bills or the prices of anything a customer bought from the merchant.

When I met with the seven groups of people from my county, I asked them to vote on whether they wanted the stamps or if they preferred to have them voted out. Since all the groups voted to get rid of them, I worked to have the stamps outlawed.

The lobbyists from the stamp companies were at the Legislature in full force, however. One lunch hour I was working at my desk, alone on the Senate floor. The lobbyist from Sperry-Hutchinson (S & H) Stamp Co. saw me and asked for a few minutes of my time. I agreed so he came in and sat at a desk next to me.

Knowing I was against the stamps, he opened his briefcase and took out a stack of signatures about four inches thick. They had been photocopied, and he wanted me to go over them. I told him that I didn't have time, adding that they were not from my district or county. Then, I explained to him that after polling my people, I had been instructed to work against the stamps. We talked for a few minutes and then he said, "If you would change your mind and go with me, I can make it well worth your while."

Very few things anger me quickly. I had just been offered my first bribe! My Swedish temper almost went out of control. I stood up, looked him square in the eye, and said, "You found your way into this Senate chamber and if you know what is good for you, you'd better find your way out."

He got up, picked up his briefcase and headed for the door. He muttered as he left, "You don't have to get mad about it."

Needless to say, word must have traveled through the lobbyists because no one ever mentioned money or indicated anything like that to me during my following six years of Senate experience.

Another hot issue that year was the Right-to-Work Bill. Simply stated, the Right-to-Work Bill said that one did not have to belong to a union to work on a construction job or for a company but it did not prevent them from joining a union if they desired. Emotions ran high. The unions adamantly opposed the bill because they wanted everyone to join, pay monthly dues and work toward better retirement and health benefits as well as fair wages.

Industry, on the other hand, generally supported the Right-to-Work because they wanted an honest day's work for an honest day's pay. Some felt the unions restricted production which resulted in a less competitive finished product.

The bill was one of the hottest issues to come before the Legislature that year. Lobbyists from both industry and labor interests were thick around and in the Capitol until the bill was put to a vote. On this issue, industry opposed labor. The bill was defeated by one vote.

My serving on the Senate Finance Committee took a lot of time. We interviewed close to fifty departments. They included such agencies as the Bean Commission, Wheat Commission, Potato Commission, et cetera. We also traveled the state wherever state agencies were located. Our visits included the University of Idaho, Orofino Mental Hospital, Lewiston Normal School, Idaho State University, the state prison, and all the agencies in and around Boise.

Our procedure included meeting with the president or department head and his budget people. They would present their budget for the following year. Then, members of the committee could question them or go look at their particular problem. This might include checking out a building problem, their water supply, heating plant or even the location of a new building. Members of our Joint House and Senate Finance Committee really had a chance to learn how the state government operated. In addition, we were able to observe and assess the efficiency or nonefficiency of the people operating state agencies. I found the experience invaluable to me as a legislator.

When I served in the Idaho State Senate, we met every other year. Our pay amounted to $10 a day while we were in session. We were also allotted $25 a day for food and housing. For a number of years, the legislators were paid $10 a day plus living expenses for sixty days only. If the session lasted longer than that, we didn't get paid for the extra days. I guess the idea was to keep the Legislature from continuing the session throughout the summer. That was changed in the 1965 session, I believe, when we finally started receiving the expense money for being there beyond the sixty-day limit.

Conservatively, I figured that it cost me more than $1,000 a year from my own pocket to serve in the Legislature. All phone calls to various agencies for my constituents came from my own pocket. We didn't have an expense account or credit card like they have today. Most of the

Early in my career as a State Senator I met with former Governor Robins (right) who preceded Governor Smylie, Jim Parsons Sr. (left), and the Sandpoint Chamber of Commerce President Don Diehl and his wife Sue. Robins, a doctor in St. Maries was the only other Governor elected from North Idaho prior to myself. The photograph was taken at the Pend Oreille Lodge located on Contest Point above Lake Pend Oreille. The lodge, which belonged to my friend Ed Hawkins Sr., later burned to the ground and no longer exists.

legislators who came from rural counties had to subsidize their income during the lawmaking session. Those who lived in Boise or who were otherwise close enough to live at home had an advantage.

Most of us didn't complain about the added expense because we felt we were serving the good people of the State of Idaho. We wanted to see a good, clean state with a superior education system, a climate conducive to attracting clean industry and agricultural development that could move our state ahead.

I ran for re-election in 1962. My opponent that time was Bob Doolittle, the same man who had defeated me by forty-three votes when I ran for the House in 1958. Again, in the primary, I ran unopposed. So was Bob Doolittle. But this time in the fall general election, I won by more than 1,000 votes.

Governor Robert E. Smylie ran for a third consecutive term. His opponent, Vernon K. Smith, ran on a pro-gambling platform. Smylie was considered a Conservative, so he had the backing of most Conservatives in the state. Smith, on the other hand, was a Liberal, and his pro-gambling stand turned a lot of church people of various religious faiths against him. In fact, they really got out and worked against Smith. This meant that anti-gambling forces had the choice of Smylie or no one. The Governor worked with the Legislature to keep us in line and, up to that point, hadn't made too many enemies.

Speaking against a piece of legislation on the floor of the Senate in 1963, I served three terms as Idaho Senator Don Samuelson. I always believed the state's tax revenue belonged to the people of the state and that any spending should be to their benefit.

I worked with Governor Smylie during my three terms in the Senate and found him easy to get along with. I still have a number of nice letters from him complimenting me on my work with various pieces of legislation such as that which came out of the Water Legislation Committee on which I chaired. Governor Smylie won the election that year by a good majority.

During this term, besides serving on the Senate Finance Committee, I chaired the Public Resources and Public Recreation Committee. I also served on the banking and agriculture committees. The session went well. We had new leadership in the Senate and several new Legislators. Several old timers had retired or passed away.

In 1964 Governor Smylie called a special session to enact legislation for the creation of a state water agency. At the time, California and several other southern states were eyeing Idaho's water. They were hoping for federal legislation allowing them to take water from Idaho's Snake River and pipe it into California and Arizona. As chairman of the public resources committee, my responsibility was to get the water agency legislation passed to prevent the redirecting of the water out-of-state.

It promised to be very controversial. Several Senate leaders told me that we would never pass it in a three-day special session.

Just as soon as the bill was given to me, I set up a committee consisting of both Democrats and Republicans. It also included people who were the most knowledgeable in water law and water rights. Bill Holden, from Idaho Falls, was my right-hand advisor. He was a nationally famous water attorney. Senator Jim McClure had some reservations about the bill, so I asked him to serve on the committee. As a Payette attorney, Jim had lots of experience with Idaho water rights.

We held public hearings to get input. The committee rewrote the bill. It was read the first time on the third day. In both the House and the Senate, all bills must be read on each of three days and voted upon on the third reading. There is an emergency clause in the rules however, that allows the rules to be suspended, the bill read three times in succession and voted upon on that same day. The emergency clause was included in the rules to cover legislation which might be needed in a hurry—the kind resulting from a hurricane, flood or fire, or from the death of an elected official. The rules were suspended and the bill was read a second and a third time. Then after some debate, it was put to a vote and passed.

In this case, we had created a Water Board and set the stage for the next Legislature to implement the Department of Water Resources for the State of Idaho.

I don't think I slept for three days during that time. I burned lots of midnight oil talking with lots of people to ensure that the concerns of everyone were considered and weighed very carefully.

In 1964 I entered the Senate race for the third and last time. My opponent this time was a school principal named Jim Stoicheff. Continuing the same plan as in past elections, my past record repeated itself. After my opponent collected two votes to my one in the primary, the tables turned in the general election. I came out on top by 2,000 votes.

When the Legislature opened in January 1965, the Senate Finance Committee played a different ball game. Rodney Hansen from Rupert was installed as chairman. We had the same tenure on the committee, but he had served in the Senate longer so the Republican leadership gave him the chairmanship. Rodney was a very liberal Republican and ran the show rather loosely. There were times he didn't appear to do his homework or lead the budget planning for the Republican party. Under his leadership, it turned out that the liberal Democrats and several of our liberal Republicans controlled the budget vote most of the time. It was a frustrating session for me, and I was glad to see it end.

All that aside, I must say there are many pleasant compensations that come one's way when involved in an elected political job. For example, I went on two Idaho State Land Board trips into the mountains. The Priest Lake and Priest River Chamber of Commerce invited U.S. Senator Len Jordan and Governor Smylie on a Land Board tour of the Selkirk Mountains north of Priest Lake. As a State Senator and chairman of the public resources committee, I was also invited. A group of about twenty businessmen, Forest Service and State Forestry personnel took us by boat up to the north end of Priest Lake. Then we left the boat and mounted saddle horses. A pack string of mules was also there to carry our camping gear. All we had to bring was a sleeping bag, camera and shaving kit.

We rode horses for four days. Each evening our hosts picked a nice place to camp along a stream or on the shore of a high mountain lake. Our meals were cooked over an open fire. Bacon, eggs, sausage, hash browns and sometimes hotcakes were served with hot coffee for breakfast. Our lunches included sandwiches and fruit. Many times we enjoyed lunch at the Forest Service lookouts we visited. In the evenings steak was served along with hash browns or raw fried potatoes. Every meal was prepared first class and was really appreciated by the men after a long day in the saddle on rocky mountain trails.

During the days we rode through stand after stand of virgin timber and cedar groves with huge trees ten to twelve feet in diameter. The Idaho State Land Board is made up of elected officials responsible for managing state land. Revenue from this land goes to our schools and to state education funds. The board consists of the Governor (who acts as chairman), the Secretary of State, Attorney General, State Auditor and the Superintendent of Public Instruction. The purpose of this trip was to show these men how the areas were being managed and to acquaint them with some of the problems that arise from time to time. It is important that these decision and policy makers see and understand what they are dealing with before they have to decide on the best policy to follow.

One of the most beautiful campsites was at Two Mouth Lakes, two small lakes in a beautiful basin connected by a small stream less than one hundred feet long. There are a number of beautiful lakes in the Selkirk Range. Harrison Lake is located northeast of Chimney Rock, a famous landmark in the Selkirks.

In Bonner and Boundary counties, the most northern in Idaho, much of the timber land belongs to the state and this trip covered the major timber stands. It is managed by the State Lands Department under the direction of the State Land Board.

When the trip ended, everyone expressed their appreciation for the courtesies shown to us on the trip. Several members of the Land Board said that the journey through the Selkirks had given them a better understanding of the resources they were charged with managing. In short, the state forestry people who were responsible for day-to-day management at the time did a great job.

The second enjoyable trip was hosted by Burt Curtis, fire warden for Potlatch Forest Lumber Co. of Lewiston. This time we took a rubber raft trip down the North Fork of the Clearwater River. Again I was invited because I was chairman of the Senate Public Resources and Public Recreation Committee. Other guests included Governor Smylie, Superintendent of Public Instruction Del Engleking, State Auditor Joe

186

Williams, and Attorney General Allan Shepherd. In addition, several legislators and members of the State Land Department accompanied us.

I was fortunate to take this trip twice, once as a State Senator and again during my first year as Governor. On this trip, they took us into Boles Cabin, a set of cabins and buildings across the river above Big Island on the North Fork of the Clearwater River. We had a great dinner that night. Each of us had an assigned bed in a cabin. The next morning a "lumberjack breakfast" was served before we took off in the large rubber rafts. The early June weather was warm and beautiful. We put the rafts in at Boles Cabin and started down the river toward Orofino. The river was very clean, clear and beautiful with no houses or buildings along on its banks from Boles Cabin to Ahasahka, just below Dworshak Reservoir. Since those days the Boles Cabin area has disappeared beneath a hundred feet of water because of the construction of Dworshak Dam. The structure certainly ruined a beautiful river and a lot of big game range.

Trips like these really helped dispel some of the frustrations that came with serving in the Idaho State Senate for six years. There were some tough times when the political power plays led to some disappointments. Overall, I was pleased with what I was able to accomplish for my constituency and for the state itself. It was truly a great experience — an education you cannot buy!

Chapter 15

Serving the State

In the fall of 1965, I became concerned about the 1966 Idaho Governor's race. Through my six years in the Idaho Senate, I had become acquainted with people that were involved in politics from every county in the state. My associations included both political parties and I had friends among the Democrats as well as the Republicans. My equipment business also helped me get acquainted with many business people throughout the state.

Through the information I gathered while traveling around the state in 1965, I concluded that it was obvious that Governor Robert Smylie would not be elected for another term. He had been in office a long time, and had also signed a bill putting the sales tax on the ballot. Everywhere I traveled, I heard the same "anti-Smylie" comments. At this point, I had no thought of running for Governor myself.

I started talking to Allan Shepard who had himself expressed an interest in the Governor's race. Allan had been elected Attorney General of Idaho in 1963 for a four-year term. He told me he couldn't afford to run at this time. Next, I contacted Jack Murphy, who had been President of the Senate and a leader in the Legislature for a number of years. Jack, however, decided he didn't want to run against Smylie.

My next potential candidate was Pete Cenarrusa, who had been Speaker of the House for a number of years. Pete was and still is a very good friend. He was a Basque sheep rancher from Carey and a very personable fellow. I later appointed him Secretary of State after my old friend Edson Diehl died from a heart attack after just six months in office. Edson had been elected Secretary of State at the same time I was elected Governor. Anyway, in 1965 Pete considered my suggestion to run for Governor for quite some time, but finally decided against it.

When Pete declined, I tried talking to another friend of mine who had been very active in politics for more than twenty years. Bill Young from Nampa had served as Speaker of the House and as a leader in the Senate for several terms. He had a law degree and was very capable. He gave the idea some thought but he too declined the challenge.

After all my politically experienced friends had turned down the opportunity to run for Governor on the Republican ticket, I decided to give it a try. Having served six years in the Senate on the Finance Committee, I knew every department in Idaho state government as well as the personnel. I was also aware of where the tax dollars came from and how they were spent.

I felt that several areas of our state's government could be improved. For example, we could take the Lands Department from politics and hire experienced professionals to manage our state land. Many agencies were still using antiquated procedures that I felt could be replaced by more efficient modern methods. I also wanted to work with the agencies to get more value from our tax dollars and move the state ahead. These were the major challenges I faced, and I sincerely believed I could solve them.

One morning in mid-January of 1966, I told Ruby of my plans to run for Governor. After coming off the ceiling three days later, she said, "Okay, I'll help you."

I think she was hesitant initially because she had not had the opportunity to get around the state and hear the opposition expressed by people at all levels toward Governor Smylie's decision to seek a fourth term. I was the one on the road all over the state selling equipment and meeting people in every community. I also think she didn't want to see me hurt if I lost the election.

To begin the campaign, I asked my old friend and dentist, Angus Snedden to be my campaign manager. He agreed and said he'd help me as much as his practice allowed. I announced my candidacy January 5, 1966, in Sandpoint. My procedure was to send out a press release to each newspaper, radio and television station, as well as to the national news media which included the Associated Press and United Press International.

The news release read as follows:

ADVANCE ! !

FOR RELEASE BY NEWSPAPERS AND RADIO

STATIONS THURSDAY A.M., JANUARY 6, 1966.

Bonner County State Senator Don Samuelson today announced he will be a candidate for the Republican nomination for Governor of Idaho, and plans an aggressive campaign for the office throughout the state.

He has served in the Idaho Senate for the past six years, during which time he has been chairman of the Public Resources Committee, a member of the Finance Committee, the Business Committee, Mines and Mining and the Aeronautics committees for two years each.

In a county that has consistently given the top of the ticket a Democratic majority, Samuelson has gained strength at each of the last three elections. He was reelected to his Senate seat two years ago by an even larger majority than previously, even though it was a landslide victory for President Johnson.

When Samuelson was first elected to the Senate, he held meetings with all segments of the economy of his county to learn the needs and desires of his constituents before the session opened. Then midway during the session he returned to the county for a series of meetings with these same groups to bring them up to date on the legislative picture. He sought and acted upon recommendations of these groups in matters affecting the county, the district and the state.

"As a senator," Samuelson said, "my efforts were much more effective because I knew what my people were thinking. If I am privileged to serve as Governor of Idaho, I propose to consult with groups representing all phases of our economy at six-month intervals to determine their problems and help with solutions. These include cattlemen, sheepmen, labor, industry, potato industry, wheat growers, farmers generally, sportsmen, small businessmen and others."

Samuelson was chairman of the committee during the special session of the legislature that placed the Water Agency legislation on the 1964 ballot. When this amendment to the Constitution was approved by the voters, he became chairman of the special committee of the 38th Legislature which hammered out the laws now on the statute books which implemented this legislation.

"I believe very strongly," he said, "that we should keep Idaho water to develop Idaho land and for the use of the people and the industry of our state. Water is our greatest and most valuable resource."

The Bonner County Senator has been identified with the economy bloc of the Senate and many times has taken the stand that Idaho should not go on a fiscal spending spree.

"If I become governor," he said, "I propose to use a staff of certified public accountants to keep track of the budgets of the agencies and work with them in an attempt to stop bad business practices, duplication or waste, in the same manner that private business must do to survive."

His membership on the Senate Finance and other committees has given him broad knowledge of the state's institutions, agencies and economy.

The news release ended with a brief personal history of my having been born on an Illinois farm, serving in the Navy at Farragut and describing the businesses that I owned and that my residence was in Sandpoint. It also summarized the community organizations that I had

been or was involved in at the time, noted my presidency in the Idaho Wildlife Federation and District Federation, and gave reference to my family, of whom I am very proud.

Next, I traveled to every county and quietly set up a committee of volunteers to work on my behalf. I had no problem finding people willing to work. Throughout the state, I found people disappointed because of Smylie's support for the sales tax. Others felt he had just held the office too long.

On my first trip around the state I stopped to see as many country chairmen as I could, as well as newspaper publishers or editors,

This was the campaign picture I used in the race for Governor in 1966.

and managers or owners of radio stations. During my travels I took notes and asked for help in setting up a "Samuelson for Governor" committee in each county. Some of the first people to join my campaign included

Nyal Rydalch, president of the Farm Bureau: Robert Compton, editor of the Power County Press; Bill Chubb, publisher of the Bonners Ferry Herald; Laurin Pietsch, Sandpoint News Bulletin; Robert S. Graves, Camas County Recorder in Twin Falls; the Olmstead brothers from Grangeville; Ted Hanawalt of the Kuna Herald; Ralph and Jean Hunter of the Meridian News-Times; John Porter of the Rexburg Journal; and Ronald Burke of the Recorder Herald in Ketchum — to name just a few.

I campaigned quietly in every county up until the State Convention in Boise on June 11, 1966. When convention day arrived, we were there with our small group of supporters.

Governor Smylie was first on the program and had hired a group of high school students. They wore straw hats with "Smylie" on the headband in large letters. They also had a small band which put on quite a show when he received the nomination.

Then it was my turn. My people, Alice Nelson from Sandpoint and Robert Robson from Shoshone County gave two excellent speeches. When my vote was taken, I had received enough votes to get on the ballot in the primary election. Those that had accompanied me to the state convention included Angus and Rose Snedden, Jim and Pricilla Judge, Jim and Alice Nelson, all of Sandpoint; Grant and Mary Kilbourne from Pocatello; Jerry and Jim Hill from Idaho Falls; and Bob and Penny Robson. A small group led by Angus Snedden started their march around the hall. It began with about six people — no band, no hats, whistles or props of any kind. On the first round, a few people joined in. The next time, a few more. The last time, the whole room was moving. Ang was a great campaign manager who was able to encourage a lot of people to join him in supporting me.

Governor Smylie and I gave our acceptance speeches, and the race was on for the primary election.

In my acceptance speech I presented my program by stating that, "I believe in a strong sense of fiscal responsibility, not only to a balanced budget, not only to the actual needs of the state, but also and primarily to the majority of the people in Idaho and their ability to pay."

Secondly, "My program would utilize the talents and abilities of the people of Idaho. I would regularly schedule meetings with the major contributors to the economy of our state to listen to them, hear their suggestions, and learn their problems. From this, we could determine how best government can assist them in helping themselves grow. I believe that our economy can grow rapidly and permanently if we can assist the farmers, business men and industry in this state. By correcting some of the problems and creating a better climate for the people who already are in business in our state, they can expand and grow and in doing this they will add more jobs for our people."

I believed my experience as chairman of the Senate Public Resources and Public Recreation Committee for six years had given me an insight into the need for the proper management and wise use of all of our natural resources. I saw the need to continue to keep Idaho water for the use of Idaho people and Idaho industry. "We must inventory, plan and develop our water, as well as fight for its use."

As I covered the state with my business concerns, I also continued to make political contacts. Time magazine really helped me get recognition. In fact, they gave me publicity that couldn't have been purchased for thousands of dollars. The magazine carried an article which, I'm sure, was meant to hurt me. It backfired.

The article stated that the John Birch Society had given me thirty thousand dollars as a campaign gift. When this hit and members of the media read it, they tried to contact me. I had left home and was in south Idaho at the time. I normally didn't call home more often than every three or four days. Therefore, I was not aware of the article, nor was anyone in the rural areas where I was working. My name made the headlines in all Idaho papers for three days. Then, just before going into Boise on my way home to Sandpoint, I called Ruby. She was upset because the press had been relentless in calling her after the article appeared.

Upon arriving in Boise, I got a copy of the article and prepared a press release. I said that it would be great if the story were true, but I hadn't seen such a contribution. Reporters asked me if I would accept a contribution from the John Birch Society and my reply was, "I will accept contributions from anyone who accepts my philosophy of government. That doesn't mean that I believe in theirs."

This hit the headlines and again I was news. Every place I went people commented and complimented me on my statement.

When the primary election was held on August 2, I won by 17,000 votes. That upset my opponent to no end. He worked against me in the general election campaign. One of the papers reported that he had been seen driving a car with a bumper sticker that read, "Republican for Andrus." When someone asked him about it, he said the car was his son's.

I had spent just over four thousand dollars on my campaign which included money collected in the counties to run ads for me during the last two weeks of the campaign.

Our phone never stopped ringing for twenty-four hours after I won the primary. We had calls coming in from all over the United States.

I had not beaten Smylie; he had beaten himself. This was my opinion even as I had tried to talk friends into running against him. Through this campaign, I maintained my strategy of not mentioning my opponent. Instead I simply presented my program and asked people to help me if they believed in what I had to offer.

In the general election, I would be facing Democrat Charles Herndon, a lawyer from Salmon, Idaho. Just a month into the campaign however, he died in a plane crash in the mountains southwest of Challis. The accident occurred in mid-September. He was flying in a chartered airplane from Twin Falls to Lewiston. The plane iced up, lost altitude and crashed on Elk Mountain between Stanley and Lowman. As I recall from news reports, several hours passed before the downed plane was located and medical personnel arrived. Mr. Herndon survived the crash but was seriously injured and later died. Apparently, the pilot had spent most of his life in the southern states and had very little experience flying in the mountains of the Northwest.

After Herndon's death, the Democrats wasted no time holding a convention and nominating Cecil Andrus to replace Herndon. As I understand it, there were some pretty hard feelings among some of the old-time Democrats who thought they should have received the nod. Bill Dee, a long-time Democratic senator from Grangeville who had served as Minority Leader for several terms, was one candidate considered. Bill was a conservative attorney practicing in Grangeville. Max Hansen was another very serious candidate at the convention. The Democrats chose

Andrus because he had tallied within 1000 votes of Herndon's total in the primary.

Andrus and his father ran a stud mill about two miles north of Orofino, Idaho. I had called on him when I was selling equipment. We had both been elected to the Idaho State Senate in 1960 and had served our respective counties and parties for the next six years.

After the primary election, I hired Bob Woods from Trestle Creek to take over my business. Carol Poelstra, one of my employees, kept the office open which allowed me to devote all my time to campaigning.

Several members of the news media predicted that I couldn't win during the primary campaign. Even after I won the primary, they continued to work diligently against me, constantly predicting that I would not win the general election. I noticed in addition that my press releases were often changed. When confronted with this fact, they always blamed such changes on the linotype operator or the secretary.

Nevertheless when the votes were counted in the general election that November, I had won by a comfortable margin in spite

Donna and Steve shared in the excitement that their father had just been elected as Governor of the State of Idaho and that their mother would be First Lady for the next four years.

of my adversaries. When the election was over and it was clear that I had won, our phone started ringing and calls came in from all over Idaho and the United States. For twenty-four hours steady the calls continued to come in, congratulating me on my victory. Needless to say Ruby, Donna and Steve were very pleased and excited. We had come back to our home in Sandpoint to vote on Election Day. That night our house was filled with neighbors and friends listening to the returns. The family members all took turns answering the phone. I received many telegrams from people who couldn't get through to us by phone. My father Fred Samuelson was living with us at the time and I'm sure that evening turned out to be a highlight of his life. It was a grand and glorious day for the Samuelson family!

I had spent $40,000 in this election. According to some sources, my opponent had spent many times that amount. The committees working throughout the state were a great help to my campaign. These included women's organizations who held coffees for me in their area. I recall talking to seven different groups in the Pocatello area in one day. I have always been most grateful to all these nice, dedicated people.

After the election, my first move was to sell my business. Griff Barlow, a doctor friend of mine, bought it. Griff and his wife Mary Jane were both medical doctors in Glendale, California. They had a ranch at Spirit Lake, Idaho. Besides being Conservative Republicans, they were very good friends.

Having sold my business, I moved to Boise and kept the apartment that I held during the campaign. After the first of the year, we could move into the Governor's house. My next duties involved putting together a budget and writing a *State of the State* message to present to the Legislature. I also had to interview people and appoint heads to various State agencies. To say I was a very busy man during the balance of November and the month of December would be an understatement.

Several people joined my staff to help out after I won the primary election. Dick Hughes was one of the first. He had a law degree and had been quite active in the Idaho Republican Party. I believe his wife was State Secretary for the party. After the election I appointed Dick as head of staff in my office and he carried my program to the Legislature. Jerry Hill and his brother Jim also joined my team from the start of my campaign. They were both very valuable advisors and workers. Jerry's responsibility while on my staff was to prepare and answer letters. Grant Kilbourne and his wife Mary were very avid supporters from Pocatello. Grant helped with finances and advertising problems from the start. He hunted for a good speech writer and came up with a fellow from Twin Falls named Doug Bean. Doug outlined and wrote speeches for me during the last two months of my campaign. Then I appointed him to help draft letters and write speeches after I was elected. Doug had a knack for writing exactly what I wanted to say to the variety of groups I addressed during my four years as Governor.

Grant Kilbourne was a good friend and advisor. He was president of

Simplot's Fertilizer Plant in Pocatello. I felt very fortunate to have a friend like Grant. He was a Conservative but a good businessman who loved Idaho. I could always talk to him.

Although I must say, the one stalwart supporter through the primary, the general election and my four years as Governor was my wife Ruby. She worked hard when we were on the road campaigning. She handed out hundreds of campaign folders and talked to numerous women's groups. During the time I served as Governor, she never interfered with anything in my office, but was always very supportive. Several times people approached her suggesting she put pressure on me to do something for them, but she would give them a stock answer, "Don was elected Governor. You talk to him. If you can convince him that you are right, I'm sure he will help you."

As Governor of a state one certainly gets enough pressure from special interest people. She felt therefore that getting more from one's wife at home is unneeded. I appreciated Ruby for honoring my position the way she did.

The inauguration took place on the Capitol steps. My family and father attended the affair and beamed with pride at my becoming

The inauguration took place in January of 1967 on the front steps of the State Capitol Building.

Governor of Idaho. After the Inaugural Ball became a memory and the Legislature had been sworn in, our work started.

During the first week of the Legislature, I presented both my budget message and the state-of-the-state speech to joint sessions of the Legislature. My message outlined some of the changes that I would propose to the Legislature along with ways we could provide better service through modernization. I also offered to work with the Legislature to bring about these changes. I proposed vocational training through our education system. I stressed the need

197

for consolidating and modernizing the State's fragmented computer system. Another issue dealt with the Public Lands Department. I advocated taking the department out of politics and putting it in the hands of professionals. This, I explained, would provide more revenue from state lands which would boost our state's education system.

I also suggested that we develop our natural resources through good management and that we hold our state spending to balance the income without increasing taxes. The voters had just passed a referendum to adopt a three percent sales tax. Since it had to be initiated, I pledged to

Presenting my proposed state budget and State of the State message to the Joint Legislature, I explained my belief that we should hold state spending to balance the income without increasing taxes. The state's Senators are seated in the front rows while the House members are seated at their desks.

work with the Legislature to ensure a balanced program for the future. Most of the comments from around the state were very positive. There were just a few complaints from some of my diehard opponents in the Boise area.

At the beginning of the legislative session, all Republican members from both the House and the Senate met with me. They were asked to work with my office in preparing legislation so we could work together in the interest of Idaho. Republicans held the majority in both houses of the Legislature at the time.

I asked the leadership on the Republican side to meet with me for half an hour each Monday morning for coffee and discussion of what would take place that week. He and the Speaker of the House, Pete Cenarrusa, would come every Monday morning for coffee.

Bill Young presided over the Senate and Jack Murphy was assistant majority leader but neither one would show up. During the first month or so, they weren't very cooperative, even though we had been good friends while I was in the Senate. I've never understood why, unless it was because I had made it to the Governor's office after spending so much time trying to get them to run.

With the help of many of my friends on both sides of the aisle, we accomplished many good changes and programs for the state. For example, we completely reorganized the State Department of Lands. It was supposed to be managed so that the revenue they generated went toward Idaho's public schools. Until I took office, the department had been operated by political appointees and there were no qualifications required for any job. We changed that and set the department up with three divisions headed by qualified professional people. The divisions were timber, mining, and agriculture/grazing. We also set qualifications for the land commissioner and the heads of the three departments. This action increased the efficiency of the department besides creating better land management of our resources. It also provided more money for our school fund.

A second major achievement of my administration was the complete overhaul of state insurance regulations. We brought insurance industry people in from all over the state and asked them to help us re-write the insurance code. When I took office, only two Boise agencies handled all state insurance covering the Capitol and all state holdings, including state universities and colleges, automobiles, furniture and even fixtures. We changed the law so that all insurance had to be put out for bids, allowing any interested agency an opportunity to do business with us. It was no longer a closed agency that benefitted a few politicians and their friends.

I have always believed that Industry and Labor should work together closely. At the start of my term as Governor, I appointed ten men from Industry and ten from Labor to meet and work together solving labor/industry problems in Idaho. About 65 people per year were dying on the job in the mines, the farms and in manufacturing firms in our state and an additional 2,500 were injured in the workplace each month. At the time, we had only two safety inspectors in our state. Therefore we increased unemployment compensation twice during the four years, added inspectors, re-evaluated safety regulations and rewrote some of the laws.

Six months before my being elected, the Idaho Savings and Loan, with its headquarters in Twin Falls, went bankrupt. Twenty million dollars in deposits were involved in that action alone. I was told that their deposit slips were inscribed "Insured in Morocco." This, in turn, led six more smaller savings and loan companies into bankruptcy, each for about a million dollars in assets.

The State Finance Department had been very lax in their audits and enforcement. I was told that we would never pay more than ten or fifteen percent back to the depositors. These people were farmers, businessmen, school teachers, students, retired people, et cetera — the very people it was my duty to serve. At the beginning of my term, I appointed Dave Silva Finance Commissioner. Dave, a young man from Coeur d'Alene, started to work on the savings and loan problem right after his appointment. He had just been appointed vice president of Idaho First National Bank in Coeur d'Alene. When he started working on the problem, he worked with a man appointed by the bankruptcy courts.

In no time a consortium of bankers and businessmen who happened to serve on the board of directors for several different banks approached Dave and offered to buy the assets of all the savings and loans for a little more than four million dollars. Dave came to my office and said, "Governor, they are trying to steal the assets."

"If you will stay with me," he added,"we can get a big share of the depositors' money back to them. If we sell out, the depositors will be lucky to get ten cents on the dollar."

I assured him that I would support him to the end. Consequently, he and the man appointed by the bankruptcy court worked together and sold the assets of the seven savings and loans. They paid one hundred percent back to the depositors of five of the smaller savings and loans, returned seventy-six percent to another small one and gave seventy-three percent back to depositors of the large company. This was all accomplished during my four-year term.

When we had refused to sell the assets to the consortium, I had a steady stream of bank directors and officials come into my office asking me to sell the assets to their group. Many of them claimed to have been my supporters. Everyone of them told me that if I didn't turn the assets over to them, they would do everything they could to defeat me in the next election.

My stock answer to them was, "No! We will not turn the assets over to you. As to supporting me in the next election, that decision is entirely up to you."

Some pretty angry people walked out of my office. One of the worst was Docky Bettis, a multi-millionaire who had given me a hundred dollars for my campaign. I had made it clear to all contributors that I was not for sale at any price and that I would do my best to provide honest and good government for everyone.

The assets for the savings and loans had been sold and the checks made out to depositors about a month before my re-election. This same consortium filed charges against the state, an injunction that prevented us from sending out the checks. We hadn't planned it as a campaign advantage, to capitalize on the situation — it just worked out that way. As soon as the election was over, they withdrew their injunction. I lost respect toward the judicial system that would issue an injunction to a bunch of people who had tried to beat the depositors out of their money. It was a good feeling, however, to know that our administration had won on this one, even though we didn't win the election.

During my four years of office, I was equally proud that education in Idaho recorded dramatic progress with vocational training getting a high priority. We also supported natural resource development that has always contributed to the economy of Idaho and provided many family incomes. We supported the modernization of the State Reclamation Agency to make it more effective and efficient. The water resources of

Idaho received new policy statements and the staff was enlarged to handle the extra load, leading to more efficient use of Idaho water. The Parks Department moved ahead by expanding facilities throughout the state.

During my administration the Department of Agriculture, under Mr. Stan Trenhaile, was in good hands. Cash receipts to Idaho farmers and ranchers amounted to $514.5 million in 1967; $546 million in 1968; and a dramatic increase to $615 million in 1969.

The Department of Commerce did a good job selling tourism in Idaho in 1966 and 1967 under the leadership of Louise Shadduck. But she resigned in 1968 to go to Washington D.C. to work for Congressman Orville Hansen. I appointed Al Minton from Pocatello to take her place as head of the department through 1970. He was a retired businessman who was very effective in bringing in new, clean industry to various locations in Idaho. He sought out companies looking for a place to expand. Then he would find a community in Idaho that had the facilities or resources matching the company's needs. When he found the right combination, he would clear it with the business community and then bring the information to me. I would then call and invite the president of the company and his key people to come to Idaho, have lunch with us and allow us to show them the location. Six different companies took us up on the deal, and six of them located in Idaho. Al Minton worked with Hewlett-Packard and was instrumental in introducing them to the potential advantages of expanding in Idaho. They didn't make the move however, until later after we had gone out of office. When they finally made the move, others tried to take credit for it.

Several other state agencies realized improvements as well during my term. As an example, we helped the Highway Department modernize and become more efficient. In addition, the Aeronautics Department built a new airport close to the Canadian line in Boundary county. They also improved and upgraded several small airports throughout the back country of Idaho's mountains. The Board of Corrections was restructured to solve prison problems. We removed this agency from politics and set regulations for the people running the prison, including the warden.

I had a great law enforcement crew. The Idaho State Police was made up of fine, dedicated lawmen, but they were very understaffed. Some counties had just one state trooper to cover three eight-hour shifts per day, thirty days a month. Consequently much of the time in those counties, there was no patrolman on duty to help with accidents or prevention. I repeatedly asked the Legislature for a few more men and more equipment. They failed however to respond to my requests.

The Public Employees Retirement System was initiated in 1970 and was subsequently made available to public school employees, county personnel and most public employees in the state.

I felt that Idaho had one of the finest National Guard units in the United States under the command of General George Bennett. I was always very proud to serve as Commander-in-Chief of both the National Guard and the Air National Guard.

During the four years in the Statehouse, I broke ground on almost every construction site where state facilities existed. Some of these included the Vocational Technical Phase II and the Mini Dome at Idaho State University, the Vocational Education Building at Lewis and Clark Normal, the Supreme Court Building and the Central Heating Plant in the Boise Capitol Mall. Also included were the Library Learning Center Addition and Physical Education Complex at Boise State University; the State Correction Institution on the new prison site; and the Women's Health Education Building, Education Building and the College of Forestry Building at the University of Idaho. These structures, along with several others throughout the state totalled

Boise Mayor Jay along with Jim McClarey presented me with a polished shovel because I broke ground for $40 million worth of State Buildings during my term at the Capitol.

more than $40 million. I am very proud of this accomplishment because much of it came from surplus money I helped create. A big share of it went to improve our state's education facilities at all levels.

Bill Robinson was head of the Labor Department for me and did an excellent job. With his help, we increased workmen's compensation twice during my term. We had been the lowest in the United States when I took office. Bill worked with Labor and Industry to accomplish this without any "bloodshed" on either side.

When I ran for re-election, Bob McFarland, head of the AFL-CIO in Idaho told me that I had done more for Labor than they had been able to do in twenty years, but because I was a Republican, Labor would not help re-elect me.

That's gratitude for a job well done!!

The Finance Department under the leadership of Dave Silva accomplished much during my term. Prior to my administration, banks in Idaho were not allowed to pay interest on state, county, school and municipal deposits. That restriction was removed and now the state and local funds, including school funds, are earning interest on their deposits. This was rewarding because it increased our state income tremendously.

In addition, the Investment of Endowment fund was shackled by antiquated restrictions and earnings of funds far below potential. Consequently, the Legislature passed SJR-4, a Constitutional Amendment. Follow-up legislation by the 40th Legislature removed unwise and archaic limitations on investments. Now, a large portion of the $75 million worth of endowment funds are earning eight to nine percent.

I started the first Governor's Indian Advisory Council in the nation. There were five reservations in Idaho. I had each one appoint two people from their reservation to meet with me twice a year. I also had my state

Our native American Indians are great people, and I loved working with them.

agency people available to answer questions and help them. They told me several times, "We don't want you to give us anything, but we would like your people to help us manage our land and help us raise good crops and livestock."

As far as the Idaho Fish and Game Commission was concerned, I made a mistake in not asking for its members to resign as soon as I took office. While campaigning, I had heard many complaints about the department. Soon after being installed, I invited the five commission members into my office and told them about the complaints I had heard. I asked them to straighten out the department. There were several areas of concern. Good men who had served on the department in law enforcement for many years were moved around the state with the hope that their resignations would open the way for more biologists. There was also a contention that the fisheries on many lakes and streams "were allowed to go to pot." Pend Oreille and Priest Lake in North Idaho were good examples. I had also heard that the department was wasting a lot of money while seemingly coming up with every way possible to raise the prices of licenses and tags. Many times I heard the comment, "The fish and game resources we have are in spite of the Fish and Game Department — not because of them."

All I got in response to my suggestions was lip service and a lot of meaningless activity. My frequent talks with the commission made very little headway. The Legislature passed laws that required all commissions to resign when a new administration took over. That made it much easier for future governors to either re-appoint or replace them with entirely new members.

When I took office, the Bureau of Public Audit was an antiquated agency operated by two nice, elderly men who had some bookkeeping experience. However they were not certified public accountants. As soon as the first Legislative session ended, I started going through a stack of their audits. I soon came to the conclusion that someone was just copying figures from one year to the next with little or no program or planning. We found other positions for the two men by transferring them to an agency that needed bookkeepers. Then we hired a certified public accountant named Gene Harder to head the department. We asked him to find several other C.P.A.'s to help him. The bureau of

Public Audits checks forty-six agencies. Gene set up auditing procedures and began auditing some of the larger agencies.

The State Highway Department was one of the first. Within a very short time, they uncovered a deal where one of the employees had set up a dummy company to move power lines and telephone lines along highway right-of-ways. He was cashing checks and depositing an average of $17,000 per month in his own account. If I remember right, he had taken more than a million dollars that way.

In one of the other departments, they uncovered another situation where a young man was just getting started. He had already taken just over a thousand dollars.

Another situation involved the state prison. I had heard that the prison board, which included three men along with the assistant warden, and the warden had been hauling groceries, turkeys and all kinds of meat out of the prison. I brought the chairman of the prison board into my office and told them to stop their activities immediately. This was shortly after I had taken office. I was told they were not taking me seriously and were continuing to haul things out of the prison. One morning without warning, I sent our auditors out. They took over the office and the files.

What they uncovered was unbelievable! One of the board members had signed out forty-three pints of whipping cream, more than one hundred pounds of meat and every month large amounts of other kinds of food. The wife of one of the prison wardens had given more than fifty prison turkeys to her friends for Christmas. It was also discovered that some expensive dresses had been charged at Anderson's Department Store in Boise to the Women's Prison. I accepted the resignation of all the board members, and with the help of the House and Senate Leadership, appointed three new members.

With the installation of the new, effective Auditing Department and the publicity about the Highway Department and prison problems, other personnel working for the State of Idaho were pretty careful about keeping their records clean.

In short, with the help of friends from both political parties in the Legislature, my administration corrected many problems and modernized the operation of Idaho's state government. I always felt privileged to serve as Governor of Idaho. It was a great honor. At the same time, I felt that I was elected by all the people. Therefore, I believed I should be a servant of the people, not a dictator. I tried to weigh all the information in front of me and make a decision that was in the best interest of the state of Idaho and its taxpayers. My door was open to everyone from both political parties, and after I was elected, the future welfare of the state received my full consideration. Serving four years as *Governor of the State of Idaho* was and still is the highlight of my life.

This was taken at my desk in the Governor's office of our beautiful State Capitol Building in Boise.

Ruby was a marvelous and gracious hostess as first lady of the State of Idaho. She made many good friends and was considered by many to be one of the finest first ladies of our state. Here she is with me as we are greeted by President Johnson and Ladybird in Washington D.C.

President Johnson met with several Governors on matters concerning the western states. I'm on the left in this photo.

Ruby put together the Idaho Heritage Committee to raise money that would provide dishes, silverware and other expensive items for the Governor's House without using Idaho tax revenues. Here she is speaking to one of the many women's groups she visited on behalf of this committee.

It was Ruby's pride in the state and importance of the Governor's job as a leader that inspired her successful effort with the Idaho Heritage Committee. Seated with her in the dining room are the several ladies who helped her with this important part of being a state's First Lady.

209

Chapter 16

Rewarding Times

A governor's responsibility can take up twenty-four hours a day, seven days a week. We are always on call to respond to state or national emergencies. I have appeared before as many as seven groups of people in one day. Many times this started with breakfast and ended with speeches to dinner parties in various Idaho cities. Sometimes I just gave brief remarks or words of welcome to out-of-state guests. Other times I spoke up to half an hour.

I always enjoyed meeting and visiting with people. I found that aspect of my job fun, especially because it gave me the opportunity to learn about various phases of the economic and social contributions of our state. My position also opened the door to several memorable adventures and trips throughout the state.

During my four years in office I felt privileged to host the Boy Scouts of America's National Jamboree in 1967 and the World Jamboree in 1969. Both events were held at Farragut State Park, where I had spent my navy years.

Louise Shadduck, then director of the Department of Commerce and Development, was responsible for bringing in the Girl Scout Jamboree in 1965 when I was still a State Senator. I spent a day at Farragut at that time meeting several scouts and their leaders. Louise was also responsible for bringing the Boy Scout Jamboree to Idaho. She was a great host for our state. Louise was also one of my best department managers and a very loyal friend. Her contributions to Idaho were tremendous and ever-lasting. I believe that she did more for tourism development in Idaho than any other person or group. She put Idaho on the map, so to speak!

Our state benefitted tremendously from the three jamborees because many of the boys' and girls' parents traveled to Idaho to be with or close to their children. They were exposed to the beautiful mountains and lakes. Farragut itself is located on the south end of Lake Pend Oreille. The park offers some of the most spectacular beauty in Idaho as visitors

During the week-long International Boy Scouts Jamboree at Farragut, I welcomed visitors from all over the world. Some 17,000 boys attended the event. For me, it was a reunion with my Navy camp as well as a finale for the times when I was Boy Scout leader.

can spot Rocky Mountain goats on the hillside just east of the park across Buttonhook Bay. Pend Oreille Lake is forty-one miles long and up to six miles wide with a good portion of it more than twelve-hundred-feet deep. It is surrounded by the Coeur d'Alene, Cabinet and Selkirk Mountain ranges. The jamborees also introduced thousands of scouts to the beauty of North Idaho. Many soon became adults and came back with their families to share their memories of the area.

During the World Jamboree, there were seventeen thousand Boy Scouts from all over the world. I took time off from other gubernatorial duties and spent almost a week at the Jamboree. I was concerned about security and wanted to make sure that everything went as planned. Bob Billington, who was Director of the Boy Scout Association at the time, was one of the nicest men I have ever met. Several other scout executives also attended the Jamboree for the full week. I moved from camp to camp welcoming the scouts from various countries. Because I had started the first hunter safety program in the United States, they asked me to give a short, daily lecture on safety with firearms. Everything went like clockwork during the week. Louise Shadduck, Bob Billington and their board of directors had planned well. All in all, the week proved to be very interesting. I was very proud of the state of Idaho and my employees who helped make it successful.

Another rewarding experience during my gubernatorial term was attending the governors' conferences. These included governors from all states and territories who worked together, regardless of party, trying to solve mutual problems. Much of the time was devoted to framing and presenting resolutions to both houses of Congress and to the President.

I was nominated and elected to serve one year on the executive board of the National Governors' Association. That year the conference was held in Little Rock, Arkansas. Governor Win Rockefeller hosted us. He invited members of the executive board, on which he also served, to meet at his big ranch for two days prior to the main conference. Governor Love from Colorado and I traveled together and were given individual rooms in his home at the ranch.

What a beautiful place! He owned an antique automobile collection. He also had a private recreation hall with a bowling alley and pool tables. For his large herd of purebred cattle, he had his own veterinarian along with a livestock hospital. The facility's operating rooms were equipped with hydraulic, stainless steel operating tables. I had never seen a set-up of such magnitude, let alone at someone's ranch.

Win Rockefeller was a very down-to-earth man whom I admired for his honesty. From time to time, he had a bit of a problem with the "spirits" but he was always a gentleman. Needless to say, I enjoyed my year on the executive board and working with Governors Love and Rockefeller.

We also had the Republican Governors' Conference and the Western Governors' gathering. Each met once a year. The Republican Conference concentrated on state-related problems and made recommendations to Republicans in the U.S. House and Senate. If the President was Republican, he was included also.

The Western Governors' Conference met annually to work on problems facing the Western states as well as day-to-day hassles, including timber, logging, grazing on state and federal lands, mining and recreation issues. We shared lots of information on how to solve our problems. Some states faced problems with their water and with the U.S. agencies like the Forest Service and the Bureau of Land Management. By working together, we could put pressure on the parent agencies in Washington D.C. to alleviate the conflicts.

All the governors' conferences were serious, hard-working sessions that helped some of our Eastern legislators understand the problems of western states. For instance, sixty-six percent of Idaho consists of federal lands not subject to state taxes. Another nineteen percent is state owned, managed under the direction of the state land board, which I chaired for four years. Take the state and federal lands away, and that leaves a very small tax base. For that reason, it is very important for states like Idaho to manage their natural resources and lands most efficiently. Sharing information through the governors' conferences was very beneficial toward this end.

During my four years as Governor, I had very few chances to do any hunting or fishing. For a couple of years I hunted ducks on the Boise River, getting up before daylight and arriving at the blind to wait for the legal shooting time set by the U.S. Fish and Wildlife Service. We would hunt until about seven in the morning, then I'd head for home, change clothes and be in my office by eight o'clock. Sometimes we would get a few ducks and sometimes just the experience of seeing the sun come up was fun and relaxing whether we got any or not. It was great to get out in the crisp morning air. It is a great way to start the day!

I had only one chance to go elk hunting during my term as Governor. My friend, Dr. Griff Barlow had a hunting camp on the North Fork of the Clearwater River north of Orofino. Griff had bought my equipment business when I was elected Governor. He was a Conservative Republican and a good friend. Griff invited me down to his hunting camp for a weekend. I left Boise after work on Friday night and drove north to Orofino and the camp. It was quite late when I arrived but Griff and several of his friends were up waiting for me.

After a good night's sleep and a good hunting camp breakfast, we were ready to try our luck in the woods. Griff asked one of his guides to go with me and show me the area. We drove about a mile out of camp in a pickup truck. We took an old logging road that led back into the edge of a good-sized basin on the side of the mountain, parked the truck and started out on foot. After hunting for about three hours, we saw some elk tracks and other elk sign along the side of the basin.

For some reason or other, my guide and I separated. He dropped down the hill about a hundred yards or so. Then we proceeded in the same direction. I was walking slowly and quietly over a small knoll when I saw movement and stopped dead in my tracks. About fifty yards ahead of me stood a fat elk eating leaves and stems from some bushes. I watched the animal for a few minutes before deciding this was what I had come for. I bagged the elk with one shot.

My guide heard me shoot and soon appeared on the scene to congratulate me and help dress the animal out. Griff had my meat cut and wrapped because I had to head back to Boise to be in the office by Monday morning. Needless to say, we served elk to our friends and guests on occasion at the Governor's house that winter.

Besides the successful elk hunting adventure, I also had the opportunity to go chukar hunting a few times along the breaks of the Snake River. One of my dentist friends, Dr. John Lundy, loved to hunt the birds. John had several beautiful Golden Retrievers that he raised and trained for hunting. Hunting chukar along the hillsides above the Snake River in Hells Canyon was great sport and provided good exercise. I always thought that was a good way for keeping in shape.

One day toward the end of August 1969, Governor Stan Hathaway of Wyoming called me. He was a good friend. Stan informed me that the committee which had selected teams for the One-Shot Antelope Hunt had called him and asked if he could find a team to replace a group that had dropped out. He asked me if I was free to take part and if I could pick a team to come along with me. A look at the calendar showed that the date was open, so I accepted.

One-shot antelope hunting originated in Wyoming in 1940 when two men from Lander came up with the idea. The state was, and still is, sparsely populated with a lot of federal lands. The thousands of antelope continued to damage farmers' crops. With this in mind, a committee was formed to write rules for the hunt. Each year five teams participated, each led by a celebrity such as a governor, U.S. Senator or movie star, et cetera. Each celebrity could invite two other men to join his team. Traditionally, the Wyoming governor heads a team every year, but he must choose different men each season.

In the competition, each three-man team had to be accurate enough to bag their antelope with one shot. If a team member shot more than once, his effort was considered a miss — even if the second or third shot dropped the animal. The three-man teams would go out in parties of four consisting of one member each from two different teams along with a driver and a guide.

The year I was invited, Governor Hathaway bagged his antelope about nine o'clock in the morning. After Stan's animal dropped, the crew pulled up through the sage brush alongside it. The guide then opened up the ice chest and passed out a cold beer to toast Governor Hathaway on his good marksmanship. The men joked and talked with their backs toward the "dead" animal when suddenly someone turned around and the antelope was gone. It had just been nicked. It had gotten up and taken off while the men were toasting. The animal was about a hundred yards away moving pretty fast, when Stan shot again. He got the antelope that time; but for the record, it was a miss because he had used more than one shot.

I had asked my old friend Clyde Ormand from Rigby, Idaho, to be one of my team members. Clyde was an outdoor writer and a great sportsman who had hunted all over North America. He and I had served on the board of directors for the Idaho Wildlife Federation and we had worked on wildlife problems together in Idaho for many years. Through this association we had become very good friends. I also chose Roger Perkins, who was my pilot most of the time that I was in the governor's office. Roger was a captain in the National Guard. He was also a helicopter pilot and instructor. Since he loved to hunt, I asked him to be on the team.

The three of us arrived in Lander on the Friday preceding the hunt. Chief Sinclair was head of the Shoshone Indian Reservation just north of Lander. The chief and his tribal members took charge of an Indian ceremony that made the team members blood brothers. They blessed our one bullet and gave each of us an Indian good luck charm to wear around our necks during the hunt the following day.

215

We stayed at the old hotel in the center of town. After being awakened at four Saturday morning, we enjoyed a big breakfast. Each team member also made a sandwich and packed his own lunch. All the groceries were furnished so we could choose what we wanted.

Then each of us was assigned a partner from another team, a four-wheel drive vehicle, a driver and a guide. We started out at daylight, which was about six in the morning and we had to bag our antelope before four that afternoon. I was lucky that morning. I downed mine at about 250 yards with one shot. My rifle was Model 70 Winchester feather-

weight in a .243 caliber. My partner on the hunt, a member of the other team, got his buck about an hour later. We dressed them out, loaded them in our vehicle and headed back to town.

Clyde came in soon after. He had taken a nice buck at 325 yards with one shot. We waited all afternoon until about half an hour after quitting time for Roger to come in. Luck did not smile upon him that day, however. He hadn't had a shot all day until just a few minutes before closing time when he shot at a buck that was running over five-hundred yards out, but he didn't connect.

Our team scored two out of three. There's an old Indian tradition that if you don't score one hundred percent between the three of you, you have to "dance with the squaws." Only one team scored three out of three so they didn't have to dance, but the rest of us did. Anyway, it was a great weekend with a lot of nice people from all over the United States. The Wyoming hosts really did their best to make everyone feel welcome.

The One-shot Antelope Committee also held a "Foo-Foo-Ra" somewhere in the West each spring. This consisted of target shooting and other outdoor competition. The spring after I took my team to the one-shot hunt all the teams were invited to go back to New York to the famous "Campfire Club." The Campfire Club had a hunting and fishing organization about forty-five minutes from Times Square in New York City. That year, it served as the setting for the Foo-Foo-Ra.

The event was co-hosted by the African First Shotters. The African First Shotters was a safari organization that hunted in Africa. They never hunted animals listed as endangered species. They financed students from African countries to come to the United States to study range and game management with the understanding that the students would work in these areas in their own country.

When we attended the Foo-Foo-Ra, we were fortunate to be invited to join a member of the past shooters on his airplane from Denver to New York. I don't remember if it was a 747, but I do know it held a lot of people.

The competition involved several tests. We had to shoot at a running bear target which ran across the range on a cable. Then we shot at clay targets thrown out of a fifty-foot high duck tower that resembled a forest service fire tower. It had electric traps that threw clay targets in three directions. Another challenge was the "quail walk." Competitors walked on a trail through a wooded area. Clay targets came flying from hidden traps, usually wherever you least expected them.

Another test was known as the "water boil." They gave each of us a block of wood, a hand axe, two matches and a small metal container with a quart of cold water and a knife. In that event, they timed us with a stopwatch while we split wood, cut shavings with our knives, built a fire and set the metal container of water on it. The task was complete when the water was boiling. One of my teammates, Roger Perkins, won that contest.

Our last challenge involved a fly rod. The officials had set out bicycle tires at different distances on the lake. Each contestant was to drop a fly inside each floating bicycle tire. The wind was gusty that day and we cast from a wooden dock which extended into the lake.

I really enjoyed the day's events and meeting nice people from all over the United States. That evening we were all guests at a banquet in a hotel in the heart of New York City. Sunday morning we headed back to Denver by plane and then on to our respective home bases.

In 1967, the first year of my term as Governor, the owner of Hoff Lumber Company at Horseshoe Bend, Ted Hoff called and asked if I'd like to go on a horseback trip through the Sawtooth Mountains. Ted and the U.S. Forest Service were hosting the trip. A group of conservationists wanted to put a large part of that area into wilderness, thus locking up the resources forever.

Much of the Sawtooth area offered spectacular scenery with numerous alpine lakes surrounded by jagged peaks. Along with these were old stands of mature virgin timber which would be lost to bugs and fire unless it was managed and some of it harvested.

I knew I would have to take a position. Therefore I decided to take them up on the offer. They furnished a good horse and most of the equipment. I had my own sleeping bag, some fly fishing equipment and some extra clothes. About a dozen men went on the trip. We started from the old mining town of Atlanta and rode for five days through the beautiful Sawtooth Range, eventually coming out at Grand Jean Park located at the west edge of the Sawtooth Recreation Area.

We set up camp each night alongside a lake or stream. With some pretty good cooks along, we ate really well. Several evenings after dinner, Ted and I rode up the mountain to lakes which were off the regular trail and did some fly-fishing. Whatever we caught, we released.

On the last day Gordon Trombley, director of the Department of Lands, sent a helicopter into the Sawtooth Mountains to get me. We had two forest fires going in North Idaho. One was the Sundance Fire, northwest of Sandpoint. The other was the Trapper Creek Fire in Boundary county, close to the Canadian line. Both were burning in the Selkirk Range at the same time.

I was disappointed to cut short the trip through the Sawtooths, but I knew the two North Idaho fires needed my attention. I arrived back in Boise by helicopter about noon and was briefed on the fires. It seemed that the Sundance Fire had been contained, and it would be just a matter of mopping up the remainder. I kept in contact with the Department of Lands throughout the weekend. Both fires were in the center of one of our largest blocks of state land. Money derived from the sale of timber and other resources goes to Idaho school endowment funds, so it was very important that we held any damage to a minimum.

We had experienced a very dry summer that year. More than ninety days had gone by without any appreciable rain in that area. I flew over the burns several times in a plane and once in a helicopter. It was frightening to see huckleberry bushes and other kinds of brush burn so rapidly — as if it were paper.

The federal government was holding hearings in Spokane, Washington, on a federal lands bill that next Tuesday. All members of the Idaho Land Board wanted to go, so I had invited them to ride with me in the National Guard C-54 airplane. We made arrangements to leave Boise Monday afternoon. Our plan was to spend the night in Spokane so we could testify Tuesday morning.

When we were about fifty miles from Spokane, I realized how close we were to the Sundance fire. I asked General Bennett if they could fly us over the fire. He agreed and headed the plane toward Sandpoint and the fire area. As we approached, we could see a large plume of smoke resembling pictures I had seen of an atomic explosion. We flew over the fire at almost ten thousand feet and could see that something had

In my room at the Ridpath Hotel, I received an early morning call from Neal Rahm that the Sundance Fire had become a firestorm ripping across the Selkirks. Some of the same ridges and draws I'd hiked with Les Gissel and Carl Grief were completely destroyed.

219

happened. The fire was covering a very large area and seemed to be heading northeast toward Bonners Ferry. There was nothing we could do, so we headed back toward Spokane, landed and went to our hotel.

Shortly after arriving, Neal Rahm, the U.S. Forest Service Supervisor from Missoula, Montana, called and asked me to come to his room. He told me he had just received word from his fire research people that the Sundance fire had turned into a fire storm, burning a swath across the Selkirk Range for more than twenty miles.

He added that their fire research plane had been flying over the burn when the fire exploded. With their infrared cameras, they had determined that one square mile of timber had burned in less than six minutes. It was also reported that the fire storm picked up burning limbs as big as my arm and carried them as far as twenty miles! The suction of the storm was so great that in some areas it actually removed all the dirt from roots of trees. Two fire fighters in the path of the storm got into a situation where they knew they couldn't out run the fire, so they crawled under the Caterpillar tractor they had been operating. Both were cremated. Two long steel I-beams supporting a bridge across Pack River had gotten so hot they melted and conformed to the contour of the ground beneath them.

Both the Trapper Creek blaze and the Sundance fire required months of mop-up. Hundreds of fire fighters spent thousands of man-hours on the burns, which kept the air smokey for weeks. Twenty-three years later, the Sundance burn is still remembered both locally and nationally. Mother Nature is a great healer though. The area is now covered with new growth, which now attracts big game as well as recreationists.

In the spring of 1969, I was invited on a three-day trip in a boat down the main Salmon River from the old town of Shoup to the Mackay Bar. My hosts were Don and Bob Smith, a father and son. They wanted to talk with me and show me why proposed Forest Service regulations were too restrictive. I believe Don Smith was one of the pioneers in Salmon River boat and float trips for hire. In addition to myself, General George Bennett, a pilot, and Clyde Ormond, my outdoor writer friend, went along. General Bennett flew me to the small landing strip at North Fork, a short distance north of the town of Salmon in Idaho alongside Highway 93.

Since it was steelhead season, we all took our fishing equipment with the idea of fishing a few stretches of water along the way. Everyone had a steelhead tag except me. I had been so busy right up to the time we left Boise that I failed to get one. It didn't occur to me however, until we stopped to fish the first time. Consequently, I used my fly rod and some small flies and went after rainbow and cutthroat.

When we arrived at the Mackay Bar where we had dinner and spent the night, Bob suggested that we go down to Shep Ranch, another resort that handled licenses and steelhead tags. Fortunately they had one and that allowed me to go after steelhead on the way back up the river. That night we ate a steak dinner and enjoyed a good rest at the Mackay Bar Resort.

General George Bennett is standing next to me in the middle. Don Smith is on the left and his son Bob is on the right. Fortunate enough to acquire a steelhead tag at the last minute, I was able to tangle with a couple of them on the way back out.

The next morning after breakfast it was suggested that we take the boat up the river a short distance and meet "Buckskin Billy," a hermit living in a cluster of log cabins he had built over the years. I spent a couple of hours visiting with him. He showed me a muzzle-loading rifle that he had built completely on his own — including the lock, screws and trigger. He also gave me a tour of his cabins, pointing out the many things that he had made. Billy was a well-educated man and a real

221

character. He was especially interested in talking to me when he found out I was a gunsmith. In fact he talked constantly.

Our trip back up the "River of No Return" was most interesting. Bob let me ride with him when he took the boat up over the falls. Clyde Ormand had his camera and took a picture of us engulfed in spray as we came up between two big rocks in the middle of the river. Later that summer Clyde's article about the trip and the picture were published in Sports Afield.

After we left the falls, we stopped at a camp where Bob and Don had once eaten lunch. We also fished on the way back up the river but didn't have any luck.

Don Smith was a great storyteller who entertained us from time to

Clyde's shot of Bob Smith and me shooting the falls on the River of No Return.

time with tales of people who had inhabited the Salmon River back country in past years. I not only enjoyed the company of all our party but I also learned a lot about the Salmon River country as well, especially the vicinity around Salmon, Idaho. A lot of interesting history was generated in that area and we were fortunate to have Don touch on a few phases of it during the trip.

Don told us about two old hermits who lived across the river from each other. They were both excellent shots when it came to wild game. But their favorite pastime, he said, was shooting at one another across the river. Whenever one would catch the other outside his cabin, he would shoot at him but never connected. They were enemies for some reason. This feud went on until one of them died of natural causes.

He also told us about a couple who lived down the Salmon River. The lady was pregnant and about to deliver, so she and her husband snowshoed in six-foot-deep snow over a high mountain pass. They continued down the other side and hitched a ride to the hospital in Salmon. They had covered more than 20 miles on snowshoes.

Don related several other interesting (but not printable) bear stories while we floated down the river eyeing bighorn sheep, elk and deer. We also saw cougar tracks in the mud, sandbars and dust trails along the river.

Don and Bob Smith had built a nice floating houseboat which they used for feeding and housing their guests on riverboat trips. They anchored it with a cable to a cove of several large trees along the river. It was clean, comfortable and self-contained because they did not want to pollute the Salmon River any more than it was naturally. In the spring the river ran brown from soil washing into it during the heavy rains and snowmelt.

The Forest Service had served Don and Bob notice that they would have to remove their houseboat from the river. Consequently, they asked me to contact the Forest Service and ask that they be allowed to keep it for their guests. I couldn't see that they were harming the river or the environment in any way, so I did make a couple of phone calls and wrote several letters asking powers-that-be to reconsider before making the Smiths remove their boat. I believe they were required to move it by the following spring.

Chapter 17

Challenging Times

In 1970 when election time rolled around, I declared myself a candidate for re-election. But being in the political race was different this time because I also had the responsibilities of my office.

Shortly after my announcement the President of the AFL-CIO made an appointment to see me. During our visit, he told me that I had done more for labor than their organization had accomplished in the last twenty years. He went on to say that the Political Action Committee (PAC) had told him that if he helped me in any way, he would lose his job.

"Because I'm Republican?" I asked.

He said,"Yes."

Having been unopposed in the primary, nothing had been done to hurt me.

I had to depend on other people to put my campaign organization together so I picked a few key players. Grant Kilbourne agreed to be my finance chairman, and he did an excellent job. Our advertising agency was headed by a man from Pocatello although the base company was in Salt Lake City, Utah.

This was my first big mistake. We had several advertising firms in Boise and one of them did a lot of work for our Commerce and Development Department. I didn't want anyone to think that state money would be used in my campaign. Soon after signing the advertising contract however, I realized my mistake. The company flew their people to Boise from time to time. Air travel consequently ate up a substantial portion of the budget. They didn't have anything at stake — they got paid, win or lose. Whereas the Boise advertising agency could keep their contract with the Commerce and Development Department if I won. I'm sure this in itself made a difference.

Ang Snedden, who had served as my chairman in the first campaign, agreed to help me again. When I ran in 1966, John McMurray was state republican chairman. John knew everyone in the state and was a great help to me. He kept the job until 1968 and then decided not to run for the office again. At the same time Gwen Barnett, whose husband Steele worked for Boise Cascade, was national committeewoman. Roland Wilbur, who worked for Potlatch Forest Industries in Lewiston, was the national committeeman. At the Republican Convention in 1968 Roland Wilbur was elected chairman of the Republican Party.

John McMurray was a great guy to work with as chairman, and my door was always open to him. When Roland Wilbur took over however, it was a different story. I very seldom saw him. Whenever I did, he seemed to have a chip on his shoulder. When it came time for me to run for re-election, he informed me that he did not intend to raise funds to help me in any way. In fact, he didn't raise one dime to help any of the Republican candidates that year. Toward the end of the general campaign, we (my staff and the people working on my campaign) tried to get hold of our state chairman, but to no avail. Later, we learned that he was in California playing golf the last two weeks of the campaign.

My Democratic opponent worked for Roland Wilbur in the Potlatch Forest Industrial Insurance Division right up to the time he campaigned for Governor. I was told that Roland Wilbur actually worked for my opponent and deliberately left the state at the end of the campaign.

I heard another interesting story from a good friend who had played golf in Clarkston with a banker. When the Idaho Governor's race came up, the banker told my friend that the management of Potlatch Forest Industries had instructed them not to let Democratic candidate Cecil Andrus' account drop below $30,000. In short, I had the consortium of businessmen, bankers, the unions, and Potlatch Forest Industries working against me mainly because I wasn't for sale.

All polls indicated that I was ahead by one point right up to the election. When the ballots were counted, I stayed in the lead right up to the end. Then the vote from the three labor-controlled areas came in—Pocatello, Lewiston, and Coeur d'Alene. When it was over, I had lost by 5,000 votes. Anyone can check election records through the Secretary of State's office and confirm my assertions.

Losing the election was very depressing for me as well as my family, staff and friends. We had campaigned hard but there was a lot of voter apathy that year. I had put in long hours and many seven-day weeks trying to improve our state government. I also did not play politics and worked with the Democrats as well as the Republicans.

I always believed in the two-party system but when elections had ended, I tried to work with and for everyone on any legislation or project that was good for Idaho. My re-election would have opened the way for several things I wanted to accomplish. One was to build a new governor's home without using any tax money. Jim Brown, owner of the <u>Idaho Statesman</u>, was going to start the fund with a $25,000 memorial to the Eilshires, the former owners. They had left the paper to him. Several other individuals also planned to donate to the project through memorials.

Another goal I had for my second term was to completely reorganize the Idaho Fish and Game Department in hopes that it would be responsive to all areas of the state. My policy has always been that everything should be "on top of the table" or out in the open. Then if mistakes were made and someone would come up with a better solution to the problem, we could change it.

After the election defeat, I gave very little thought toward my future. My first priority was Ruby's health as we discovered she had developed cancer. My total focus became just getting her through all the treatments and cancer surgery.

This period once again confirmed my belief in the Good Lord having His hand on my shoulder because Ruby recovered fully and I got a better job, too, with a lot less stress. It also paid two and a half times more money! I covered four states instead of one. As Secretarial Representative of the United States Department of Transportation, my responsibilities, particularly with the Alaska Pipeline, put me on a lot of airplanes and in many hotels and motels throughout Alaska, Washington, Idaho and Oregon — the states under my jurisdiction.

The nicest part was working for top people in each state and on the pipeline, even though I did put in long days. At times, it seemed that my home was in an airplane.

Right after losing the election, Ruby and I hosted the Republican Governors' Conference in Sun Valley. John McMurry acted as conference chairman. I thought he did an excellent job of putting the conference together. He and his friends raised the money. He also made arrangements for gifts for all our visitors and their wives.

A few days before the conference, Ruby had gone through a medical check-up. The doctors determined that she had uterine cancer and should start radiation treatment immediately. She talked them into waiting until after the conference to start the procedure.

As soon as it ended, she checked into St. Luke's Hospital in Boise and started with radium implants to kill the cancerous cells. She had two implants about three weeks apart. She also underwent surgery during early March. They removed the cancerous area and found no live cancer cells. Ruby had gone through a pretty rugged six weeks.

During this time, we had to move out of the Governor's house by the first of January. I found a nice house on Hummel Drive and bought it. With the help of many good friends, we moved to our new home. When Ruby was discharged from the hospital, our son Steve and I took care of her. Steve was living with us and going to college in Boise at the time.

I was out of a job and my wife was a very sick person who had a fairly long road to travel to gain back her strength and her health. I didn't do much in the way of looking for a job until Ruby recovered. She was my first priority.

In late spring that year, I bought a plane ticket and headed for Washington, D.C. Richard Nixon was President and there was a vacancy as Secretary of Interior. I went to see Rogers Morton, chairman of the Republican Party, and asked him about the job.

Rogers said, "Don, the President called yesterday and asked me to take that job. I accepted this morning but it hasn't been announced yet."

The next morning's papers carried the headline of Nixon's choice. I visited with Rogers in his office for about half an hour during which he told me about several jobs that were coming up. He told me that he would help me with any of them I wanted.

I returned to Boise. About two weeks later, Rogers called me and asked if I would like to head the Bonneville Power Commission in Portland, Oregon. I told him I didn't know the first thing about electricity and would rather wait until a position dealing with land or natural resources came open. Rogers understood my reasoning and assured me he would let me know when there was an opening.

One day in May, I received a call from Wells McCurdy in Seattle. He had been a Mobil Oil distributor in Sandpoint before moving to Seattle. Since that time he had gotten involved in shopping centers.

Wells told me about a very interesting job opening up in Seattle. The title was "Secretarial Representative for the United States Department of Transportation." If I took the job, my office would be in the Federal Building, and I would have the responsibility of the four states of Alaska, Washington, Oregon and Idaho. I would represent the Department of Transportation on the Federal Regional Council in Region Ten.

The responsibilities of the job, Wells said, involved several agencies under the Department of Transportation. These included the Seattle and Alaskan districts of the Coast Guard, the same two districts of the Federal Aviation Administration, the Federal Railroad Administration and the Alaskan Railroad, the Federal Highway Administration (which covered all four states) and for two years, the National Transportation Board — before it became an independent agency.

John Volpe was the Secretary of Transportation under President Nixon at the time. During my term as Governor, I had gone to Japan with him when he was chairman of the National Governor's Conference. We spent seventeen days in Japan on a trade mission. We also attended the Japanese Governor's Conference, where I gave a talk on transportation through an interpreter. John and I had become very good friends.

After Wells McCurdy called me, I took a day or two to think about his idea. Then I decided to call John Volpe and ask him about the job.

"I'd like to have you in the job," he responded immediately . He told me to write him a letter and enclose my resume, which I wasted no time in doing. About two weeks later the phone rang. One of John's administrative assistants named Barry told me my application had just been approved by Mr. Volpe and had been sent on to the White House for approval. Ten minutes later, I received a call from the White House. The official informed me they had just approved my application and that I was appointed to the job of Secretarial Representative of the Department of Transportation in Region Ten. My office would be in Seattle, Washington.

Pipelines are under the Department of Transportation, so I had responsibility of the big Alaska Pipeline that carried oil from Prudoe Bay to Valdez. That meant spending a week each month in Alaska for the next six years and seeing the pipeline emerge from a survey line to its completion. I also visited all the camps and watched the bridge being built over the Yukon River. It was fascinating to watch buildings up to nine stories high being transported to the Port of Prudoe Bay on barges.

My job also involved working with the governors of all four states and with the department heads of each transportation department. My first office was in one corner of the Health and Welfare Building in Seattle. When the new Federal Building was built, I was assigned a suite of rooms on the 36th floor, right under the Coast Guard offices. A secretary manned the office eight hours a day five days a week. When my first secretary, Margaret Ike, retired, Darlene Elston took over and worked for me until I retired at the end of 1976.

From the very beginning, I was assigned a lieutenant commander from the Coast Guard to act as my administrative assistant. The first one was Lt. Commander Dave Irons, who was definitely an officer and a gentleman. Another fine man, Lt. Commander Richard Brower, served under me in the same position later on. They assisted me by representing the Department of Transportation on the Federal Regional Council. They prepared for each monthly meeting of the federal agencies in the region. Both my good assistants were promoted to Captain when they went back to their regular duties in the Coast Guard after serving me.

I did a lot of traveling in this job. I was assigned a car to travel Washington, Oregon and Idaho but otherwise, it seemed like I lived in a hotel or an airplane most of the time. I took numerous trips to Washington, D.C., and attended meetings all over the United States. I was elected vice chairman of the Federal Regional Council and served in that capacity my last two years with the department.

Once, I spent a very interesting week in Kobuk, Alaska. It involved one of the larger mining companies. I had been working with them on a large silver-copper mine which they had developed north of Kobuk. They had dug a one-thousand foot shaft and had the necessary equipment to raise and lower men and other equipment as well as bring up the ore. The ore was estimated to be worth more than a billion dollars but there were no roads close to the area, no railroads nor any water transportation.

229

I was invited to come to the mine and make recommendations on a transportation method for getting ore out of the area. The mine was fifteen miles north of Kobuk, inside the Arctic Circle. Federal Aviation personnel of Alaska had to fly supplies or equipment into Kotzebue. In doing so they flew over the Dahl Creek Airport about three miles from Kobuk. I made arrangements to ride to the Dahl Creek airstrip. Then, I asked a very good friend, Ivan Stewart, to meet me and take me to the mine.

Ivan had one of his crew meet me at the airport. It was Friday afternoon, and I had planned to spend the weekend with Ivan and his crew at Jade Camp. I spent Saturday and Sunday helping around camp. Ivan had assigned us the job of building an outdoor toilet to haul up to the jade mine. At the mine, huge jade boulders were loaded on rock sleds and then pulled about twenty-seven miles to the camp, where they were cut into smaller chunks. To cut them, the crews used eight foot Diamond drag saws, which operated twenty-four hours a day. Circular diamond saws were used to cut the jade into smaller pieces. The electric power came from a large generator connected to a Pelton wheel. Water from Dahl Creek turned the Pelton wheel.

The jade was put in heavy burlap bags which were limited to seventy pounds each. These were then transported to the Kobuk Post Office and mailed to Anchorage for further treatment, a process which took place in Stewart's Photo Shop on Fourth Street just back of the Anchorage Westward Hotel. Ivan's wife Oro operated the photo shop. Since that time, I've spent many hours on visits to Anchorage with my good friends, Ivan and Oro Stewart.

Meanwhile, back at the jade camp...when we finished the toilet, we spent some time hiking up Dahl Creek looking for jade. There had been quite a bit of placer gold in Dahl Creek before it was dredged. The dredging people had left a certain area for the old prospector however, who spent his final days there panning for yellow gold. The area was right next to our camp, so Ivan suggested that I take his gold pan and give it a try.

There was gold. In fact, I came up with a few nice colors in the first pan. I had on a heavy jacket with long sleeves and a hat, but the mosquitoes were about the size of hummingbirds and almost as thick as a swarm of bees. Even though I had doctored my face and hands with Cutter's Repellent, they still flew into my eyes, nose and mouth whenever they found an opening. I stuck with it through three pans and then had to quit and get back to camp and behind some screens.

Monday morning Ivan took me down to a road where they had a four-wheel-drive Jeep. Then he took me up to the mine. The mining engineer had been expecting me. After showing me my quarters for the next few days, we went into the dining area for a briefing about the mine. During the briefing, I was told that mine officials had considered building a two-mile-long airstrip through an area covered with sand dunes that was close to the mine. Then they planned to concentrate the ore and haul it out in Boeing 747 freighters. As I remember it, they planned to haul about 250 tons per load. The engineer also told me that the plan was feasible but would cut their profit margin down to where it just wasn't worth it.

I spent several days flying all over the area in a helicopter. He had a crew drilling on another silver-copper ore body with the potential of being as large as the first one and worth another billion dollars plus.

Toward the end of the week I returned to Fairbanks on one of the mine's supply planes. When I arrived back in my office, I made a report to the secretary concerning my recommendations for transporting the ore out of the mine area.

The recommendations covered several other aspects of transportation. I had learned about a bed of steam coal that extended to a depth of eighty-seven feet. It was just a short distance north and east of the mines. I proposed construction of a mine mouth coal-fired power plant that would provide electricity for Nome, Kotzebue and all the rest of the native villages in the area. Those communities all used diesel power plants which were dependent on fuel that had to be flown in at a great expense. The terrain was relatively flat or sloped toward Cape Darby and Norton Bay, so I suggested that an electric railroad be built from the mine down to Cape Darby where the water was deep enough for ore barges. The ore could be loaded on the railroad cars, hauled to the port at Cape Darby, loaded on ocean-going barges and from there taken to smelters any place in the world. My report was sent to the Secretary of Transportation and a copy was sent to the mining company.

Nixon's administration changed about that time however, and to my knowledge nothing was ever done with that report. The new President, Jimmy Carter, assigned Brock Adams to the position of Secretary of Transportation.

Before that my job required long hours each day and sometimes on weekends. I built up considerable leave time and found opportunity to use it on two interesting and pleasant trips.

The first was a seventeen-day trip to Mozambique on the southeast side of Africa. It was a camera and hunting safari and members of the Wyoming One Shot Antelope Hunt were invited to go with the African First Shotters.

It certainly wasn't free however. The seventeen days cost Ruby and me approximately $5,000, though the amount included airfare, hotels, guide service and most of our meals. My hunting license and game tags added another $150 to the tab.

Besides sponsoring African students at American colleges and universities, the African One Shotters have three other major policies. They do not hunt any game on the endangered species list. They expect each member to be proficient enough to bag their game with one shot. And they want all their members to be good sports.

When the time came, Ruby and I left Seattle and flew to Kennedy Airport in New York where we met the rest of the group with their wives and families. We had two celebrities in our group. They were astronauts Jim Lovell, one of the group who had gone to the moon and Donald "Deke" Slayton, who had headed the astronaut program for NASA and who picked the crews for each flight. He also was a crew member himself and served as part of the crew that flew with the Russians. Both were fine individuals. Ruby and I enjoyed being with them.

From Kennedy Airport we flew to Amsterdam, Holland where we spent one day on a one hundred-ten-foot cruiser in the North Sea. It was rough that day, kicking up twenty-foot waves. Some of the crew did some bottom fishing while others of us shot trap off the top deck. The trap was located on the deck below us, and the clay birds were wild in that wind. Each of us shot three strings of ten or a total of thirty birds. I guess the weather and the wind put me on my toes because I shot the high score of

27 out of 30.

Our friend Laurin Pietsch, publisher of the <u>Sandpoint News Bulletin</u> had a son, Kent, living with his family in Amsterdam. Kent worked for a Swiss banking firm there.

Laurin had written Kent and told him when we would arrive and where we would be staying. Kent and his wife took the day off and gave Ruby and me a tour of the city that included a boat ride on the canal system. The flowers were beautiful throughout the city and our tour included several historical sites plus a nice lunch in a unique restaurant. That was a special treat that we hadn't anticipated thanks to Kent and his wife.

The next morning we left Amsterdam on KLM Airlines for Johannesburg, South Africa. We stopped for fuel at Kasanka about midnight and found that the airline had arranged for several of the shops to be open for us to buy souvenirs. Ruby bought an ivory necklace and earrings featuring carved elephants. In Johannesburg, we stayed in a nice hotel and enjoyed a banquet that evening.

Next, we boarded the plane for Lorenco Mark, the capital of Mozambique. Then it was on to Bira. From there, we loaded busses and traveled about twenty miles to a tourist facility at the Gorengoza Big Game Refuge.

The dirt road from Bira to the game refuge twisted and turned its way through some farm country where cotton was the main crop. The last half of the trip took us through a wooded area that led to the resort facilities on the Gorengoza Game Refuge. About halfway through this area, we came to a stream about one-hundred feet wide. The bus eventually stopped and we all piled out and walked across a foot bridge to the other side of the stream. Meanwhile, the bus was ferried across the stream by manpower. About twenty Africans with poles took the ferry and bus across. Several men on the far side pulled on a rope attached to the front of the ferry while the others used their poles.

When they reached the other side, they drove the bus off the ferry, we climbed aboard, and were on our way again. It had taken an hour to cross the stream, but no one seemed to be in a hurry.

The hunters were divided into two groups. One bunch flew to the hunting area about one hundred and fifty miles away from the big game refuge where the rest of us stayed to await our turn. I was in the second group. For three days we spent our time on a camera safari, riding in Volkswagon buses with the tops open. We saw hundreds of game animals each day and managed to take some very good pictures. Some of the game included herds of cape buffalo, wildebeest, hartebeest, impala, sable, lions, elephants, hippos and zebras.

The cape buffalo is similar to our American buffalo in size and stature. The most notable difference is its set of long horns. A hartibeest is the color of a Jersey cow but has long legs and unusual horns that turn inward. I would guess that a mature hartibeest weighs five to six hundred pounds on the hoof. Impalas are small antelope with crooked horns that weight about one hundred pounds. The sable is one of the most graceful and beautiful animals in Africa. It has a a blackish-grey coat with a white spot on the throat. Its long, tapered horns seem to reach over the length of the animal's body. An adlut sable weighs up to two hundred and fifty pounds.

While observing the game, we heard a story about a man who had taken a Land Rover to town for supplies. On his way home, he had evidently run off a plank bridge and crashed. The next morning they found one of his boots with a foot in it. The lions and the rest of the jungle animals had found him first. The speculation was that he had gone to sleep at the wheel or might have stopped too long at one of the taverns in town.

Finally the time arrived for me and my crew to fly out to the hunting camp. Although Ruby didn't hunt, I had made arrangements for her to accompany me. She rode on the seat above and back of the pickup cab between my white hunter and me. He was a Portuguese named Jack Silva. He met us at the landing strip in the jungle and transported us to the hunting camp. We traveled a narrow dirt road for about three hours and arrived in camp in time for lunch. Then we boarded the pickup and headed out on our first half-day hunt.

After traveling about half a mile from camp, Jack stopped the pickup. There was a target set up against a tree about a hundred yards away.

"Your rifle has traveled a long way, so it would be best to check it out and see if it is still sighted in," Jack told me.

I agreed so I slipped a shell into the chamber and squeezed off a shot at the target.

Jack was watching the target with his ten-power binoculars. "Okay, let's go hunting!" was all he said. He seemed pretty pleased so I assume I hit the center.

While we were stopped, I told Jack I wasn't down there to kill all the animals in Mozambique. I was interested in just mature males. I had a license for seventeen different species. "If we see an animal on my list which isn't a mature male and I pass it up," I assured him, "I won't be mad at you if we don't see another one."

"Okay. That's fine with me," he replied and we were on our way.

We had a pickup truck with an African driver. There was a rack on top of the cab with a heavy foam cushion where we could lay our guns, cameras and binoculars. Rubber bungicords across the cushion kept our guns and equipment from bouncing off the foam. A seat was mounted back of this on top of the stock rack. It was wide enough for three people. I rode on the left, Jack rode on the right and Ruby sat in the middle. A second seat was fastened to the box on the back of the pickup. Two other African's rode there. One was a game spotter; the other, a skinner.

The skinner cleaned and dressed the game we bagged each day after which it was transported back to camp where it was then cut up and distributed to the natives in a small village right next to our safari camp. The natives came to the meathouse each night when we arrived back at camp. Our people finished cutting up the meat and gave it to the people who lined up with pans, large leaves, or whatever they could find to carry the meat home.

Late in the afternoon the first day, my guide spotted four cape buffalo at the edge of the jungle. All of us but Ruby piled out of the pickup. She got into the cab. We started stalking the buffalo as they moved through the jungle. We continued for about an hour and kept spotting other buffalo. Eventually we determined we were following a herd of twenty-five or so. Finally, they stopped in a clearing at the edge of the jungle.

With Jack leading the way, we crawled through the brush on our hands and knees until we got to a point within one hundred fifty yards from the herd.

Jack was looking them over with his ten-power binoculars. He whispered to me, "There are two big bulls in the bunch. The one in the center is the largest."

The big one was facing us, so I held on the small white spot on its chest and pulled the trigger. When the gun went off, the herd stampeded. The dust was so thick we couldn't see anything. Jack got up and took off, yelling, "Come on!"

The bull had gone down when I hit it; but as we ran toward it, we could see it was trying to get up to follow the herd. I shot again to ensure the animal stayed put. It wouldn't have been necessary but Dave had warned we didn't want to have to track a wounded cape buffalo in the dark — so I was only making sure. My rifle was a Model 70 Winchester magnum .300. I used 180-grain Nosler bullets to shoot the cape buffalo, .but for other game, I used 180-grain Winchester pointed soft points. Both were very accurate when shot and did the job they were designed to do.

With the buffalo down, Jack sent the driver back for the pickup and Ruby. We took pictures and then the animals were dressed out and loaded into the pickup. We then drove back to camp.

When my guide measured the horns, they were thirty-nine and a half inches. Forty inches would have put them in a record class but for me it

Ruby and me with my near-record class Cape Buffalo.

236

was a fine trophy.

We shared our camp with Harold and Ruby Dahl and an elderly gentleman named Rick. They were all from Denver. That evening when we arrived back in camp, there was a nice campfire burning outside the dining hall, and our three new friends were waiting for us. We enjoyed a "happy hour" for awhile standing around the campfire before we headed to the dining hall for dinner.

After a good night's sleep, we were awakened by a young African in a white coat who delivered a cup of coffee to our cabin for each of us. After washing and dressing, we headed for the dining room and a nice breakfast. It was still dark when we finished eating. We loaded our equipment onto the pickup, climbed into our seats and took off through the jungle, just as streaks of light began to appear in the Eastern sky.

That day we covered a lot of country. I bagged a water buck (which measured 29¹⁄² inches), a bush buck, a reed buck and an oribe before we were through. The bush and the reed buck were both about the size of a mule deer, weighing maybe one-hundred and fifty pounds each. They had dark grey to black hair and carried slightly curved horns with a half

Like the buffalo, my water buck measured half an inch shy of being record class, but for me it was a trophy of a lifetime.

237

twist. The oribe, a very small antelope, weighed only about twenty pounds. The small size of the Oribe and their speed make them a difficult target when they run through the bush. I felt lucky to have bagged mine on a dead run with one shot.

When we returned to camp that night, the campfire was going and we sampled finger steaks from my cape buffalo. We cooked them ourselves on sticks, much like we would have if we'd been roasting wieners. Boy, were they delicious!

After about thirty minutes of happy hour by the campfire, we were invited to another great feast in the dining room. The room was a fairly large, round, screened-in building with a thatched roof and concrete floor. It included a nice kitchen on one side and a large dining area with beautifully decorated tables and nice chairs. It was quite a surprise to us, being way back there in the African bush.

The last day of the hunt began the same as the others with the early breakfast and us out of camp just before the break of day. I had mentioned to my guide that I would like to get a zebra, so we spend most of that day hunting for one — to no avail. About mid-morning, we watched seven hartibeests out in the center of a big plain. The grass was about as tall as our pickup cab. We maneuvered to within about five hundred yards of them before they spotted us, stopped and formed a small bunch. Jack looked them over with his ten-power binoculars.

"They are about five hundred yards," he said. "The one in the middle is a big bull. Do you think you can hit him?"

I said I could and held the sights on the spot I needed to hit. Just after I squeezed the shot off, the hartibeest went down and the other six took off. We drove over to where the animal had been standing. There it lay. A clean shot had dropped it in its tracks. The men went to work immediately to dress out the meat and load it on to the pickup.

On the way back toward the jungle, we jumped a couple of warthogs. A big boar was bringing up the rear as they ran up a creek bed, heading toward some tall grass and weeds about two hundred yards away. My first shot went over the top of the boar, but the second connected. He had a nice set of tusks. After dressing and loading him, we headed back into the jungle.

About three o'clock that last afternoon, my guide detected movement through the jungle ahead of us. It turned out to be a herd of female impalas. They would pass through a small opening ahead of us.

"If there is a buck with them, he will be about twenty-five yards behind them," my guide said.

Sure enough, we spotted one lone impala a short distance behind the herd of does. The females went through the small clearing and my guide said, "When the buck goes through, get him."

When the buck appeared, he was on a dead run. I swung my rifle and shot. There was a puff of white hair but he continued on his way in high gear. It sounded like I had hit him dead center, but I ran into the jungle a few steps and spotted him going across a small clearing. I shot again and put him down.

When we walked up to the animal, Jack reached down and picked up its tail. I had severed it about two inches from the base with my first shot. There was only a small piece of skin holding the tail on the buck. No wonder that first shot had put him into high gear! It was a fine, mature impala. We took pictures, dressed and loaded the meat and headed for camp.

On the way back, we came across a beautiful sable buck and two does. He had an impressive set of horns, too, that curved back almost touching his tail. He stood broadside to me, silhouetted against the sky about one hundred yards away. But sable were not listed on my license so I couldn't shoot him.

Soon after that we were back to camp for happy hour, dinner and a good night's sleep. That was our last night in the African jungle.

The next morning after breakfast we flew back to the game refuge and then to Johannesburg, Holland, New York, and home to Seattle. The trip was seventeen days of unforgettable experiences for Ruby and me.

In the spring of 1976, my doctor in Seattle recommended that I have a prostate operation, stating that he had seen many cases like mine turn into cancer if they were let go. I decided to follow his advice. The surgery took place at Swedish Hospital, where I stayed for ten days. It took almost a year to get my strength back, even though I walked to work and all over town every day.

That summer I met a man in Fairbanks, Alaska named Bill

Waugaman. He was a master guide and had been assigned a hunting territory in the Wood River Range and its drainage southeast of Fairbanks. Bill said he would take me Dahl sheep hunting that fall if I would get a sheep license. We set the date in September and I applied for a week of my vacation for that time.

Bill's wife had passed away with cancer that spring. They had a beautiful daughter and a sixteen year old son, Eds. Bill wanted to take the boy on the trip to serve as our wrangler. I brought my rifle and hunting gear with me, leaving them with friends until Friday night when I went home with Bill and stayed with him in his beautiful home on a hill west of Fairbanks.

The day before, Bill had hauled Eds and the horses down to a road that led back into the Wood River Range. The road was close to the Usebelli Coal Mine about fifty miles south of Fairbanks. Eds took the horses up the trail to Bill's base camp, which was a nice log cabin with a small landing strip next to it. The next morning we had a pilot fly us into the landing strip and the cabin. After breakfast with Eds, we loaded the horses and headed up a creek bed for about six miles, where Bill had a spike camp. We encountered an average of one moose kill every half mile. The wolves were thick in that area and there was no management program to keep the predators in balance with the game. The spike camp consisted of a clearing and two 55-gallon steel barrels that contained a lot of staple food such as salt, pancake flour, sugar, syrup, etc. One barrel had a big canvas tent, lantern stove, gasoline and other camping items. We found the clearing but the barrels were gone. Later, Bill discovered the barrel with the tent a short distance away in the brush, but it took a while to locate the one with the food in it. The bears had rolled it about a hundred yards down into a swampy area. The barrel was lying on its side and water had leaked through the seal. A lot of staples that we had been depending on were spoiled.

After finding the barrels, we set up camp and made dinner. We had one beautiful sunset that evening. It was one of the most breathtaking I have ever seen. After dinner we watched a couple of caribou feeding on a hill about a hundred and fifty yards from camp. The hillsides were beautiful with various colors of vegetation and the Wood River Range itself was breathtaking in the fading light of evening and the growing shadows.

Sunday morning we awakened early, had breakfast, saddled the horse and headed toward the mountains about a mile away. We rode up a wide, rocky creek bottom to some benches at the foot of the mountains. When we got there, Bill motioned us to be quiet and stop our horses. He piled off his and carefully climbed the creek bank to where he could see over the top. He motioned for us to leave our horses and join him. Approximately one thousand yards away was a group of about twenty sheep, feeding. Among them were several rams. One appeared to be an extremely big fellow with a curl of about one-and-one-half.

There was no way for us to get closer without being seen, so Bill suggested we retreat and hunt in another area before coming back again. Then, we might find them closer or in a position where we could stalk them. So we moved out and up the northeast side of the range for the rest of the day. There were no more sightings though we hunted several areas. Then one morning we started up a creek bottom we had traveled the first day. When we reached a spot about half a mile from the end of the draw, we saw four rams feeding along the grassy slope at the bottom. We stopped the horses around the backside of a bend and waited until the sheep fed out of sight.

Then Bill suggested we ride up a short distance and take off on foot keeping a ledge of rock between us and the sheep. This we did with Bill in the lead and his son and me following close behind. All went well until we came across a patch of wet grass on a steep hillside about a hundred feet from the rock that we wanted to reach. Bill and Eds had vibram-soled boots and went across the wet grass with no trouble. I had a pair of LL Bean chain-tread Pac's. When I hit the grass, I went down and had to pick my way across the grassy area. Bill had his ten-power binoculars out and was peeking around the rock looking for the sheep on the other side of the creek. Still looking through his binoculars and thinking I was right behind him, he said, "There are four sheep on this side also." But only Eds heard him. I caught up to them shortly after his comment, so when he turned around, he assumed I had heard about the four on this side. He informed me that one of the rams was the big one we were looking for.

I found a rock ledge where I could stand and rest my rifle over the top.

With the big ram in mind, Bill suggested that I get up on it. I peeked around the rock and saw four sheep on a rocky point about five hundred yards away. Still thinking one of those rams was the big one Bill was talking about, I climbed up onto the ledge and very carefully laid my rifle in a position toward the four rams. Bill whispered, "The big one is on the left."

I held for a five-hundred-yard shot and squeezed off.

"You missed! Shoot again!" Bill said.

I knew I had missed. The four I was looking at were now running up through the rocks, so I responded, "Bill, if I couldn't hit him standing at that distance, I could never hit him running!"

Then Bill realized I hadn't seen the four rams on our side of the creek. They were only about one hundred yards from us when I shot. But they took off at the sound of the gun going off. We followed them the rest of the day, but never caught up with them.

The next morning Bill told Eds and me that we were almost out of food, thanks to the bears. We had been picking wild cranberries and blueberries to supplement our meals, but Friday would be the last day that we could hunt. Friday was the next day.

After supper, we took a short hike around the camp to watch several caribou on a hill about three hundred yards away. They were feeding and making their way through the country. We also spotted a good-sized black bear, too, feeding in a blueberry patch.

Back in camp, Bill told Eds and me some interesting stories of the sheep hunts that he had taken in Asia. After a good night's sleep in our spike camp and a good breakfast of hotcakes and coffee, Eds saddled our horses. Bill and I put things away and washed dishes. This done, we mounted the horses and started up the same creek bottom we had traveled the first day. There wasn't a sign of any wildlife moving anywhere we could see. Finally we reached the spot where we had stopped the first day, where Bill had found the herd of twenty sheep about a thousand yards out — too far to shoot.

Bill got off his horse to climb up the creek bank and look over the area again. Just after he dismounted, he noticed a nice ram on the other side of the creek almost at the top of the rocky ridge.

"Get off your horse and get your sights on him," he said. "This may be your last chance on this trip."

I slid my rifle out of the scabbard and lay down in the creek bottom with the rifle and scope headed in the direction of the ram. Just about that time, the ram started to move up over the ridge.

Bill made a loud, shrill whistle and the ram stopped squarely on the top of the ridge and looked back at us. I held the cross hairs of the scope on his shoulders and pulled the trigger. Bill was watching the ram with his binoculars.

"You hit him!" he shouted. About ten seconds after I shot, the ram tumbled head-over-heels down off the ridge. He stopped about a hundred feet from the bottom when he wedged against an outcropping of rock. Eds climbed up and freed him from the rock, after which the animal tumbled all the way to the creek bed.

I had hit him just back of the front shoulder. The bullet had gone into the brisket, through the heart and out the top of the shoulder. That gives an idea of the angle I was shooting while lying in the creek bed. He was a mature nine-year-old with a full curl to his horns.

All three of us were very pleased with our luck that last day. After

Taking this beautiful Dahl Sheep on the last day of the hunt made it one of the most memorable hunting trips I've had.

taking pictures, we dressed and loaded the sheep on one of the saddle horses and headed for camp. We skinned and dressed our prize, saving the cape. Later, I had the head mounted by Kleinberger Bros. in Seattle.

We stayed in camp that night. The next morning after breakfast, we packed the two barrels with the tent, stove and other gear. After sealing them, we left them under a tree at the campsite. We then loaded the meat, hide and horns on the pack horses and climbed aboard our saddle horses for the six-mile ride back to Bill's base camp and private airstrip. Our plane picked us up the next morning and Eds started back down the trail with the horses.

Sunday afternoon, I flew back to Seattle to begin another week in the office and recount the week that I had just spent in the beautiful Wood River area of Alaska. Bill and Eds Waugaman were two of the finest people that I have ever had the pleasure of hunting and camping with.

Chapter 18

Led to Live in Idaho

"... a country boy...a shetland pony...a phantom jet more than 1000 m.p.h."

Several of my friends and members of my family encouraged me to write my autobiography because of my seventy-eight years of interesting and varied experiences. I am grateful to have had the privilege of living through more than seven and a half decades of change — that which was greater than any like period in the history of our great country and probably the world.

Throughout my lifetime, I have seen and participated in numerous changes in transportation alone. I rode a pony to school every day as a boy. That mode graduated to the horse and buggy or wagon. Next, I remember the Model T Ford touring car that I drove to high school which also served as a school bus for our neighbor children. There was my '28 Chevrolet coupe followed by my Model T pickup. The pickup was less than a year old and looked brand new when I had it. It was shiny black with a black canvas top. I had several other cars including a 1929 Ford coupe and a sedan after I was married.

This earliest photo of me taken in the winter of 1914 shows the bobsled we used for transportation when snow was on the ground.

With a desire to take to the skies, I enrolled in pilot training and eventually flew a J-3 Cub airplane, a Taylorcraft, a Stenson Stationwagon, Bell and Jet helicopters, C54 twin engine aircraft, and a Leer Jet at more than 500 miles per hour. When I was governor of Idaho, I had the opportunity to ride in an F4C Phantom jet from Mountain Home Air Force Base. We reached a speed of 1040 miles per hour and I had the

245

controls for about forty-five minutes at speeds around 550 m.p.h. I flew over the Capitol Building and took pictures with the cameras operating in the jet.

A few years later, when I was with the United States Department of Transportation, the U.S. Coast Guard regions in Seattle and Alaska were within my area of responsibility. This again provided me with the good fortune of riding with the Coast Guard on fishery patrols over the Bering Sea west of Alaska. Our means of surveillance was the Double Rotor Sikorsky helicopter, one of which I had the thrill of flying for more than an hour over the waters southwest of Juneau, Alaska.

All of these experiences came my way because I had a private pilot's license and loved to fly. For a country boy who started out riding a shetland pony and eventually flew in a phantom jet more than 1000 mph, I feel as if I've seen some pretty major changes during my lifetime.

I also feel very grateful to have enjoyed good health and a kind and loving family. This goes back to my four grandparents who were born in Sweden. They came to the United States between 1860 and 1880. When they arrived, they were all single. My grandfather Swan Peter Samuelson came from Norkoping, Smoland Country, Sweden, in the 1860's. He married Christina Adelina Borquist on March 4, 1875. His bride had emigrated from Vena, Smoland County, Sweden, in 1867.

My mother's parents were William Erhardt Johnson and Anna Olive Larson. Anna came to this country with her mother, Anna Christine (Bjorklund) Larson from Visst Ostergotland through Stockholm, Sweden. She arrived in the United States in 1885 and worked as a housekeeper and at other jobs for a year or so while saving her money. When she had enough for passage for her Swedish boyfriend, she sent for him to come to the United States. They were married in 1887, shortly after his arrival to America. They had six children, three boys and three girls. One was my mother, Nellie Matilda Johnson.

Grandfather Johnson worked as a farm laborer for a short time after coming to America. When he married my grandmother, he started a painting and interior decorating business in Woodhull, Illinois. This was a small farming community of about six hundred people located one hundred sixty miles southwest of Chicago. He pursued that work until he passed away in September, 1935.

This family picnic photo was taken in 1918. My grandparents, Bill and Anna Johnson are on the right. My folks are behind them next to me standing. My sister Aileen is in front and that's my uncle, Fred Swanson on the left who married mom's sister Dora. Dora took the picture.

I worked with Grandfather Johnson from time to time when my father didn't need me on the farm. I sanded, steel-brushed buildings, painted barns and outbuildings and houses. It was enjoyable working with him and for him because he liked to whistle while he worked. I have lots of fond memories of the times I spent with Grandfather Johnson, who was a pleasant, soft-spoken man. I always knew when he was coming to the barn before ever seeing him because he was forever whistling those happy tunes. Grandfather Samuelson was a farmer, too, a tradition he followed from his own family in Sweden. He moved to Woodhull when my father took over the farm, the place where I was born.

Woodhull was a farming community with only a couple of grocery or general merchandise stores. I can remember the button shoes and the big round block of Longhorn cheese and the big cheese cutter that cut off wedges for the customers. I also remember the barrel of dried lutefisk that sat in the aisle of one of the stores.

Besides the merchantiles, Woodhull had a Ford garage, a grain elevator, a lumber yard, a doctor's office, a dental office, two pool halls, several restaurants and a number of churches. These churches included the Methodist, Presbyterian, Swedish Lutheran, and Catholic.

My dad was confirmed in the Swedish Lutheran Church, so we worshiped there for a while when I was young. There were two services on Sunday morning, one in English and the other in Swedish. My mother was raised a Methodist though, so when we moved closer to town, we changed to her church. The first time I remember attending a religious service was at the Clover Chapel, a nice white building with cedar siding and a bell tower on the top. It also had beautiful stained glass windows on both sides. Behind it was a huge cemetery where the first settlers in that area had been laid to rest.

The Samuelson farm was seven miles from town. We usually came to town by horse and buggy, but in the winter we used a bobsled. I was six and one half years-old when Grandfather Samuelson died, so I don't remember him too well. He fell down an extremely steep inside-cellar stairway and broke his hip. Gangrene set in, and he died two weeks later in the year 1920. Grandfather Samuelson's death came before penicillin or any of the bacteria-killing drugs that we know today had been developed.

Living seven miles out with just horse and buggy for transportation, my folks seldom went into town more than once a month. Consequently, in my first few years, I didn't get to see my grandparents too often or for very long at any one time.

Both my grandmothers were good cooks and especially adept with many of the favorite Swedish dishes: homemade bread, Swedish pancakes, polt, ostakaka, Swedish cookies and cakes.

Polt, one of my favorites, is an interesting concoction. Whenever we butchered a hog, my mom prepared a large bowl or pan with several cups of rye flour. Then, when dad cut the hog's throat, they'd catch the blood which was then stirred it into the rye flour with a large spoon. Then came more flour until it became too thick to stir. They had a large kettle of boiling water ready on the stove and large spoonfuls of the mixture were dropped into the boiling water. When cooked, polt looked like dumplings. When they were done, mom would set them out on a cookie sheet or cake pan to dry and cool. Then she would slice them and put them into an iron skillet with raw milk and butter and fry them until they were a bit crisp. Then they were ready to eat. I loved them and still do.

Besides the obviously pleasant memories of their culinary abilities, I remember both grandmothers as kind, gentle and hardworking ladies. I always enjoyed going to see my grandparents.

Whenever I had to attend a school activity in the evening while I was in school, I stayed with Grandmother Samuelson. It was always a treat because she knew exactly what I wanted to eat, and she enjoyed fixing my favorites. I loved her homemade black bread and Swedish rolls in particular. I don't think she ever ran out of cookies either. I guess she looked forward to my visits because she had become lonely living as a widow for so many years after Grandfather Samuelson's death.

My parents, Fred Samuelson and Nellie Johnson, were both born at Woodhull, where they lived and died. The only time one of them lived elsewhere was the eight years my father spent with Ruby and me in Idaho from 1961 until 1969, after which he returned to Illinois where he passed away June 16, 1970.

Both my parents went to school in Woodhull. Unfortunately, my father was only allowed to finish the third grade. Then his father needed him on the farm, and that was the last of his education. Dad somehow learned to read and write though. He read the newspapers from cover to

cover as well as magazines and a book now and then. He was a hard-working man, who labored long hours every day. For years during the farming season, we would get up at four in the morning to milk eight to ten head of cows; feed, curry

That's my father on our hay rack wagon with his favorite team of horses, Midget and Queen.

and harness the horses; feed the cattle, hogs, and chickens. Then we'd have a breakfast of bacon, eggs, potatoes, bread and jam at five-thirty and head for the fields around six or six-fifteen. We came in for lunch at noon and went back to the fields until five in the afternoon. Then we did just about the same chores in the evening as we did in the morning, ate supper late, and went to bed around nine. On several occasions I remember going out and shocking oats, barley or wheat by moonlight until ten or eleven o'clock, just in case of rain during the night because it would cause the grain to mold. Once it had been shocked, the grain could dry out if it got wet without getting mold.

In my dad's prime it was nothing for him to pick three triple-top box wagon loads of corn a day by hand — that's over 180 bushels! Then he shoveled it into the corn crib completely by hand. He would keep that pace up until all the corn was out of the fields and in safe storage.

Before my mother and father were married, dad worked as a carpenter with Fred Johnson, the brother of my grandfather William E. Johnson. Dad was always building something at home or at the neighbors' between harvests or during slack farming periods in later years.

If my memory serves me right, my parents became acquainted while dad was working for Fred. Dad and mom went together for about a year before marrying on July 16, 1910, in Woodhull. They had three children, but the first, a girl, died at birth. I was the second child and was born on July 27, 1913. My sister Aileen joined us on July 17, 1916.

After my parents were married, they started farming Grandfather Samuelson's 160-acre farm outside of Woodhull about seven miles. Since our only mode of transportation outside of walking during the first six years of my life were horseback riding, horse and buggy or horse-drawn wagon and bobsled, I grew up walking a lot and spent many hours on the back of a horse.

My grandparents were honest hardworking people who went to church as real believers and took part in community betterment projects and helped their neighbors and friends when people like that suffered from sickness or injury or experienced fire or storm damage. They would help with farm work or rebuild a building that had burned or damaged in a storm with nothing but donated labor.

My folks were the same way, always helping neighbors and friends. Because dad was a carpenter before he started farming, he was always helping neighbors and friends build or rebuild their barns, corn cribs and out buildings just to be neighborly.

Of course my mother and the neighbor ladies put together meals whenever such a project was in progress.

Both my parents were honest, hardworking Swedes. My mother never had an idle moment. She was always knitting, sewing or crocheting, even when watching television or listening to the radio in the years before TV.

My parents set a good example for me. I don't remember an instant where they had problems or trouble with other people. They were well thought of by their many friends and neighbors.

As I reflect on the early years of my life, I recall many things that sort of headed me in the direction my life took over the years.

I loved hunting and fishing, of course, and camping from a very early age. Fred, Roy and Rex Komer, a cousin Chester Odean and I started camping on Edwards River about six miles from our home and did so at least a week each year. We caught fish with our hands as well as with hook, line and worms. We were all in the eight to twelve year-old range at the time. After that I worked on the farm with my father where I learned to run a trap line and shoot well.

Those early years developed my interests in outdoor sports and planted the idea that it would be fun and interesting to be in the sporting goods business. I honestly believe that the Good Lord guided me into those areas that seemed to fit my abilities so well.

When I was in the fourth or fifth grade at the Woodhull grade school, I remember reading a book entitled, History of the State of Idaho by C.J. Brosman. It was full of photographs and several things impressed me. I developed an interest in Idaho from that book that never left me. It was as if the wildlife, lakes, mining and the mountains of Idaho were calling me. For some unknown reason, it seemed, I was being directed toward Idaho from that very early time.

There was a chapter in that book on Indians that also interested me. Little did I realize then that in years to come many many Indians of those very same tribes would become my good friends. It was my strong interest in the Indians of Idaho that prompted me to start the first Governor's Indian Advisory Council in the United States. Two members from each of five reservations met with me and my department heads twice a year during all four years I was in office.

I remember the photograph of Idaho's State Capitol building on page 169. But I could not have realized then that I would some day, many years later, occupy the office of the Governor in that beautiful building.

Another picture from that book that stuck in my mind was on page 99. It was the Bunker Hill & Sullivan lead smelter and refinery. How could I suspect I would spend much of my life within one hundred miles of that same place, the richest mining area in the United States?

These are some of the reasons I sincerely believe I was guided to the west and specifically to the state of Idaho.

In 1943 I enlisted in the Navy while living in Davenport, Iowa. I expected to be sent to the Naval training station near Chicago, but instead was put on a train headed west and the first thing I knew we were unloading from the train at midnight in Athol, Idaho! I didn't know it then, but we were only about twenty-six miles south of Sandpoint, where Ruby and I have made our home since the end of World War II.

Yes, for many reasons in recent years it has appeared to me that all along I have been guided in the things that led into such wonderful experiences for me and my family. And of those many times when I was somehow spared from disaster, surely it was His hand on my shoulder.

When I sold my interest in the Pend Oreille Sport Shop in 1958, I had the urge to move on in my business life. That's when I started Don Samuelson Equipment Co. covering Idaho, Montana and ten counties in Washington as my territory. My income doubled. I was my own boss again and could move my business ahead as I saw fit.

But that same year I became concerned about the way our country was headed. I felt I had no right to complain though, unless I tried to help straighten things out. That was the beginning of my career in politics. I lost my first election to the State House of Representatives by only 43 votes but won the next three terms in the Idaho Senate.

Now it all seems to have been part of a plan to put me in a position to lead this great State of Idaho as Governor.

Though I lost the bid for re-election at the end of my four year term, it seemed to me the Good Lord once again was watching over me because right after the election Ruby developed cancer and our family was very concerned for her well being. It was His hand on our shoulders that pulled Ruby through her ordeal. That was twenty-two years ago and she's still with me.

Through the trying days of her illness, I was biding my time taking care of Ruby. Almost as soon as she was on her feet again several opportunities opened up for me. I took that job of Secretarial Representative for the United States Department of Transportation in Region Ten with renewed enthusiasm. With responsibilities that spanned several government agencies in Idaho, Washington, Oregon and Alaska plus the big Alaska Pipeline, I had plenty to do. And not only was the job interesting, but it paid two and a half times the Governor's salary as well. Though I put in long days and seemed to live on airplanes and in hotels more than at home, I worked with a lot of nice, top level people.

Looking back it all seems like a dream come true, that my life has followed a master plan to help the state of Idaho and this great country of ours.

During my years in the state Senate and as Governor I looked at government money in the same way that I did my own. I understood that it was the taxpayers' and property owners' money and that it should not be wasted. I believed that government should be run like a business. Not in the sense of showing a profit but for the purpose of providing necessary state services at a reasonable cost.

I tried to appoint or hire the most qualified people available to me regardless of their political or religious affiliations. I tried to encourage my department heads to work closely with the people under their responsibilities, making sure that they kept the citizens, taxpayers and property owners of our state in mind and that they provide the services our people needed without over-regulation or restriction.

My years as a member of the Senate Finance Committee brought me valuable insights into how the various departments were being operated.

Again, it was His hand on my shoulder that allowed me as a freshman Senator to serve on that important Senate Committee because that gave me an excellent education in regards to where Idaho's tax dollars were being spent, for what and by whom.

I tried to encourage all of my people to keep things out in the open and on top of the table so everyone could see what we were doing. That way if we were making a mistake, a lot of people could call it to our attention and it could be corrected before it went into law and took effect.

I tried to set an example, never taking my privileges as Governor beyond any other citizen of the state. I even made sure that the car with the number one license plate never went over the posted speed limit.

Most all of Idaho's State Police officers at the time were very good friends and I didn't want to embarrass them by stopping the Governor for speeding or disregarding regulations that everyone else was supposed to adhere to. I never felt that being Governor gave me privileges beyond those of any other citizens of Idaho.

Chapter 19

Since Our Retirement

Ruby and I seem to have the wanderlust. Since we retired we have taken a number of trips to various parts of the world.

When Jimmy Carter was elected in November of 1976, the Alaska Pipeline had just about been completed. Since the administration turned from Republican to Democratic, I decided it was time to retire. When I notified the Secretary of Transportation, I learned that the six years spent with the department along with my military service qualified me for a relatively small retirement benefit. My retirement took effect December 31, 1976.

We had renters in our North Boyer home in Sandpoint, so we notified them that we'd like our house back by March 1, 1977, which was no problem for them. On March 7 with the help of friends, we loaded a U-Haul truck with our possessions and once again headed for Idaho. We had been waiting for more cooperative weather. That morning we woke up to snow. We drove through six inches of the white stuff on Snowqualmie Pass, but with the load on the truck, made it without chains.

Ruby followed me driving our 1970 four-wheel-drive Chevrolet Blazer. After coming down the east side of the pass, we had good roads for the rest of the trip. When we arrived home, several friends, including Les Gissel, Harlan Walker and Cap Davis, helped us move back into our house. We spent the next several months re-decorating and making incidental repairs.

It was good to be back home in Sandpoint, which is located on the northwest shore of Lake Pend Oreille in North Idaho. We have a view of the Cabinet Range of mountains to our east, and we sit at the base of the Selkirk Mountains, which extend from Canada sixty miles to the north. Just over the mountains as the crow flies is another beautiful body of water, Priest Lake. Both lakes offer breathtaking scenery and some great fishing. Dolly Varden and Kamloops trout are common in Pend Oreille, while Mackinaw trout weighing up to fifty pounds attract fishermen to Priest Lake.

Having been in the sporting goods business in Sandpoint for fourteen years, I had hunted and fished all over North Idaho. Now that I was retired, I decided to get back to my first love of fly fishing. One of my favorite North Idaho streams was the North Fork of the Coeur d'Alene River southeast of Sandpoint. One of our favorite campsites was the abandoned Beaver Creek Work Station at the mouth of Beaver Creek.

Sometimes as many as five families would take campers, trailers or tents and head up Dry Creek to DeLyle Forks and then down Buckskin to the North Fork for a weekend of camping and fishing. Probably our most consistent companions were Harlan and Margaret Walker.

Once the camp was set up, we would take my four-wheel drive up over the mountains and down to the other side of the river. It was between seven and eight miles back to camp by the river.

Then Ruby would drive the Blazer back to camp. Donned in hip boots and ample fishing gear, Harlan and I would fish our way back to camp. We did a lot of catch and release, keeping only enough to have a good fish feed for dinner. The weekends spent at that campground were always enjoyable.

Among our choices for other favorite campsites was one along Pack River above Samuels (approximately fifteen miles north of Sandpoint). For a few years we could catch nice rainbow, cutthroat and an occasional eastern brook trout in the river. Then after one year for some reason, we seldom caught anything over six inches. With our policy of catch and release, I know we didn't clean out the stream. Caribou Creek is one of Pack River's tributaries in that same area. Again, we saw the same trend. The fish we caught gradually became smaller over the years. We haven't been back.

Another of our favorite spots was on the Moyie River at the Meadow Creek Campground about twelve miles northeast of Bonners Ferry. The Moyie is a beautiful stream, which flows out of Canada and empties into the Kootenai River about six miles above Bonners Ferry. With its clear, cold water, the river varies in width from fifty to one hundred feet. The majority of fish caught in the Moyie are rainbow, although I once hooked a nice eastern brook trout there. The Meadow Creek Campground is still well kept. It's a great place to relax with the rippling waters close enough to your camp site to put you to sleep at night.

Since retiring, I have also spent lots of time fishing with my sidekick Les Gissel, who retired from the state Fish and Game Department. Les was our local game warden. We've fished Idaho streams from as far south as the Clearwater River and north to the Canadian line. Over the years we've given up backpacking for four-wheel-drive vehicles. We've also done some hunting and just plain looking for signs of wildlife along the trails in the back country. Many a day was spent on top of mountain ridges enjoying the scenery. Neither of us has to kill game to enjoy ourselves on hunting trips. We do take a deer or an elk occasionally, but only with the idea of never wasting an ounce of it.

One area Les and I have particularly enjoyed is the High Drive overlooking the east side of Lake Pend Oreille. We've not only hunted and fished there, but we've also enjoyed some prospecting. I've always been interested in mining gold, silver and precious gems. Back in the 1950's, Les, Jim Breinich and I did a lot of prospecting on our days off. That was during the hunt for uranium to fuel nuclear power plants. Since retiring, Les and I have continued to keep our eyes open for minerals on our fishing and hunting trips.

A short time after my return to Sandpoint in 1977, I was invited to come to Parma in Southern Idaho to hunt pheasants on Don Weilmunster's ranch. Don mentioned that he had a big ranch between Montour, Pearl and Horseshoe Bend. The ranch had gold and silver prospects and old mines all over it. When he learned of my interest in mining, Don asked me to help him open up and develop some of the old mines.

I spent a lot of time with him going over his 30,000-acre ranch. After looking at mining maps, I went through the state mine inspector's reports as well as the federal mining reports in Spokane. I also found information on many of the mines by looking through records at the state historical society in Boise.

One set of claims known as the "El Paso Group" is reported to have three-hundred thousand tons of ore blocked out in it. The ore averaged half an ounce of gold per ton, and the silver varied from six to one-hundred ounces per ton. The development of these claims occurred between 1900 and 1920. At the time, the process of separating silver and gold from sulphide ore was very difficult.

This has changed in recent years with several new processes known as leaching. Bio leaching, for example, introduces micro-organisms which eat the sulfide and release the gold and silver. Because of this new process, I have been very interested in contacting a company versed in the procedure to look at the property.

During retirement, I have done a little gold panning and occasionally worked a rocker and sluice box. It's still a big thrill to see those yellow flakes show up in the pan or riffle. I don't expect to get rich at mining, but it's a great recreation. Who knows...some day it may pay off big!

Another of my favorite activities is trap shooting. After opening the Pend Oreille Sport Shop, I got involved with the Sandpoint Gun Club. Our trap ground was east of the Great Northern railroad tracks. We shot out over Lake Pend Oreille. I soon became the club secretary and provided all the shells and clay birds at my cost. Some club members included Harry Hupp, Bill Parker senior and his son Bill, Art Kalk, Louie Schnell, Laurin Pietsch, Stan Maxwell and Fred Schedler.

During my last year as Governor in 1970, a good friend Curt Berklund called and invited me to join the Shoshone Indian Trap Shooting Club. I met Curt when he and his folks ran a lumber mill at Cottonwood, Idaho. I was selling rock drilling equipment and fire extinguishers. Curt's mother ran the office and I enjoyed a cup of coffee with her when I stopped at the plant. After I left the Governor's office and went with the Department of Transportation, Curt was appointed Director of the United States Department of the Bureau of Land Management and lived in the Washington D.C. area. I had the priveledge of working with Curt on several projects during those years and stayed with him and his gracious wife Adele and their family when my travels required that I go to Washington D.C.

The Shoshone Indian Trap Shooting Club shot at Sun Valley the last full week in June every year. Due to other commitments, I could only attend one day that year and only one other time before I retired. But since then, I 've missed only one shoot because of a conflict of interest.

The club is made up of men and women from all over the United States and Canada. The majority however, live in the western United States. It was started at Sun Valley in 1949 but moved to Jackson Hole,

Wyoming, about ten years ago. It is now held on a beautiful spot between the airport and the Grand Tetons. Ruby and I look forward every year to the week with our many friends at the beautiful Jackson Hole Gun Club. We take our trailer and stay at the gun club for more than a week some years. I have arrived early the last two or three years to participate in the Wyoming Registered Shoot. Although Ruby doesn't shoot, she looks forward to going every year. We see a lot of old friends from all over the United States and Canada. The highlight is seeing these people and just having fun. Although one's score is secondary, it's always nice to present a good one.

We have also joined the Hi-Yu Indian Club, which usually meets in mid-September in Yakima or at Sun Mountain, Washington, and sometimes in Spokane. Many of the members are Shoshone Indians. We always enjoy spending the week with these fine people.

Besides my recreational activities, I have enjoyed being involved in the Bonner County Historical Society. In the spring of 1981 another member, Bud Moon, called and asked if I would consider serving on the organization's board of directors. After some thought, I consented and spent the next six years on the board, serving one year as president.

I took a deep interest in the society and during one year raised more than $10,000 in cash and materials to fill in the second floor of the museum for more display space. When I was president, we had a violent storm one night which caused a big fir tree to crash into our building. It tore a hole in our archives room where all the records and newspapers were stored.

After being notified by the Sandpoint police, I had to go to the museum at ten o'clock that night, climb up on the roof in the wind and rain, and cover the hole with plastic to protect the irreplaceable items inside. I think I finally arrived home about three in the morning.

We completed several projects during those years. One involved taking an old cabin apart log by log and putting it back together next to the museum. The structure is finished on the outside, but it needs to be restored inside. We also began a project to move an old water wheel into town from Hoodoo Creek about twenty miles southwest of Sandpoint. It came from across the road close to the Seneacquateen Cemetery, a pioneer burial ground west of Sandpoint. It was given to the Historical Society by Mr. and Mrs. Bell, residents of the Hoodoo area.

The water wheel supposedly furnished the first electricity in Bonner county. For that reason, we wanted to preserve it. Two fellow board members, Paul Rechnitzer and Glen Judge, and I hauled the old wheel into my yard and took it apart. Parts of the wheel were rotted out, so we replaced all the spokes. The board then planned to construct a chain link fence around it to prevent curious children from being hurt.

I raised $500 for the project by convincing both Northern Lights, Inc. and Pacific Power and Light Co. to donate $250 apiece. Glen Judge furnished the lumber for the spokes and paddles, and John Pucci did the concrete work. Bill Overland repaired the large wooden bull wheel.

At the time of this writing, none of the money raised for restoration had been used. We hope the present board will use the funds to complete the chain link fence so that Paul, Glen and I can finish the project. It's been a lot of work, but we all felt an urgent need to salvage and repair this important artifact.

Although I am no longer on the board of directors, I still have a deep interest in preserving the history of Bonner county and northern Idaho.

In 1981, Ruby and I received an invitation to visit Stoneridge Resort, a timeshare condominium complex about forty-five miles southwest of Sandpoint at Blanchard. We fell for their sales pitch and bought two studio apartment weeks set up for four people. We bought two prime time units.

Although we have never stayed in our unit, we have traded our two weeks for other apartments all over the world. This certainly got us out and moving.

One of the first exchanges took us to Cedar Lake Resort on the Gold Coast, a short distance from Brisbane, Australia. We rented a car and drove all over the area with Ruby's brother Bob and his wife, who accompanied us. It was interesting driving on the wrong side of the road. In Australia and New Zealand, the steering wheel is on the right side of the car, and you drive on the left side of the road.

The country roads had either a blacktop or concrete strip in the center where people drove until they came to a hill or curve. Then, they moved over and drove with one wheel on the pavement and the other in the ditch, so to speak. Since our insurance only allowed for one driver, I drove. During the two and one-half weeks of touring Australia and New Zealand, I logged more than two-thousand kilometers driving on the wrong side of the road.

Our condominium had two bedrooms, a nice living room and a kitchen overlooking a small lake. During the week we spent there, we traveled the back roads through the farming areas and spent some time at the beach on the Gold Coast. The resort owned a house on the beach where we could change into our bathing suits. It was a beautiful sandy beach that stretched for miles both ways. It was also topless, which was a bit of a shock at first. After a few days however, we accepted the situation as normal for the area.

When our week ended, we returned to Brisbane and flew to Melbourne where we rented another car and took a road to Ballarat, an old mining town. We toured an interesting gold museum which had small individual display stands containing samples of gold from different creeks in the area. It was interesting to observe the difference in color and size of the gold coming from each creek or mine.

We stayed in Homestead Motels during our travels out of Melbourne. Each night we were given a quart of milk, coffee and tea along with our unit. After staying in one of their motels for three nights, they gave us a card qualifying us for a ten percent discount from then on. Instead of $25 a night, we paid $22.50. The Homestead motels were clean and very comfortable.

We spent eight days making a circle north and west of Melbourne and finally returned to turn in our car. From there, we flew to Sydney, changed planes and flew to Christchurch, New Zealand. Again, we rented a car, then drove to the south end of the island through a number of beautiful towns and over many one-way bridges, some half a mile long. Some of the bridges had turnouts where you could pull out of the way if you met another car. Just a short distance from Queenstown, we came to a one-way tunnel that was one mile long and built on a ten percent grade. A stop light at the entrance controlled traffic going through.

The mountains in New Zealand are rugged, high and beautiful. We saw thousands of sheep grazing along the steep, green hillsides.

Queenstown was a beautiful town nestled in the mountains above one of the fiords. We bought tickets for a boat ride up through one of the fiords where we saw many beautiful waterfalls tumbling over cliffs several thousand feet above us. The vegetation was fresh and green. Crystal clear water fell freely in some places and over rock walls in others.

After leaving Queenstown, we drove up the west coast through the beautiful rain forest. Just a short time before we went through this area, it had experienced a terrific rain storm, the worst in one hundred years. We found construction crews still filling approaches to bridges and repairing the roads everywhere. The high water mark was at least six feet above the bridges in some areas. After completing our trip up the coast, we went over a mountain pass to the east and back to Christchurch. From there, we flew to Sydney and caught a flight home.

We enjoyed both the scenery and the wildlife of the Land Down Under. Although we saw only sheep and a few white-face cattle in New Zealand, we spotted kangaroos, wallabies, koala bears and numerous varieties of beautiful birds in Australia.

Another time-share condo trip took us first to Edinburough, Scotland, where we enjoyed a few days before our scheduled week in Avimore. This gave us time to spend in Edinburough, which is rich in history. A nice hotel in the middle of the town served as our housing.

We walked many miles during the two days we spent there. Once we walked up to the castle on top of a pretty high hill where several queens and prominent people had been beheaded. We also had lunch and dinner in some of the unique restaurants in the old Port of Edinburough. Friday evening Ruby and I had dinner at a nice restaurant close to our hotel. After dinner, we walked through a mall shopping area and then went to the hotel. The next morning we boarded the train for Avimore.

Soon after arriving at our room however, Ruby became very ill. She was suffering from severe gas pains and soon lost her dinner. We were up until three in the morning before she finally went to sleep. Because of Scotland's nationalized medicine, it was hard to get a doctor. Ruby did have a package of Pepto Bismo tablets, which seemed to help.

The next morning we started the two hundred mile train trip to Avimore, even though Ruby wasn't feeling too well. We arrived there about noon, rented a car, and drove to the resort, which was less than a mile from the train depot. Our first priority once we found our condo was to buy a few groceries. With Ruby still not feeling well, we just took it easy the rest of the day. Sunday morning we had breakfast and planned to tour the area around Avimore. Ruby was still ill, so we read the Sunday paper and did very little. By that afternoon, she was worse.

Upon reaching a doctor, we were told to meet him at the clinic. By the time we arrived at the clinic, Ruby was so miserable that it took us 10 minutes to get her out of the car and into a wheelchair. After an examination, the doctor told us she had food poisoning. He gave her an intravenous shot and sent us back to the condo. That evening he came to see her, and by that time, the shot seemed to be taking effect. She still did not feel too good, so he told us to stay close to home and relax for a couple of days.

After following doctor's orders and seeing that Ruby was back to normal, we drove around the lake where the Lock Ness monster is supposed to be. We also visited a wool shop and the tourist center which featured a large map dotted with red pins showing the areas where the monster had been sighted. On our drive around the lake we kept a close watch, just in case the monster decided to surface, but no luck.

After leaving Scotland and arriving back in Idaho, we decided to take our Nomad trailer and circle the state to visit old friends. Ruby still hadn't fully recovered from her ordeal, so we headed for the Big Hole River in Montana to relax and fish for a few days while she recouperated. We parked the trailer at the Anaconda Sportsmen Campground on the Big Hole River, and I fished for one day. That evening after dinner Ruby became deathly ill. About ten, I propped her up with pillows in the Blazer and headed for the hospital in Anaconda.

I had to drive slowly because every time we hit a bump, Ruby cried out. We arrived at the hospital about midnight. The doctor on duty checked her and said she simply had a hiatal hernia. He gave her a shot and said she should be okay. I asked the hospital personnel three times if I could leave her there while I returned to the campground to get our trailer and take her home. They refused and the doctor said the shot would keep her pain down for about 12 hours.

We left the hospital and drove back to camp, arriving at the trailer about three in the morning. The shot had done little to minimize her pain, so I drove slowly to avoid chuck holes and other bumps. As soon as it was light, I hooked up the trailer. We headed to Anaconda where we picked up the freeway to Missoula, took Route 200 from there through Thompson Falls and on to Sandpoint.

Ruby was in terrible pain. Several times she told me that she didn't think she would make it home. At Plains, Montana, I called our doctor Robert Carlson in Sandpoint and told him I had a very sick girl. He told us to come to his office, and I asked him to have a wheelchair ready for Ruby. We arrived about three thirty that afternoon. Dr. Carlson took one look at Ruby and told me to take her to the hospital. Once she was there, doctors Carlson, Cope and Neher checked her over and ran several tests and scans.

I hadn't had any sleep for forty-eight hours and was pretty exhausted. I asked the doctors if I could go home to rest a bit. They said to go ahead and that they would call as soon as they had completed the tests. No more than half an hour passed before the phone rang. The diagnosis was pancreatitis, an inflamation of the pancreas. She also had about a quart of blood and fluid in her stomach cavity. They said an operation was necessary to avoid peritonitis which is an inflamation of the smooth serous membrane that lines the abdomen. If that were to happen, they said, it could be very dangerous.

The cause of pancreatitis came from one of the arthritic medications that Ruby had been taking for several years. I suspected that the cause might be traced to one or more of the medications that she had been taking. I contacted our pharmacist and found that one of them described the danger of pancreatitis with prolonged use.

The surgery went well, and I went home to bed about 3 a.m. after being assured that Ruby would be okay. Her full recovery took about six months, but we thank the Lord that our doctors made the right decisions.

Needless to say, our experience with the time-share condo in Scotland didn't exactly go as planned. Once Ruby recovered however, we continued our jaunts, going to places like Palm Springs, California; Stowe, Vermont; Jackson Hole, Wyoming; Wolfborough, New Hampshire; Big Canoe Resort in Georgia; Scotsdale, Arizona; Spain and the Canary Islands. We've also vacationed in Sebastion, Florida, and Caloosa Cove Resort in the Florida Keys.

I have had a complete physical exam every year of my life since I was sixteen. In October of 1987, while performing my annual physical, the doctors suspected colon cancer. Several tests confirmed their diagnosis. After checking in to the hospital on a Sunday, I went through surgery the following morning. Dr. Neher took about 16 inches of my colon which contained the tumor. Fortunately, the cancer had not spread to any other organs, so I didn't have to go through chemotherapy or radiation. For that I was most grateful. Again, I felt the touch of a hand on my shoulder. I am grateful for keeping up my annual checkups and for having doctors like Carlson and Neher. Besides that experience, I have had cataracts removed from one eye. Otherwise, my health has continued to be excellent.

We had purchased a mobile home in Apache Junction, Arizona, in 1986. Our plans had been to spend several months there during the winter. In 1988 however, we didn't get to leave home until the twenty-first day of January because the doctor wanted to make sure I was okay.

I was pretty weak when we left, but we made the trip without problems. I spent most of that winter just reading and trying to build up some strength. We headed for home about the first of April to get the taxes completed by the deadline.

On the evening of April 13th, we had dinner at Connie's Restaurant in Sandpoint with our good friends Paul and Pat Parks. Pat sold real estate for Century 21. She mentioned she had a piece of property with one hundred feet of lake frontage close to Bottle Bay on Lake Pend Oreille. The property had a modified A-frame shell on it. Someone had built the shell, put exterior plywood on the top and two sides, wafer board on both ends and then covered it with fifteen-pound felt. The owner had then moved to Wyoming.

We decided to go out and look at it the next morning. The building was a mess. Water had swelled the particle board floors, and the lot was so covered with weeds and brush, you couldn't walk through it. Yet it was a good spot close to the water with a beautiful view of the lake and the Cabinet Mountains. It looked like a great challenge, so we went back to town and made a cash offer. It was accepted.

A young carpenter, Greg Walker, helped me put the cabin together and finish it. I contracted to have a brown steel roof put on first. Then, Greg and I put composition shingles on both sides and T 1-11 siding on both ends, except the bottom floor toward the lake. Greg finished that with redwood and glass. We also built a complete bathroom in one corner downstairs and completed the kitchen area on the other side. I then designed a stairway in another corner.

We finished the remodeling project by the fall of 1989. The last step was to put down linoleum in the bathroom and carpet the rest of the house upstairs and down. After we'd finished, Pat and Paul Parks got a lot of our friends together for a housewarming. Since they couldn't get in without a key, they had to let me in on the deal. Paul made a large pan of spaghetti, and the other guests brought potluck dishes and a bottle of wine. I was told to bring Ruby out at exactly four o'clock Monday afternoon. I told her that I had to meet a man in Coeur d'Alene on business and wanted her to go with me. Although she wasn't very enthusiastic, I eventually talked her into the trip. We started out about three-thirty. While going over the Long Bridge across Lake Pend Oreille, I told her that I had to go by the cabin to pick up a gallon of carpet adhesive to take back to a store.

When we rounded the curve where we could see the driveway, Ruby said, "Look at all the cars! Someone is having a party and we weren't invited!"

When we got closer, she exclaimed, "Our door is open! I wonder how it got open?"

As we pulled into the driveway, everyone filed out. Ruby was so excited she didn't know what to do or say. Twenty-four of us had a grand spaghetti feed and enjoyed great company.

Probably the highlight of our retirement was participating in the 1990 Idaho Centennial. As a former governor, I was appointed honorary chairman, along with two other living past governors, Robert Smylie and John Evans.

One evening in early June, Jim McNall, one of our local county commissioners called and told me I had been selected to represent Bonner county as grand marshall at the main Centennial Celebration in

Boise which was to take place from July 2nd to the 4th. I told Jim I would be honored to do so.

We traveled to Boise from Jackson Hole, Wyoming, where we had been attending the Shoshone Trap Shooting annual gathering. Ruby had been invited to share the honors with me. After a two-day trip pulling our trailer behind us, we checked in at the Statehouse Inn and joined the other grand marshalls from other counties throughout the state.

I saw many old friends with whom I had served in the Legislature and others with whom I had worked as Governor. Ruby and I were involved in two parades and a steam train ride from Nampa to Boise.

July 3rd was a busy day. A bus stopped at the Statehouse Inn at eleven forty-five and took all the grand marshalls to Nampa, where we boarded the steam train and had soft drinks and snacks. At one fifteen in the afternoon, the train started for Boise. We arrived at the Union Pacific Depot on the south end of Capitol Boulevard. Antique autos furnished by the Boise Antique Car Club took us down the boulevard to the Idaho State Capitol.

Our very good friend, Bert Colwell, drove us to the Capitol in his 1914 Overland four-door Touring Car. Bert and his wife Winnie are longtime friends. He had been head of state communications during my term as Governor.

When Bert let us out in front of the Capitol, Ruby and I had to report to the Centennial Committee and get our badges. A few minutes before three that afternoon, we were ushered out to the Capitol steps, where we stood in the sun for more than an hour. When the ceremony ended, Bert took us to his home for a quick dinner. Winnie had prepared a delicious turkey and barbecued spare ribs. As soon as we had finished eating, he took us back to the hotel in his Cadillac. At seven o'clock that evening, we boarded the bus for Bronco Stadium at Boise State University and attended the evening ceremony there which was capped off with a fantastic fireworks display. I was involved in the ceremony because of my status as honorary chairman.

On July 4, the grand marshalls were treated to a Boise tour-train excursion and lunch in a park. We also visited the old Territorial Prison, and while traveling down Warm Springs Avenue, heard the names of many famous Idaho families who had lived there. At four that afternoon,

Bert picked us up at the hotel again in his 1914 auto, and we found our spot in the parade line-up. The parade route was three miles long. I've never seen so many people along a parade route anywhere. They were twenty deep down both sides of the street in many places. As soon as the parade ended, Bert dropped us off at our hotel, where we had dinner and a good night's sleep. The next morning we headed north to our home in Sandpoint.

Ruby and I felt honored to be selected as grand marshalls from Bonner county and as honorary chairpersons of this wonderful birthday celebration for our state. An added pleasure was seeing and visiting with many old friends whom we had met during our years of public service.

Chapter 20

Good Friends

December 15, 1989, started out to be a pretty nice day. Ruby and I were beginning our annual trip to Arizona. We had packed our things in the 1987 Ram Charger the day before and planned to leave home about six in the morning. As the day started, there was no snow or ice on the roads. It was a clear, nice winter morning.

We packed up the last couple of items and drove to Coeur d'Alene for breakfast. I filled the gas tank on the Charger, and we headed south of Highway 95 for Boise, where we had planned to stay a day or so with our son Steve and his family.

About twenty miles south of Coeur d'Alene, we were cruising along at just over 50 mph when we came to a curve in the road. The curve faced south, and there were no trees or any form of shade on the road. I saw no sign of ice or snow on the road, but suddenly our vehicle headed straight across the road toward the opposite shoulder. I tried pumping the brakes, but the vehicle failed to react. When we hit the shoulder, the Charger broke out of the icy pavement, and I headed it down the wide shoulder. We had hit black ice!

I thought I had the vehicle under control, but loose gravel on the shoulder of the road caused it to slide sideways and catch a signpost. The signpost tipped out of the ground and started us rolling over a twenty-foot embankment. We hit the driver's side first and then completely rolled over to a stop.

Frightened and crying, Ruby was hanging in her seat belt above me. I unbuckled my seat belt and then reached up to unfasten Ruby and let her down. The windshield was completely shattered, and we were both covered with glass. I reached up and tried to open the door, but it was locked. Then, I noticed the electric window buttons and pushed the one for my window. It worked.

I crawled out the window and then reached in to get Ruby. At that point, a young man named Jerry Johnson was driving by and saw me crawling out. He stopped and came down to help Ruby and me get up the bank and into his warm car. Someone had called the medics. They were there within just a few minutes. I had a black eye and had cut my nose, which bled all over me and Ruby. They patched me up and checked Ruby to find out the origin of the blood, but soon realized it was mine. The medics told us that six accidents had occurred on that curve during the prior two-week period. One couple, unfortunately, had been killed after colliding with a logging truck. We were very lucky that no one was in the other lane of traffic as we went across the road.

The Idaho State Police and the Kootenai County Sheriff's officials soon arrived, and Ruby transferred to the warm police car so Jerry Johnson could be on his way. About an hour after our accident, ISP Corporal David Cordova walked out on the road to measure where we had started to slide. The officer couldn't stand up in the road because it was so slick. About 15 minutes later, the sanding truck made several passes over the curve; it covered less than a hundred feet of the highway. One of the paramedics who lived close to the accident scene told us that whenever humidity was high in the winter, the wind or air currents would coat that curve with black ice.

That was my latest close call, which Ruby shared with me. We had always used our seat belts and were most thankful to have developed that habit.

Our Ram Charger was towed into Coeur d'Alene. When I called my insurance company, they insisted that Ruby and I have a checkup at the Sandpoint hospital. Although Ruby was shaken up a bit, she had no injuries. I must have wrenched my neck with the seat belts during the roll because it was pretty stiff and sore for a week afterward. The Ram Charger was totaled. Both the insurance agents and our doctor wanted us to take it easy for a few days, so we stayed home until December 21st.

Then we started again in our Oldsmobile and stayed the first night in Riggins with our friends Bill and Mary Carter. The next morning we drove to Boise and spent the Christmas holidays with our son Steve, his wife Karen and their two boys. It was a wonderful Christmas, knowing that someone was watching over our shoulders one more time. The day after Christmas, we loaded the car and headed for Apache Junction.

On January 11, 1990 we left the Phoenix, Arizona airport at seven o'clock in the morning headed for Madrid, the capital of Spain. We were accompanied by our good friends and neighbors Dave and Nancy Lewis. Ruby and I did not speak Spanish, but both Dave and Nancy had spent much time in Spanish speaking countries. It was great to have them along as our interpreters.

We changed planes in Madrid and flew on to the island of Tenerifi at three o'clock in the afternoon on January 12th. We rented a car and drove to our resort, the Harbor Club, where we had a time share apartment. We were supposed to have a double apartment for four people but somehow there was a misunderstanding and our apartment was too small. The manager of the resort took care of the problem though by giving Dave and Nancy another apartment.

The first night at the resort all of the new arrivals were guests at a cocktail party held to help us get acquainted. January 14th we had lunch at Arona and spent some time walking around Las Galletas. The next day we drove to Santa Cruz and all around the Island. We couldn't believe the amount of new construction going on, mostly on resorts.

Someone told Nancy about an interesting trip up over a mountain pass. There was a native restaurant along the way where they suggested we have lunch. We found the road narrow and very steep in places, very winding; but it was black topped and had good-sized stone barriers on the downhill side for safety. The road led us up the mountain to Santiago del Liede and six miles along the ridge and down through a saddle to the little mountainside village of Masco where we had lunch at the restaurant which was located just off the road on the side of the mountain. It was a beautiful trip in a typical rural mountain setting. The person who had suggested the idea had been right, too, as we enjoyed a good lunch.

Another interesting day was spent at Puerto de la Cruz where we did a bit of shopping and had lunch. Ruby and I had been guests of Spain while I was Governor in 1969 and had spent a week traveling throughout the Canary Islands. I didn't remember seeing snowcapped mountains on that trip so it was a shock to see the top of Mount Teide (only 3718 meters high) covered with beautiful white snow. In fact there is a ski area on the mountain.

When our week was up on the Canary Islands we flew directly to Malaga, Spain on the shores of the Mediterranean Sea. We rented a car there for two weeks and drove about sixty miles west to Estepona where the Club Bena Vista was located. We stayed in a beautiful two bedroom modern apartment, nicely furnished, with kitchen and living room, just a short distance from the Mediterranean. It was our home for the following two weeks.

For most of the first week we traveled to the interesting areas that were close enough to visit and came back to our apartment at night.

One of the first trips was to the Rock of Gibralter. We drove around the rock where we saw the colony of "Gib" apes that live on the rock — creatures that are born without tails. We also walked through some of the tunnels to where the old cannons are placed with their muzzles pointing outward through holes in the rock. They had been set in strategic spots to help protect the entrance to the Mediterranean Sea and the military stationed on, in and near the rock.

Sunday we drove to a flea market in Estapona. We found it different than we expected and very interesting. Monday we went to one of the oldest cities in Spain, Ronda which had a population of about thirty-six thousand. The city was a very picturesque place, built on top of a rock outcropping.

Ronda is divided by a gorge one hundred meters deep with an interesting stone and concrete bridge joining the two sides of the city. One of the bridges across the gorge is called the *Arab Bridge*, the other and older one is the *Roman Bridge*. The oldest bull ring in Spain is located in Ronda. We spent the day touring the old churches, cathedrals and other old Roman and Arab buildings. Another item of interest was the old Arab baths.

About twenty-five miles from our apartment was the town of Mayas. A nice couple from our hometown of Sandpoint have an apartment there where they spend about six months each year. We called and made arrangements to meet them and have lunch together. They were very gracious and showed us around town. Ruby bought a beautiful hand-knit sweater and Nancy bought a coat in one of the shops. It was a very interesting town built on top of a hill. We had lunch at an outside restaurant. It had been a very interesting day for us.

At this time we had covered most of the places of interest that we could drive to in a day so we decided to leave our apartment for a few days and travel to some of the old cities that were established by the Romans and Moors several centuries ago.

We traveled through some beautiful farming country past millions of olive trees which were all over southern Spain. The first stop was at Jerez where we bought tickets and went to the horse show. We saw the famous Andalusian Dancing Horses, whose reputation dates back to the 17th century. It was a great show and the horses were beautiful.

When we left Jarez we drove to Seville. Nancy and Dave found the Hotel Simon, an 18th-century home full of antiques. It was owned by Spanish royalty who used it a month out of the year and made a hotel out of it the rest of the time. We were advised to be very careful when we were in Seville because there was a lot of crime. We had no problems however and found no indication of any trouble while we were in town.

The third largest cathedral in the world is in Seville. Built in the 15th century, it is a hundred and sixteen meters long and seventy-six meters wide. It has five Gothic naves with a huge crossing where the main alter stands with its magnificent grill. The Peredos is the largest in all Christianity. It was covered with gold and remains one of the most beautiful things I have ever seen.

In another area we found a pure silver alter made and carved out of ten tons of silver. Seville was a very interesting city with a lot of beautiful buildings and artifacts dating back to Roman times.

Leaving Seville we drove to Cordoba, another Roman city. We visited several museums and the Alcazar de los Reyes Christian Castle where Columbus made a deal with Queen Isabella to explore routes to America. We went into the actual room where that historic event was supposed to have taken place.

From Cordoba we drove to Granada, another Roman city in its day. We spent most of one day going through the Alhambra, a fort-like area up on the side of a high hill or mountain. The Romans developed a water system that still works and keeps many of the fountains spewing water the same way as when they were built. This area housed and fed 40,000 men. It was a very beautiful area, well kept as well as being an important part of history.

We visited Cathedral Socustia Y Museo too — where Queen Elizabeth and Ferdinand are buried. We also visited the large Catholic church,

Real Capilla de Granada, where we saw the caskets containing the bodies of Queen Isabella, Ferdinand and their son and daughter. In one of the cathedrals we saw the stone casket (mounted on the shoulders of four soldiers) that is supposed to have the body of Columbus inside.

When we left Granada we headed over a back mountain road to our apartment on the Mediterranean. We spent the last couple of days playing cards and resting up for our return home.

Dave and Nancy took Ruby and me to the airport at Malaga and then they went to Morocco in northern Africa for about a month. Ruby and I flew to Madrid, from there to New York, then onto Spokane and finally "home at last!" It was one of the most interesting trips we have ever been on — thanks to our good friends Dave and Nancy Lewis — who were very kind and helpful to both of us.

In October Ruby and I loaded the Bronco with a few clothes and a bit of ocean fishing tackle and headed east. We spent Thanksgiving with my sister, Aileen and her family in Illinois. From there we headed south to Florida where we spent several days with my aunt Charlie Ruth Miller at Auburndale, Florida. The weather and roads were beautiful all the way.

On the first of December we headed south again to the Caloosa Cove Resort on the east side of the Keys and on the shore of the Atlantic. We had a week at this beautiful resort and invited our friends Paul and Pat Parks to spend the week with us. They had a time share week reserved at the same place and invited us to stay with them. The resort was located about half way out to Key West.

Paul and I did quite a bit of fishing off of the old bridges along the Keys but without much luck. We caught fish that were not good to eat.

We spent one day with Paul and Pat's motor home driving through the Everglades. We took pictures of a lot of birds and several alligators.

When the two weeks ran out we worked our way north to Atlanta, Georgia. Ruby's niece and husband, Bruce and Murial Truelove, live at Dawsonville, about 50 miles north of Atlanta. We spent a week and Christmas with them at their lake home. They took us around their area during the day, played pinochle in the evening and had a great time.

Right after Christmas we headed for Tucson, Arizona, where we rented a park model in an RV park for two or three months.

About the time we arrived in Tucson arthritis hit Ruby real hard. By the first of February it was so bad she was in constant pain in one hip and elbow. I called the Mayo clinic in Scotsdale and made an appointment for her. We spent about three days at the clinic and found out that her right hip and elbow were in very bad shape. The doctors recommended they both be replaced.

Our doctor was Dr. Conn, a Rheumatoligist from Rochester, Minnesota, who was filling in for a doctor on vacation. He suggested that we go to Rochester and have the operation done there.

To make a long story short — we went home the first of March, I took care of my income tax, and on the 13th we drove to Rochester. Ruby went into the clinic between the 18th and 20th. She had a complete hip operation on the 21st and a complete elbow operation on the 27th. Seven days later we were in the Bronco headed for home.

It's been over a year since the two operations and Ruby is doing great. No pain in the hip or elbow.

My turn came next. When Ruby recovered enough to get around good I decided to have a spur removed from my heel. I made an appointment for the operation to take place about the middle of May.

The operation didn't take long and I thought that I would be over it soon. The surgeon had to cut the tendon on my heel to get part of the spur out. He gave me some pretty strong pain pills and I had to sit with my foot up for three days or so. Friday evening as I started to eat dinner, I began to feel terrible. I had a cramp in my left side. By about seven-thirty I was really hurting and began to break out in a sweat.

I told Ruby to call our doctor. He was out of town but his answering service told her that his partner Dr. Cope was on emergency duty at the hospital and to take me there. Ruby couldn't start the car so I got in our Bronco and drove myself to the hospital — Ruby went with me.

Dr. Cope checked me over and decided that I should be sent to Coeur d'Alene because our surgeon, Dr. Nehr, was out of town and Dr. West in Coeur d'Alene was filling in for him.

There are two ambulances in Sandpoint and both of them were out so the doctor asked Ruby if she knew anyone that could take me. She thought of our friend Dave Lewis. Dave had just walked in the house when Ruby called. He came right over, picked us up and on to the Coeur d'Alene hospital emergency room we went.

I was so sick I don't remember much about the trip. I remember going under a lighted area and I remember sirens and flashing blue lights of a police car. An officer stopped Dave because we were traveling so fast. As soon as the officer found out what was happening he led us into the hospital emergency area, himself. Apparently he had called them because the whole crew was there ready to take me in.

Dr. West took one look at me and said, "We better get something going and fast!" They inserted a tube through my nose and then I was taken to x-ray, and from there into intensive care where I stayed for four days. During that time I went through all kinds of tests . Finally, it was determined that I had a blocked small intestine. Luckily it straightened out without surgery and I was allowed to go home.

My foot continued to pain me so I didn't get to participate in my favorite sport — stream fly fishing. I went twice all summer and my heel hurt so bad while I was fishing that I had no fun.

In September my doctor said it was unusual to have the pain last that long, so they x-rayed my heel and found a small piece of floating bone. He said that wouldn't be a problem, that he would just slip it out.

NOT SO! When the doctor went in to get the bone chip, he found that my body had rejected a suture and built a sac around it. So I was on the operating table for over an hour.

That was a short time before deer hunting season. I only went deer hunting twice and they were short trips because of the strain the frozen ground put on my heel.

Six months after the second operation my heel was getting back to normal—just in time for the 1992 fishing season.

Ruby and I are thankful to have survived those early months of 1991 and are glad that it is now part of history.

Looking back through the past seventy-nine years makes me aware of many wonderful things that have taken place in my life. Both before I met my wife Ruby and through the many blessings she and I have shared during the fifty-six years since we married.

We were blessed with two children who have made us proud to be their parents. Donna and Steve have been successful in their own right and added two grandsons and two granddaughters to our family. Steve and Karen have two boys, Mike and Rick. Donna has two girls , Debbie and Dianne.

Starting the Pend Oreille Sport Shop in 1946, right after World War II, was a great challenge. I resigned from a good civil service job in Davenport, sold our home, bought a cattle truck and moved family and all of our worldly possessions to Sandpoint. With very little money Ruby and I started the sporting goods store.

Working long hours and being honest and fair to our customers helped us survive some pretty tough times. For many years we only took enough out of the business to pay the bills and buy groceries.

I developed a policy from the start to keep my prices as low as possible and stand behind my work as a gunsmith as well as the products we sold. Building a good reputation was the first order of business and the best advertising I could have done. I have always believed that it takes a lifetime to build a reputation but only one unethical or immoral incident to destroy one forever. I sincerely believe that treating my customers fairly and as friends had much to do with my being elected to the Idaho State Senate for three terms and Governor of Idaho for four years.

I am grateful and proud that I was able to carry on the tradition of honesty and fairness throughout my political career. I had the distinct feeling that the good Lord was with me and guiding me throughout my campaign for Governor and the four years that I served in that position.

Throughout my whole life I have not been afraid to change to a job more interesting or challenging. When the changes were made in every instant that I remember, it was with a sincere and positive feeling that it was the right move at the right time. That great hand on my shoulder gave me the assurance that what I was doing was right for me, my family, my State and this great country that we are priviledged to be a part of.

Ruby and I feel very fortunate to have had so many wonderful experiences and friends. Through my jobs and our interest in traveling, we have made friends all over the United States and Canada as well as many other parts of the world. But we are most grateful of all that throughout our lives someone has kept His hand on our shoulders.